Social Work and the Body

Social Work and the Body

Nadine Cameron
and
Fiona McDermott

HV
41
·C265
2007

First published in 2007 by
PALGRAVE MACMILLAN
Houndmills, Basingstoke, Hampshire RG21 6XS and
175 Fifth Avenue, New York, N.Y. 10010
Companies and representatives throughout the world.

PALGRAVE MACMILLAN is the global academic imprint of the Palgrave Macmillan division of St. Martin's Press, LLC and of Palgrave Macmillan Ltd. Macmillan® is a registered trademark in the United States, United Kingdom and other countries. Palgrave is a registered trademark in the European Union and other countries.

ISBN-13: 978-1-4039-4330-9
ISBN-10: 1-4039-4330-3

This book is printed on paper suitable for recycling and made from fully managed and sustained forest sources. Logging, pulping and manufacturing processes are expected to conform to the environmental regulations of the country of origin.

A catalogue record for this book is available from the British Library.

A catalog record for this book is available from the Library of Congress.

10 9 8 7 6 5 4 3 2 1
16 15 14 13 12 11 10 09 08 07

Transferred to Digital Printing in 2011

Contents

Acknowledgements   vii

Part 1   The Body in Social Work

1 The Body in Social Work   3

2 The View from Neuroscience   23

3 Social Bodies   63

4 Social Work and the Body: Towards a Theoretical
   Framework   79

5 The Body Cognizant Social Worker in Action   91

Part 2   Implications for Practice

Introduction to Part 2   111

6 Social Work, the Body and Mental Health   113

7 Social Work, the Body and Child Protection   141

8 Social Work, the Body and Aged Care   167

9 Social Work, the Body and Health Care   189

10 Social Work, the Body and Alcohol
   and Other Drugs   209

Conclusion   229

Glossary   233

References   239

Index   261

Acknowledgements

We wish to acknowledge the support and interest of our colleagues in the writing of this book, especially those in the School of Social Work at The University of Melbourne, and Lynda Campbell, Alun Jackson, Jane Miller and Janet Spink for helpful comments and discussions. Our families and friends have been valuable (and tolerant) companions in this journey, and we are very grateful to them. In particular, however, we wish to thank each other for an intellectually challenging, stimulating and above all enjoyable process of collaborative thinking and writing.

Part 1 The Body
in Social Work

1   The Body in Social Work

When in early 2003 we discussed with colleagues, students and social work practitioners our idea of placing the body at the centre of our thinking and practice, we were met with arguments and anxieties that this was a backward step – a reductionist approach and an attempt to go into domains which were 'not social work's concern'. These anxieties and concerns are, in our view, manifestly misguided, but the voicing of such concerns does alert us to the importance of demonstrating just how and in what ways the human body does indeed lie at the centre of social work thinking and practice. It is our contention that only by placing the body at the centre will we achieve both a unity within social work theorizing and practice and ensure that its unique contribution to the human sciences – and to human lives – will be maintained.

Why the body matters in social work

Social workers work with bodies and are themselves 'bodies at work'. Our bodies think and feel, move and talk, laugh and cry. Our bodies are creative: through them we can make things, destroy things and enhance or hinder their growth. Just as true is the fact that our bodies are vulnerable: they age, they sicken, are constrained and incarcerated. It is through our bodies that we communicate and on the basis of their appearance that we judge and are judged by others. Seen from one perspective, the limitations, capabilities and needs of the human body determine the nature of our entire social world.

Already it sounds like we are connecting, if not equating, intentionality, consciousness, identity and personhood with the body – and, in fact, we mean to do so. It is on this basis that we argue that addressing social inequality and helping individuals

3

achieve a better quality of life require that the body not only be considered but be accorded a central place in social work theory and practice.

Placing the body at the centre of theorizing and practice is vital to social work's espoused mission and purpose. At the forefront is recognition of social work's practice interests. While social workers work across a variety of domains with a variety of situations in a variety of ways, bodies are central. In health and illness, child welfare, ageing, housing and community development, how the body is afflicted, treated, cared for, supported and nurtured is of primary concern. Social workers work with people who are excluded and marginalized, for example, with refugees, those who experience psychiatric and physical disability where stigma and bodily and emotional vulnerability are markers of human distress. Social workers work with existential problems concerning the nature of the self, personal identity, the quality of life, the meaning of life and of death. Very importantly, social workers are frequently in positions of authority over others, with influence to regulate and place others' bodies under surveillance, especially those who are vulnerable or considered to pose risks to the 'wider' society. As Tangenberg (2002) points out, social work's tendency to separate the material body from the intellect colours the majority of social work theory and practice which assumes that the role of social workers is often to use intellect and skill to regulate the bodies and behaviours of those who are in some way out of control or overwhelmed by the vicissitudes of life.

Improving public health and developments in medical understanding and technology have seen a demographic shift to a longer-lived population – at least in Western liberal democracies. This means that social workers will increasingly be working with the health and social issues of an ageing and more often disabled population. Clearly, where the frailty of the body and the economic and political issues this raises are more prominently on the agenda, social workers have an added impetus to develop their theoretical and practice knowledge and skills. This requires an increasingly sophisticated understanding of the body.

Contemporary developments in biology and neuroscience in particular require our attention. These are fields which are making rapid advances in understanding the workings of the human body with significant and profound implications for how we think about what bodies are, what they can do and what can be done to them. These technological achievements bring in their train not only key philosophical questions about how we are to understand our bodies but also profound ethical issues relating to what life itself is.

Where is the body in social work?

The body is present in social work theory but hard to find. It is assumed within the person-in-environment paradigm and is central to the model of the life course. Nevertheless, it is invisible – taken for granted, unproblematized and untheorized 'for itself'. The human body is certainly not at the theoretical centre, despite the fact that 'the person' has traditionally been placed in the foreground of social work theorizing (Chambon 1999: 58).

In 'looking for the body' in social work theory we can usefully examine the ways in which social work's theoretical and practice models have conceptualized the nature of 'being human'. There are what we might call four primary preoccupations or themes within social work theory and practice which are identified below:

1. a view of human beings as individuals, active agents in their own lives;
2. a recognition of the influence of social structures in constraining and enabling human action;
3. an awareness of inequalities which characterize social life;
4. an interest in and focus on working to ameliorate the situation of those who are marginalized, excluded and vulnerable.

For each of these, social work has drawn primarily on four theoretical positions: systems theory, ecological theory, social constructionism and critical theory. Interwoven amongst these four 'pillars' are structural functionalism, psychological theories, especially psychodynamic and cognitive behavioural. Social work has also incorporated explorations into postmodernism and critical postmodernism (Pease and Fook 1999).

We now want to look at each of these four preoccupations in our quest to find the body.

1. A view of human beings as individuals, active agents in their own lives   Within social work the nature of the person at the centre of theoretical and practical concern is one who 'contains' a separate mind and body. This hearkens back to social work's origins in the post-Enlightenment modern period. Being a 'person with a body' is presupposed and taken for granted and rarely problematized. Likewise, the environment is understood as surrounding the person but distinct from the body, although the interactional and transactional relationships between person and environment have been much debated and elaborated.

Given the essentially unproblematic way in which the person is conceptualized, a focus on human growth, change and adaptation across the life course from conception to late life retains a sense of the universality of human bodies. A distinction is made between heredity and environment, with each contributing to the development and adaptation of the person. The human body is seen as if on a trajectory from conception to late life during which, in a uniform fashion, the physical body grows and declines. Changes in the body are, by and large, internally driven and determined by genetic and inherited characteristics.

Psychological theories, especially psychodynamic and cognitive behavioural theory, and more recently postmodern approaches to understanding behaviour and the human psyche predominate. The importance of social constructionist perspectives in emphasizing the centrality of meaning-making to people have gained in importance in contemporary social work practice with individuals and families. The emotions have not been subject to theoretical interest or analysis, other than through the lens of psychodynamic theory in particular, and explorations of psychopathology drawing from psychiatry. Social constructionist emphasis on the importance of understanding the meaning of events and experiences has also 'covered' for an absence of attention to theory pertaining to the emotions.

Although little theoretical attention has been paid to theories of the subject within social work, there has been a continuing practice interest in the 'use of self'. This has been applied specifically to social work practitioners and draws on psychodynamic concepts of transference and counter-transference with recent contributions from critical theory and postmodernism emphasizing the importance of reflexivity (Payne 1998; Miehls and Moffatt 2000). Concern with notions of 'use of self' refer to the social workers' capacity to draw on understanding of their own selves, their identity as social workers, their knowledge about how to *be* social workers, their experience within a particular set of circumstances and their ability to use this available emotional and cognitive information at the service of the client or the confronting situation.

'Use of self' is, however, not confined only to cognitive and theoretical considerations. In introductions to the skills required to practise as social workers the actual use of our bodies in interacting with service users is emphasized. Particular attention is given in teaching social workers the ways in which we communicate empathy, interest, positive regard, genuineness and authenticity in our voice tones, facial expressions, eye contact and bodily positioning. Often teaching tools include videos, role plays in front of other students and observation through one-way screens. This emphasis on the visual and the spatial use of our bodies, especially our faces and gestures, highlights the significance of non-verbal communication. In this regard, social work has drawn on the sociological insights of Goffman (1969) and the Symbolic Interactionist school, where analysis of how we present ourselves to ourselves and to others and the meaning that non-verbal communication holds for ourselves and others, is a central theoretical concern.

However, within social work there has been a tendency to focus on this aspect of use of self as comprising one of the skills in the social worker's 'tool kit' rather than as of particular theoretical interest. This perhaps refers to dualistic mind/body conceptualizations, the suggestion being that one has to – and indeed must – exert control, using the body as an instrument to bring about the outcomes desired by the mind or self. What is left unexplained, both in theory and practice, is what actually determines or influences the experience the social workers have of themselves and which, in relation to the exhortation to make 'use of self', they are required to draw upon.

In summary, the person who is at the centre of social work theorizing is an active, self-determining individual with a separate mind and body, who is equipped with a conscious and unconscious mental life and for whom the meaning of behaviour is important.

Humans can, through observation and technique, use their bodies in order to communicate and build relationships with others. Their bodies (facial expressions and gestures) are tools by which means others may be influenced.

2. Recognition of the influence of social structures in constraining and enabling human action   The environment furnishes the social and material context to which humans must adapt and respond if they are to develop to their fullest potential. The ecological model has traditionally provided social work with a theoretical base which emphasizes the interaction between people and their environment, and in contemporary social work, theorizing is represented by the ecosystemic perspective (Mattaini, Lowery and Meyer 2002). However, contributions from critical theory have directed attention to the influence of social structures in constraining and enabling social life. This reciprocity is a key tenet of social work's perspective and reflects the profession's ongoing struggle to integrate and synthesize the contributions of the ecological model and critical theory in explaining the mechanisms through which social structures impact social life. As social work's theorization of the subject is essentially a social rather than embodied one, the conceptualization of the relationship between actor and structure is reliant upon somewhat descriptive and vague accounts of the ways in which transactions and interactions occur between actors and structures.

3. Awareness of inequalities that characterize social life   Social work emerged out of an interest in remedying the inequalities in life chances that humans encounter. Its particular understanding has been to focus away from pathologizing individuals and blaming them for the difficulties that beset them (see Mullaly 1997; Allen, Pease and Briskman 2003). For this reason, the focus on person-in-psychosocial-context has been the hallmark of social work as a profession and has enabled it to attend to the importance of power (and the lack of it) in perpetuating social, economic and political inequalities. Because of the conceptual difficulties noted above, namely difficulty in analysing, theorizing and demonstrating how person–environment transactions take place, social work's focus has been on identifying and naming the nature and effect of the impact of social structures on the material and social well-being of individuals. Little attention has been given to identifying the impact of inequalities on the bodies of people, an exception being the work of Ellis and Dean (2000) who have sought to provide a corporeal or body-focused perspective on social policy. In general, however, emphasis has been placed on analysing the meaning of the experience of marginalization and its consequences in terms of access to social and material resources.

4. An interest in and focus on working to ameliorate the situation of those who are marginalized, excluded and vulnerable Social work has since its earliest days espoused a mission to change the social, economic and political structures which oppress. Intrinsic to this has been a belief in the malleability of people. The capacity to achieve change in individuals – and for social workers to work to achieve change – has been theorized and understood largely with the help of psychological theories rather than in relation to the body itself. While some recognition has been given to those environmental factors which might impede an individual's capacity to adapt or result in his maladaptation (e.g. the experience of stress or trauma during childhood), little attention has been given to the ongoing malleability or to the limits of change possible for the human body over the life course.

Social action and community development have been very important to social work's mission and represent key practice sites for efforts to influence and change the context and/or environment. However, as we noted earlier, social work remains theoretically weak in explaining the person-in-environment nexus, both in terms of the environment's impact on 'lived reality' and humanity's role in changing and/or maintaining the environment (Kondrat 2002). Social work, however, has paid significant attention to the role of social workers, emphasizing the importance of considerations by social workers of themselves as embedded in structures which impact on their being and their practice. This does remain at an abstract or psychologized 'level' rather than an embodied 'level'.

These four preoccupations or themes are brought together in the central concern accorded to the concept of person-in-environment.

Person-in-environment

The concept of person-in-environment is generally acknowledged as central to social work's focus, interests and practice. It has been most comprehensively delineated by Germain and Gitterman (1996) as a holistic view that people (and other biological and social processes) and physical and social environments can be 'fully understood only in the context of the relationship between and among them, in which families, and groups, and physical/ social environments continually influence the operations of the other' (1996: 6).

Person-in-environment has been subjected to critique and theoretical reformulation within social work in order to address particular shortcomings. These include its tendency to place greater attention on the person rather than the environment (Besthorn 2002); a failure to incorporate a perspective which is sensitive to difference, for example, in relation to black people (Robinson 1998); disability (Thompson 1998); and women (Kemp 2001). In Kemp's words, person-in-environment 'glosses over important differences in people's environmental experiences, particularly ... social identity ... race, ethnicity, class, gender, and sexual orientation' (2001: 1). In so doing, a non-differentiated, universal and anonymous person is placed at the centre of theorizing. It is also a perspective which exemplifies social work's traditional separation of mind from body, heredity from environment, and locates it closely within the social constructionist paradigm.

Some of these writers have also been critical of the fuzziness, under and over-inclusiveness of elements comprising the environment presupposed in person-in-environment formulations.

Germain and Gitterman's (1996) concept of environment is wide-ranging. It includes economic, political, social, historical elements, the effects of poverty and discrimination, physical settings, the natural world, the built environment, social networks, organizations, and culture (values, norms, beliefs). Others such as Ungar (2002) and Besthorn (2002) suggest additions to what might be included in the environment which go beyond the geosphere, hydrosphere, atmosphere and biosphere, and include what they refer to as the noosphere, that is, the deeply felt, transcendental and spiritual or metaphysical connection between humans and nature itself. This concept of 'deep ecology' drawing from ecofeminism (Hawthorne 2002) suggests that the boundaries implicit in person-in-environment be removed, enabling understanding of a concept of the human self as participant in a 'relational total-field'.

THE BODY IN SOCIAL WORK

Kemp (2001: 5) argues for inclusion of a concept of space itself – a 'critical spatial perspective' – to open up and foreground the view of the environment as an active social process through which meaning is generated and identity constructed. A key criticism noted by Kemp (2001: 4) is that social work's prevailing perspective on environment relates principally to phenomena which are observable; hence her argument for the inclusion of a spatial perspective. However, we might also add that elements or phenomena which may be outside awareness and/or are unobservable, for example, the unknown intentionality of others, or the functioning of the immune system, or long-term geological or historic processes, are also absent.

Kondrat (2002) takes issue with person-in-environment's conceptual failure to demonstrate the ways in which humans act to construct and maintain the environment. She advocates incorporation of Giddens' (1984) structuration theory, arguing that this theory enables us to think about the ways in which actors and structures mutually inform and refer to one another. Structuration theory's understanding of power as inhering in rules and resources which constrain and enable human action proposes a useful means of including power as a central dimension in micro–macro relationships which is only weakly theorized within current person-in-environment formulations.

Person-in-environment is understood in social work with reference to concepts of human development across the life course. Notions of the human as a biological organism adapting, changing and accommodating to the environment draw on an ecological view of the human person's 'biopsychosocial development within diverse environments and cultures' (Germain and Gitterman 1996: 21).

In tandem with the life course model is a conceptualization organized along the 'stress and coping paradigm' (Germain and Gitterman 1996: 10). Here it is proposed that transitions from conception to late life, are attended by periods of stress which require individuals to make use of personal and environmental resources to successfully move from stage to stage. Inadequate resources and/or a stressor that is perceived as beyond the person's coping capacities may result in maladaptive behaviour and problematic outcomes. Social constructionist perspectives emphasize that how stressors impact individuals will largely depend upon how those individuals interpret them.

The concept of resilience – the ability to go on through life despite difficult experiences and adversity always being present in the environment – has also been important within social work theory. Resilience refers to 'the continuing articulation of capacities and knowledge derived through the interplay of risks and protections in the world' (Saleeby 1996: 299). While recognition is given to the interconnection of gender, neurobiological, familial and environmental factors in promoting resilience, many questions remain and have heightened significance for social workers in a range of practice settings: is the capacity for resilience innate? Why do some people recover or even prosper in adversity while some do not? Are some people more resistant to trauma than others? Does the age at which traumatic experiences occur make a difference to recovery? Why do individuals differ in their resilience when faced with the same stressor?

Attempts to answer these questions have, largely, focused on psychological and behavioural explanations, with emphasis placed on identifying both risk and protective factors found, for example, in individuals' strengths, or in social or community assets. What has yet to be convincingly developed within social work theory is an approach to resilience which draws on multidisciplinary research and adequately integrates biological perspectives such that the influence of genetics, cognition and concepts of neural plasticity inform and enhance our understanding of resilience.

So, to summarize, within social work theorizing we can find a number of different ways in which the body has been conceptualized:

1. as separate from mind;
2. as separate from environment;
3. as a biological organism which has its own set path through life;
4. as a biological organism which adapts, changes and develops. This is understood primarily within social constructionist rather than biological terms. The stress and coping paradigm rests heavily on the view that the individual's experience of trauma and recognition of problems of transition from stage to stage are referenced to their perception of the character of these external events and the availability of resources to manage them and adapt to environmental demands satisfactorily. It is in this sense that diversity amongst people is manifested;

5. as synonymous with a person who cannot be understood except in relation to context and environment – person-in-environment. What is meant by environment remains fuzzy; it can be expanded or contracted. What constitutes environment is the subject of debate.

Person-in-environment and the life course model do provide useful guidelines for practitioners in thinking about their work with clients, which tries to avoid psychologizing and pathologizing their experience by proposing a concept of human life and action as embedded in complex and interacting micro and macro dimensions. However, the absence of understandings of the biological workings of the human body and the prevalence of dualistic theories about the body limit its theoretical sufficiency.

Thus, the explanatory power of formulations of person-in-environment and the life course are limited with respect to questions of (a) how different life trajectories may be explained; (b) how the environment actually impacts on humans as biological organisms; and (c) how humans actively impact the environment.

The absent body in social work

To this point, social work has failed to develop any significant practice theories pertaining, either exclusively or in part, to bodies. There are many possible reasons for this. One such reason may be that defining the body is, in itself, a difficult task. The term 'body' may be used to refer to a range of different concepts which have only a limited number of things in common. The main kinds of bodies, under which several other, more specific kinds may be subsumed – the physiological and the socially constructed – are distinguishable in terms of their informing epistemologies, their relationships to subjectivity and the broader concerns with which they are associated.

It is the physiological body – the body as delineated by biology – in relation to which social work theory has so far been largely silent. It would be untrue to say that the professional literature has overlooked the physiological body altogether, but it has mostly been in relation to illness, disability and other forms of bodily 'aberrance' that physiology has been evoked. Social work lacks a strong literature on physiological aspects of a range of phenomena such as emotion, cognition and sensation which are common to all human experience and which have, nevertheless, been explored from a variety of psychological perspectives by the profession. This remains so despite the discoveries neuroscience continues to amass in regard to such things as how cognition and emotion interact, and upon which physiological systems, emotion and consciousness are dependent.

The wide berth that has been given to biology by social work is, in some respects, understandable. Feminist theory has drawn attention to the extent to which the unequal position accorded to women in Western societies has been justified on the basis of dubious biological discoveries. Other gross injustices have been justified through 'bad science' – theories with only small grounding in empirically testable knowledge. In previous centuries, members of particular ethnic groups were deprived of learning opportunities because of the biological 'proof' that they were intellectually inferior. It is a serious error, however, to take particular political interests that draw upon science for validity as the agenda of science itself. And just as important a consideration is what injustices social work clients may have met with as a result of the social work profession's lack of familiarity with even basic biological principles.

It is not only potential inaccuracies and distortions of biological science that concern social workers. Social workers have many misgivings about the discipline itself. For example, many social workers see biology as inherently 'reductionistic' or attempting to explain all human phenomena in physiological terms. A related understanding is that taking a biological perspective on human problems involves ignoring individual differences and discounting subjective experience. A considerable proportion of social workers also appear to believe that explaining a problem from a biological point of view is the same thing as 'medicalizing' it.

Other fears held by social workers about the threat biological perspectives pose for social work may be based on

- misunderstandings or misinformation about the nature and capacity of human brains and bodies;

- misguided assertions that a concern with the separateness (in time and space) of individuals is a rejection of the belief in the power of social structures to oppress and disempower;
- beliefs that behaviour is immutable because it is animated and motivated by biological forces;
- anxiety that morality and respect for the less able-bodied/able-minded will be undermined and a 'survival of the fittest' mentality will be reinforced;
- concerns that biological differences amongst bodies will perpetuate prejudice and racial and ethnic oppression.

The rejection by particular social workers of biology may be based on a fundamental suspicion of positivist research methods, those upon which biology is reliant. Biology takes the body as an inherently stable, predictable and measurable entity, or what Turner (1992) refers to as a foundationalist view of the body. Various social workers and sociologists have been at pains to point out that scientific knowledge, no less than any other kind of knowledge, is a social product. Despite claims to the contrary, and as Busfield (1996) states, scientific knowledge is far from value-free.

The obscured body in social work

The theories grounding social work practice have also served to obscure the body. In the contemporary era, as we have noted, four theoretical traditions vie for position – systems theory, ecological theory, social constructionism and critical theory.

These four are frequently uneasy bedfellows, each of them opening a window onto social reality but in so doing denying other views. While more recent formulations propose adoption of an 'ecosystems perspective' in an attempt to draw person-in-environment closer together and encourage 'transactional practice' where person and environment are recognized as inter-connected (Mattaini, Lowery and Meyer 2002), the resulting perspective is far from a unifying one. Instead, it would seem to create contradictions and paradoxes which offer the practitioner fragmented guidance for action.

We meet these contradictions, tensions and paradoxes head-on when faced with the assessment task – a key and defining social work activity. Most assessment protocols comprise lists of personal and environmental factors which are considered to affect social functioning or create social problems. However, these lists generally lack an integrating theoretical base (Mattaini and Kirk 1991) and presuppose that the social worker's perspective will be informed principally by these four theoretical streams, maintaining throughout a separation of person from environment, and mind from body. Thus, as Hepworth, Rooney, Rooney, Strom-Gottfried and Larson suggest, (2006: 206), the practitioner will make their assessment based on, first, understanding physical, emotional and cognitive processes within the client, and second, physical and social factors within the client's environment.

What makes the assessment process so difficult is not only the competition for attention amongst systems theory, ecological theory, social constructionism and critical theory perspectives but the lack of a central target for investigation. Many domains of human behaviour and many elements at the exo, macro, meso and micro levels of the environment presumed to impact behaviour are the object of observation and enquiry, but their target – the embodied person – remains always slightly out of focus. We are left none the wiser about how it is and in what material and actual ways environment and human body interconnect even though this interconnection is espoused as our primary focus. Gilgun (2005) has drawn our attention to some of these material impacts in her suggestion that social workers adopt what she has called the RSGB assessment which is based on four strands of descriptive non-experimental research – Resilience, Schema Theory, Gender studies, and descriptive Brain Research. While she describes well the processes through which social workers go in arriving at assessment, the lack of a central focus for assessment or a hierarchy of issues or objects for attention returns us again to those familiar assessment protocols comprising lists of factors which require attention.

As it presently stands, person-in-environment assessment protocols are problematic because they (a) lack an integrated theoretical basis; (b) are not clear in demonstrating how and where and in what ways person and environment influence and shape each other; and (c) do not provide a central focus for the social worker's attention, nor even a rationale for the absence of such a focus.

Our argument in this book is that it is the human body which must be placed at the centre of our attention – and in a way which does not reduce the importance of insights derived from systems theory, ecological theory, social constructionism or critical theory. Rather, we are proposing that a focus on the body strengthens the validity and usefulness of these theoretical perspectives.

Finding the body in social work

We are asserting that the human body is simultaneously biological and social and that the separation of mind from body, and biological body from social effects which seems to characterize contemporary social work theorizing is problematic. Bodies and minds are not separate entities: indeed from a phenomenological perspective we recognize our body as the basis for our being in the world (Nettleton and Watson 1998; Howson 2004). Placing the body (simultaneously biological and social) at the centre of attention, theorizing and practicing more adequately reflects both the nature of lived experience and the currents of contemporary thinking within the social and neurosciences. Importantly, it needs to be noted that, in most instances where the term 'biological' appears throughout this book in reference to findings or areas of academic endeavour, we are referring more specifically to neuroscientific findings and the area of neuroscience. However, we deliberately use the term 'biological' to emphasize the difference between social scientific approaches to the body and those others in which we are interested.

Human bodies are a source and a resource of society (Shilling 2003). The physical structures of our body – brain, musculo-skeletal, endocrine, circulatory and respiratory systems – are what we use to build, explore, develop and exploit the environment. Importantly, our mental and technological capacities enable us to go beyond the so-called natural world, modifying and changing our bodies. Reproductive technologies, medical interventions which prolong life even when brain stem death has occurred, organ donation and transplantation challenge taken-for-granted notions of the body as static in structure and meaning (Seymour 1998; Howson 2003). Debating these issues in relation to contemporary social work theorizations of the life course problematizes the nature and meaning of the body itself and, despite posing ethical and moral dilemmas, also impels us to think differently about the materiality of the body and its supposedly universal journey across the life course.

Human bodies are sites and places where we witness the effects of society. From the insights of critical theory we become alert to the ways in which social norms and institutions set the parameters in which action occurs, enabling us to think about the ways in which structures of power organize the human collective, positioning some of us to do better than others. For example, poor distribution of the world's food resources results in starvation for some with highly visible effects on human bodies. Again, people diagnosed with HIV AIDS die in Africa whilst in New York they live well with good management of what has become a chronic illness. Marginalization and rejection is located in and on the bodies of those who are stigmatized and denied their rights as citizens. As we will discuss in later chapters, oppression and vilification can and does alter people's physical dispositions and capacities for action (words do hurt us). Social norms, institutions and discourses have a real impact on the bodily being of all of us.

Shilling (2003: 93; see also Burkitt 1999) offers an analysis of the body 'as simultaneously biological and social (in order to) provide a starting point ... for going beyond the limitations of naturalistic and social constructionist views of the body'. The biological body is in this most important sense 'unfinished' at birth: the meaning it holds for ourselves and others being socially constructed, 'enmeshed within and transformed by social relations' (2003: 176). This means that the relationship between our body and our sense of identity is simultaneously physical and social. The insights of feminist scholars, for example, have demonstrated well how gender is implicated in the construction and maintenance of social inequalities and thus in the constitution and development of society (Butler 2004; Grosz 1994, 1995).

While the approaches of perhaps less mainstream scholars such as Butler (2004) and Grosz (1994, 1995) almost 'etherealize' the body, their emphasis on the body as socially constructed offers a challenge to those views of the body as static and universalizing which are found within social work theorizing. In Butler's work, this emphasis on the body as being able to be constructed differently and as holding the potential to challenge the status quo or taken-for-grantedness of bodily locations in networks of power prompt us to think differently and to entertain the possibility of alternative constructions. Our relationships with others can thus be said to be embodied as well as social.

We are not advocating adoption of approaches to the body which 'de-materialize' it: on the contrary, our intent is to (re)establish the material, flesh and blood body at the centre of social work theorizing and practice. In this chapter we have been re-visiting the theoretical basis of social work and have been arguing that its attempts to integrate a position which adequately accounts for the nature and effect of person-in-environment relationships have suffered from a failure to do this. While we are in agreement that the four theoretical streams underlying social work's perspective retain their significance and salience, part of this failure can be attributed to lack of knowledge about or understanding of the ways in which bodies work.

Because our interest is in drawing together biological and sociological perspectives on the body in order to move towards a practice-oriented theory of the body for social work, we do not focus on 'alternative' or 'holistic' body therapies in abstraction. Whilst these might be referred to at various points because they offer helpful practices for changing or enhancing bodily conditions, our view is that they very often are based on dualistic conceptualizations, where 'mind' is charged with the responsibility for changing 'body'. Of course, we recognize that such practices as meditation and relaxation, and behaviours such as exercise and eating nutritious food, are vital to the maintenance of bodily well-being. However, our argument throughout this book is that the dichotomy between mind and body is a false one: psychological therapies, for example CBT, are thus acknowledged as having equal utility as – and indeed being – 'body therapies'.

The structure of this book

The book is divided into two parts. The first offers an extended discussion of those theories and issues pertaining to the body that are of greatest relevance to social work, whilst the second offers examples from a range of practice areas of how 'thinking body' can extend and augment practice.

In Chapter 2, 'The view from neuroscience', we focus on the body as defined by the biological sciences, what we might also think of as 'the private body', the counterpart to the social body. In this section, we provide answers to important questions such as, what is really known about mind, brain and behaviour. And, what have the fields of social and affective neuroscience learnt about such things as emotion, cognition and memory that means social workers should 'think again' or 'think differently' about the bodies with which they work?

In Chapter 3, 'Social bodies', we discuss some of the contemporary debates within sociology which are concerned with analysing and theorizing the body. These accounts sit well with what we have identified as the four central themes or preoccupations within social work theory and practice (as discussed earlier in this chapter) but augment them in ways which may enrich social work theory and practice. We introduce debates about the relationship between the body, self and identity; bodies, meanings and lived experience; bodies, discourses and texts. Of particular interest in this (necessarily brief) exploration is the work of Goffman (1959, 1963), Foucault (1977, 1978), Merleau-Ponty (2002), Grosz (1994, 1995), Butler (2004) amongst others.

In Chapter 4, 'Social work and the body: Towards a theoretical Framework', we draw together the main themes discussed in the previous chapters. In this chapter we suggest ways in which intersecting perspectives from biology and sociological theories on the body can construct one part of a new theoretical knowledge base for social work. This chapter offers theoretical constructs drawn from biology and sociology to enable a new way of conceptualizing the body which remains committed to social workers' interests in the person–environment nexus. We propose, through the metaphor of a camera lens, that the layers and dimensions of our material and socially constructed environment – some of which we are aware of and others of which we are not – can assist us in understanding how person and environment affect and are affected by each other. The implications of this conceptualization are to enable us to better comprehend the ways in which our bodies shape and are shaped by the social and material world.

We offer two mutually informing constructs. The first refers to the body cognizant social worker whose practice exemplifies an integration of physiological and social constructionist perspectives.

The second concept is that of corporeal capacity. Here we propose a framework for practice which recognizes our location as environmentally embodied beings, each with our own inherited strengths and weaknesses, shaped by the experiences and environments to which we are exposed (and to which we contribute) during our life courses.

Chapter 5 'The Body Cognizant Social Worker in Action' opens with what we have called the Body Cognizant Assessment Guide or BCAG. This is an assessment tool which demonstrates how the concepts of corporeal capacity and body cognizant social work may be exemplified in practice situations. This is followed by a description of the body cognizant social worker in action. It offers a view of the micro processes as well as the attention to details of those environmental and corporeal factors which impact the worker–client relationship and direct the social worker's focus. How the BCAG might be used to explore the client's location in micro, meso and macro environments is discussed. The importance of the social worker understanding the relevance of the client's and her own corporeal capacity will inform strategies and interventions. She will also bear in mind the client's stage of development, corporeal history and its implications for the achievement of change. Brief reference is also made to other practice methods – group work, community development, policy – and to the implications of body cognizant practice for professional development.

Part 2, Implications for Practice is organized by fields of practice and explores themes discussed in Part 1 of greatest relevance to each practice area.

Chapter 6 'Social Work, the Body and Mental Health' opens with discussion of issues relating to mental illness and emotional well-being. This chapter is more detailed than those following because it explores current knowledge arising from neuroscientific research pertaining to those brain regions and pathways as well as hormonal and neurocircuitry involved in the biology of mental disorders. This information is not only of central significance to social workers working with people with mental illness but is also vital to understanding practice in other areas such as child protection, ageing, health, and alcohol and other drug field. We envisage that readers will return to this chapter for clarification of issues relating to brain physiology when they encounter them in Chapters 7 to 10, which are thus shorter in length.

Each of the chapters in Part 2 brings together theory and research findings from sociology and biology as they refer to the substantive issue which is the focus of that chapter. The implications for social work practice from a body cognizant location are sketched. Each chapter concludes with a relevant practice example analysed from a corporeal capacity point of view, using the BCAG.

2 The View from Neuroscience

If the 'social body' comes into and recedes from focus in social work literature, the physiological body is even harder to find. The major practice theories upon which social work is reliant have provided little consideration of biology, and there are few professional journal articles that focus exclusively on the relevance of the physiological for social work. This provides some indication that social workers, in their daily practice, are largely unmindful of the physical body. In particular, social work lacks a strong literature on physiological aspects of phenomena such as emotion, cognition and sensation. It is on this set of concerns that this chapter focuses.

The wide berth given to biology by social work is, no doubt, related to assumptions about the general irrelevance of bodies for social work. As mentioned in the previous chapter, many social work theorists – including many of those who claim to reject mind–body 'dualism' – frequently refer to mind and body as though they were materially distinct from one another. (See, for example, Saleeby 1992; Tangenberg and Kemp 2002). A consequence of this belief is that the investigation and remedy of emotional suffering, delusional mind states and the like – those things that might be said to belong to 'mind' – is thought of as the province of one kind of profession, and anything dealing with nervous and immune systems, and hormones and so forth, another; usually the 'medical profession'. But what does it really mean to think of mind and body as separate, and where does this idea comes from?

Mind, brain and philosophy

How minds and brains are related has been under debate amongst theologians and philosophers for centuries. Before then, debate was concerned with how souls relate to bodies, the soul having once been considered the generator of not only moral behaviour but also consciousness. The earliest Greek philosophers did not distinguish between body and soul, but Plato, in the fifth century BC, believed that individuals' psyches or souls continued to exist after their physical bodies had expired. Aristotle, on the other hand, thought that psyche and body were not materially discrete and could only be distinguished conceptually. Throughout the middle ages, the common view was that souls and bodies were unified 'substances' but that only the soul was capable of living forever (LeDoux 2002: 16).

Unlike those theories of many of his influential predecessors – which were largely based on cosmological understandings – Descartes' theories of the mind–body relationship took account of both faith and science. Descartes, writing in the seventeenth century, believed that the mental and physical are different kinds of substances that meet in the part of the brain known as the pineal gland. Descartes equated the soul, or psyche, with consciousness and claimed that only humans had conscious control over their behaviour. In Descartes' conceptualization, the soul, or mental substance, had a causal relationship to the body; that is, behaviour sprang from the will or the psyche. The body, however, could not, in turn, direct the mental. The psyche/soul had another role; according to Descartes, it communicated with God (Voss 2002). Due to the significant logical flaws in Descartes' arguments (One question that may be asked: if mind and bodies are different kinds of things, how do they interact?), this substance of dualist per-spective has, within philosophical circles, long since lost favour. However, whilst most individuals are unfamiliar with the intricacies of Descartes' arguments, the idea that mind and body are distinct has retained general influence throughout the West. One reason for its continuing popularity may be that it offers support for the idea of immortality, a concept that is inherently appealing to humans.

Contemporary philosophical debate around the relationship of mind to body is currently dominated by functionalist, materialist and identity theory views. The first sees thoughts and feelings as a kind of software to the brain's hardware, or mind as a function of the brain. Eliminative materialists see conscious thought – what we think of as mind – as a kind of epiphenomenon; that is, mind as a kind of irrelevant by-product of an organism's efforts to keep itself alive. Those who argue for a type identity relationship between mind and brain believe the two are directly equatable or, in other words, that highly specific types of brain activity will always give rise to the same kinds of thoughts (see Kendler 2000 for a concise overview of philosophical positions).

Most biologists or, in particular, neuroscientists, occupy what philosophers call an 'explanatory dualist' position. That is, most believe that whilst mind and brain can be distinguished *discursively*, they cannot be differentiated materially, that 'mind' and 'brain', in other words, refer to different perspectives on the same object, with the former referring to a first person or psychological perspective and the latter to a third person or biological perspective. (Unlike other theories, it does not seek to answer the so-called *hard* problem of *why* brain gives rise to mind.) This position is supported by evidence that certain types of neural patterns reliably coincide with certain thought patterns, emotions and behaviours, and that types of damage to the brain result in predictable behavioural or cognitive deficits (Kandel 1998). Grasping that mind and brain refer to the same object allows comprehension of a wide range of important concepts such as that the distinction frequently made between physical and mental illness is essentially a false one: mental illness is no more or less physical than, say, diabetes; the difference is in terms of how each manifests physiologically. A question that the inseparability of mind and brain throws up for social work is: how to determine what and how much social workers need to know about the body? Whilst we do not provide a definitive answer to this question here, we discuss concepts and findings from biology and, in particular, neuroscience, that are useful to the social work endeavour.

Why the brain and not just the mind?

If thoughts and feelings, and brain functions are different sides to same coin, cannot what we learn about thoughts and feelings through studying the brain also be learnt through phenomenological investigation? In other words, why examine thoughts and feelings from a biological perspective at all? Indeed, it must be noted that much of the contribution neuroscience has made to the understanding of human psychology has been by way of providing support for theories already developed by sociologists and social and cognitive psychologists. In fact, the reason that a biological perspective becomes important is that although we may think we 'know our own minds', much of what gives rise to particular of our thoughts and feelings are things of which we are unconscious. The psychological unconscious differs considerably from the Freudian unconscious. Whereas the latter refers to mental objects that, through the process of analysis, can be brought to awareness, the psychological or biological unconscious contains those things that, by virtue of the brain's organization, can never be accessed. Damasio refers to a range of things that make up part of this unconscious. These include dispositions individuals have acquired that lie dormant, the 'quiet remodeling' of such dispositions and the knowledge informing homeostatic processes (2000: 228). Researchers such as Bargh and Chartrand (1999) have shown that a range of mental functions, including attitude and evaluation formation, as well as emotions and motivations, occur non-consciously and automatically. Their findings are discussed further below.

Social psychologists can infer a certain amount about why and how certain mental processes occur unconsciously, but biologists have the advantage of being able to literally see inside our heads. Neuroscientific research has helped determine such as how emotion informs decision-making, and that emotions are a 'whole body' process that could not have been deduced through the application of traditional social scientific research methods, namely introspection and social inquiry. Nevertheless, the ability of biology to shed light on psychology is relatively recent.

Research on the biological bases of human thought and so on, as noted, is largely focused on the brain but, prior to the twentieth century, a barrier separated study of the brain from the rest of biology; where the 'language' of biology was biochemistry, the brain was mostly understood in neuroanatomical and electrophysiological terms (Kandel and Squire 2001: 118). A series of breakthroughs during the last two decades, however – including the discovery of how, at the molecular level, cells differentiate, communicate and change in response to stimuli – has allowed the brain to be examined and understood much as other organs are. At the same time, the relationship between biology and psychology has been redefined.

Tools of neuroscience

Neuroscience or the neurosciences are focused on the study of the nervous system and, in particular, the brain. Affective neuroscience is dedicated to studying the neural substrates involved in the production and regulation of emotion. Social neuroscience is interested in working out how other people 'get under our skin'. Today, these areas of knowledge contribute as much to our understanding of emotion, conscious thought and memory as the social sciences, which is not to say that neuroscientific knowledge is complete. Just as there are many questions about social behaviour, emotions and the like, that the social sciences have yet to answer, there are still significant gaps in neuroscientific knowledge. But where the expansion of social scientific knowledge has arguably slowed in recent times, the continual refinement of neuroscientific research tools suggests we can expect important new discoveries from this field for some time yet.

The main research tools currently used by neuroscientists are neuroimaging, and post-mortem and animal studies. Animal studies are important to neuroscience for the reason that rodent brains may be subjected to manipulations that, due to ethical reasons, human brains may not. Whilst the human brain is by no means identical to the brains of rodents, or even those of other primates, all brains of mammals share a number of important similarities. There are areas of the human brain (in particular, in the neocortex) that other animals are thought not to possess – those areas associated with language, for example – but as Le Doux (1999) points out, brain evolution is basically conservative; most brain regions and systems have been preserved in their basic structure and function over a millennia. The ways in which rat brains and human brains process sound, for example, are highly comparable. As such, the study of rodent brains has led to important hypotheses about human physiology and pathophysiology. (See Panksepp 1998 for a full justification of the use of animal studies.)

Post-mortem studies are crucial to the work undertaken by neuroscientists, having provided the 'gold standard' for the diagnosis of a range of disorders (Davidson et al. 2002: 488). Like other research methods, post-mortem studies can provide information about the origins and physiological characteristics of a disorder, as well as those genes that are potentially implicated in a disorder's development. Examination of post-mortem tissue offers the only means through which those alterations in neural circuitry that give rise to psychiatric disorders can be examined at molecular and cellular levels.

Neuroimaging is the most recent of research methods open to brain scientists. Neuroscientists currently employ a number of neuroimaging technologies, each of which provides its own kind of information about the brain. Positron emission tomography (PET), one of the earlier imaging methods, is still widely used in a range of research and practice contexts. By measuring the brain's blood flow – which increases in line with the brain's metabolism – PET is able to indicate which areas of the brain are working hardest on particular tasks. Functional Magnetic Image Resonance (fMRI) also measures blood flow (Andreasen 2001: 136). Electroencephalography (EEG) measures brainwaves, the patterns created by neuron oscillation (see Kandel, Schwartz and Jessell 2000: 914 for detailed description). Magnetoencephalography (MEG) also picks up neuron oscillation, through detection of neurons' magnetic pulsing. Neuroimaging equipment continues to undergo improvement, with size of brain areas able to be examined at one time continually expanding.

Neuroscience and social work goals

Discussed in the previous chapter were ways in which sociology can contribute to social work's understanding or conceptualization of the individual person in their psychosocial world, human beings as active agents, and the influence of social structures on human life, as well as social work's practice with the vulnerable and marginalized. Recent findings from neuroscience also have much to offer social work theory and practice. In particular, neuroscience helps to clarify the following:

• the factors that help determine differences between individuals in terms of their levels of resilience, their temperaments, and so on; and how the psychological 'world' and the micro and macro environments are related – in particular, it corrects the belief that environment and person are easily separable;

- the extent to which human beings can be considered 'active agents' or masters of their own destinies;
- how social structures impact humans' health and well-being, and contribute to keeping some individuals marginalized and/or vulnerable.

Below we offer neuroscientific findings relevant to these concerns. Prior to this, we provide a brief overview of brain structure and function. This next section will be a little difficult to absorb all at once but will be useful to refer back to for clarification of particular terms and so on to be encountered later in the book.

How the brain works

The brain is composed of different regions that are more or less important for different tasks but that generally do not perform any major function on their own. Rather, the various brain functions are dependent upon particular circuits of neural cells, or *neurons*. There are billions of neurons in the human brain. These cells communicate with each other directly through a process called *neurotransmission*, to be explained presently. The core of each cell is referred to as the *cell body* and performs a number of important functions such as storing genetic material and manufacturing proteins. Extending out from the cell body are *nerve fibres*, of which there are two kinds, *dendrites* and *axons*. Axons are input channels, and dendrites, output channels. Normally, cells have only one axon, but each axon branches several times thus allowing a single cell to contact many cells at once. In most instances, axons carry messages to other cells by making contact with dendrites, but sometimes they connect with other axons or even cell bodies directly.

'Messages' sent by neurons are in the form of biologically produced electrical impulses known as *action potentials*. An action potential is initiated at the point of meeting between a cell's body and its axon. It travels down the axon to the terminal where chemicals referred to as *neurotransmitters* are stored. The chemicals are released by this first, or presynaptic, cell into the synapse; the synapse being the space that exists between cells. The neurotransmitters cross the synapse and bind to spines or other portions of the receiving cell which, in this context, is called the post-synaptic cell (see Figure 2.1). The receiving points on cells are referred to as *receptors*. The energy from just one cell is usually not sufficient to trigger a response in another. In cases where several presynaptic cells make contact with the post-synaptic cell at around the same time, however, an action potential in the new cell will be generated.

Just as certain parts of the brain or types of brain activity need, at times, to be stimulated, they need, at other times, to be checked. For this reason, whilst some neurons are *excitatory*, others are *inhibitory*. The main role of *projection* neurons, those neurons that can send messages to neurons some distance from themselves, is to 'turn on' the next lots of neurons in a (neural network) hierarchy. *Interneurons* only send messages to those that are neighbouring and process information within a specific level of a neural network. A major function performed by these neurons is to decrease the chance that a post-synaptic neuron will fire an action potential.

The main neurotransmitter – neurotransmitters being those chemicals through which one neuron triggers a response in the next – used by excitatory neurons is an amino acid called *glutamate*. The main neurotransmitter used by inhibitory neurons is *gamma-aminobutyric acid* (GABA). Whether a post-synaptic cell fires or not is largely dependent on the interactions between GABA and glutamate. Too much glutamate activity in the brain is dangerous; it is associated with vascular disorders of the brain as well as epilepsy. Overactivity of GABA can also be detrimental.

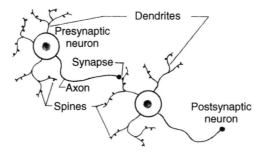

Figure 2.1   Neurons

Brain activity is also highly dependent upon chemicals called neuromodulators, of which there are different kinds. There is some controversy over which chemicals should be referred to as neurotransmitters, and which modulators, however the following are classified, here, as modulators for the reason that that they generally have slower acting and longer lasting effects than the kinds of neurotransmitters just described. Like neurotransmitters, neuromodulators are chemical messengers that are released from one cell and go on to affect others. Also, like neurotransmitters, they can be excitatory or inhibitory.

Neuropeptides can increase or reduce the effect of those neurotransmitters which are released from the same sites. Generally, peptides are more functionally specific than other neurotransmitters. Particular neuropeptides are crucial to different emotional systems. Among the better known peptides are endorphins.

Monoamines, which are most likely to be considered merely as neurotransmitters (and, at times, in this text, are referred to as such), have been a particular focus of affective research in previous years. The monoamines include substances such as serotonin, dopamine and norepinephrine. They are found in few areas but can project to a wide range of areas in the brain. Like other modulators, monoamines can aid or inhibit the actions of glutamate or GABA. Monoamines can produce state changes in a number of brain regions at the same time.

Hormones, with which readers will have some familiarity, are also modulators. They differ from the other classes already mentioned in that, in most cases, they are released from bodily organs into the circulatory system before travelling on to the brain. The brain also produces hormones. Amongst the most important hormones is *cortisol*, which is released from the adrenal gland. Examples of other hormones are *estrogen* and *testosterone*.

What is interesting and perhaps important to note is that the same transmitters and modulators can be involved in different functions. Le Doux states, 'what makes a sound different from a sight, a memory different from a perception, a fear different from a desire is not so much the chemistry involved but instead the specific circuits in which the chemicals act' (2002: 61).

Amongst the more important components of cells are *genes*. Genes have two main functions, one of which is to dictate specific features of an organism, the other of which is to manufacture proteins. Proteins are organic compounds central to the structure and function of all living cells. Many social scientists are only familiar with genes' first role and thus understand genes to be static determinants of individuals' broad characteristics. It is ignorance of genes' second function, discussed further below, that is the source of many social scientists' resistance to learning about the role of genes in shaping mood, personality and so forth. Far from being static, however, in their second role, genes are continually being influenced by environmental factors. The continual changes in the amount and kind of proteins expressed by genes are what allow the brain to change in response to new learning, medication response and so on. In other words, changes in neuronal firing or connections between neurons are only possible because of the adaptive capacity of genes.

Structure of the brain

As mentioned, cells assemble into particular brain regions that are more or less important for different tasks. Some of the most important regions are as large as a few centimetres and others are microscopic. That particular brain areas are more involved than others in particular tasks is not to say, however, that brain functions are localized. From the late eighteenth century until many years later, it was believed that the brain was divided into areas that were entirely responsible for particular functions and capacities. This was partly because stimulation of different parts of the brain with electrodes tends to result in predictable behavioural and emotional responses. We now know that the brain is considerably more complex than this and that most brain tasks require the proper functioning of complex neural circuits, many of which run from the lowest to the highest parts of the brain. So, whilst damage to very specific areas of the brain can result in the loss of particular abilities, this is only because such damage represents disruption to parts of relevant neural circuits. Specific kinds of damage that correlate with particular disabilities and psychological and emotional conditions are discussed in the second part of this book.

The human brain is composed of several major regions. These include the *cerebrum*, which is composed of the left and right cerebral hemispheres and a thick bundle of fibres called the *corpus callosum* that joins the two halves. The outermost layer of the cerebrum is the *cerebral cortex* (cortex means 'outer part'), which allows the most complex aspects of information processing and decision-making in humans. The cerebral cortex is divided into specific regions, including *frontal, parietal, temporal* and *occipital* lobes. The frontal lobes are most involved in planning, remembering, and other abstract thinking tasks and the parietal lobes in integrating sensory information and aspects of visuospatial processing. The temporal lobes perform functions associated with language and memory. The *cerebellum*, another important part of the brain, is also involved in certain types of cognitive functions as well as a range of motor functions. The *diencephalon* contains the *thalamus*, which plays a significant role in relaying information from sensory receptors to other brain areas, and the *hypothalamus*, which performs a range of regulatory functions aimed at maintaining homeostasis, or internal equilibrium. The *mesencephalon*, or midbrain, relays impulses between higher and lower parts and of the brain and is also important for optic and auditory reflexes. The *pons* conveys information from the cerebrum to the cerebellum and is important to the control of voluntary movement. The *brainstem* is the main means by which the higher parts of the brain send information to and receive information from the spinal cord and peripheral nerves (see Figure 2.2). It is vital for a range of important functions such as breathing and control of heart rate. Other more specific brain regions and their functions will be discussed further throughout this text.

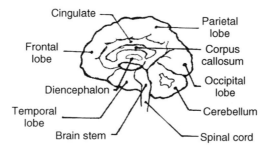

Figure 2.2 Human Brain

It is important to note that the brain changes throughout the life course of an individual in both crude or generalized and minor, individualized ways. Throughout this book we discuss some of the ways in which the brain responds to environmental and, in particular, social environmental stimuli.

One significant determinant of differences between individuals is sex. Factors that are consistently inherited in a sex-specific fashion are those on the sex (XX and XY) chromosomes. In humans, a gene on the Y chromosome, called SRY, causes the embryonic gonad to develop into a testis rather than an ovary. Testes secrete hormones that act on specific cells in the body and brain that cause them to develop in either a masculine or feminine fashion. Male and female brains differ in terms of their hormonal environments, with female brains generally being subjected to more estrogen and progesterone and male brains to testosterone. Male and female brains also show minor differences in structure and in function; men and women have been shown in some studies, for example, to use slightly different parts of their brains for certain language tasks (For example, Jaeger, Lockwood, Van Valin, Kemmerer, Murphy and Wack 1998). Some studies also have found men and women to differ slightly in terms of their abilities, with men often having been found to have superior spatial skills (see, for example, Tlauka, Brolese, Pomeroy and Hobbs 2005). Rogers, however, argues that differences in abilities are fractional and/or just as likely caused by social factors as inherent biological differences (Rogers 1999, chapter 2).

The extent to which behavioural differences between men and women can be explained by differences in hormonal milieu or structure is a matter of some controversy. Rogers argues that differences between male and female brains are not of a sufficient size to explain the very different roles and behaviours that men and women have, to date, adopted, and, further, that we cannot be certain that structural and functional differences are not themselves caused by behavioural or environmental factors (Rogers 1999). Reinisch and colleagues have suggested that biological and environmental factors have a 'multiplier effect', that genetic and hormonal factors cause small differences in the behaviour of males and females but that these differences become 'augmented by successive interactions between the individual and the social environment' (Reinisch and colleagues in Rogers 1999: 131).

Regardless of such issues as the direction of causation there are important differences between male and female brains in terms of their responses to medication and so forth. Neuroscientific research is only just beginning to uncover, and take into account, the differences between male and female brains. Thus, whilst the findings on emotion, memory and other factors presented below are assumed to be applicable to both sexes, it is possible that future studies will reveal one or another to be relevant to men or women exclusively.

Environment

As mentioned in Chapter 1, a central perspective of social work is that clients should be seen as 'persons-in-environment'. Yet 'persons' and 'environment' have been highly under-theorized within social work theory and, certainly, not been adequately considered from material perspectives. Material or biological perspectives on persons and environment are useful for social work for many reasons, not least of which is that they shed light upon how the two interact.

Because *social* environment, more so than any other kind of environment, is of interest to social work, it could be argued that social workers need to know little about 'physical' or non-social environments. But this would only be true if social relationships alone impacted individuals' social capabilities, self-esteem and general well-being. In fact, certain broader environmental hazards also affect these things. Particular chemicals used in manufacturing may cause developmental delays (Koger, Schettler and Weiss 2005), and 'noise pollution', great psychological stress and so on (Evans and Kantrowitz 2002). We do not claim social workers need to understand the mechanisms through which a full range of environmental phenomena impact individuals. Rather, we argue that by having a more nuanced understanding of environment, social workers can be more alert to the kinds of dangers that exist in clients' surrounds.

How we define 'environment' is, in part, dependent upon our purpose for defining it. Social work's main interest in environment relates to its effect upon individuals and social groups. Biological theorizations most useful to social work, then, take environment to be any determinant of an individual's well-being that is distinguishable from those things innate to an individual. In fact, establishing the relative contributions made by genes and environment, or nature and nurture, to those things relevant to welfare – 'medical' illness, temperament, and so on – is very difficult. The best means of trying to disentangle the relative effects of these are twin and adoption studies. Twin studies involve the comparison of monozygotic twins (who have the same genetic profile) and dizygotic twins (who have different genetic profiles) for rates of concordance for particular traits or illnesses. Adoption studies compare genetic and adopted children from the same families for trait concordance.

Meaney argues that it is nonsensical to talk about the relative contributions of nature and nurture to given characteristics. This is because, as mentioned above, genetic expression is determined, in part, by environmental factors. More specifically, genes are regulated by hormonal and neurotransmitter activity, and such activity is influenced by an individual's social or broader environments. In Meaney's words, genes and environment are in constant dialogue (2001: 50). He states 'at no point in life is the operation of the genome independent of the context in which it functions' (2001: 52). The ability of environment to impact genes becomes clearer upon consideration of such conditions as phenylketonuria. Phenylketonuria, which can result in particular kinds of brain damage, is caused by the absence of a gene crucial to the digestion of a certain amino acid in the food. The condition can, however, be prevented from emerging where individuals avoid, from an early age, ingesting phenylelanines (Cacioppo, Bernston, Sheridan and McClintock 2000: 830). Findings from a range of studies using mice and primates suggest that rearing or care experiences can also impact genetic expression in such a way as to prevent the emergence of particular negative cognitive and social characteristics (Bennett et al. 2002; Weaver et al. 2004).

In a long-term sense, the interactions between genes and environment are particularly complex. Individuals' temperaments, for example, can be affected by such things as chemicals they were exposed to in utero or as children. The temperaments individuals develop will, in turn, cause them to create certain kinds of environments in which they will encounter experiences or objects capable of further modifying their physiology, or temperament, and so on. An individual may be, for example, subjected to excess cortisol (discussed in more detail elsewhere) in the womb thus causing her to develop an anxious temperament. The individual's excessive anxiety may lead her, as an adult, to move to a high security environment, such as a gated community. The reduced social contact she experiences as a result of where she lives and other aspects of her environment may serve to exacerbate her anxiety, thus triggering an illness that may not have emerged had she lived in a different kind of community, and so forth.

Understanding that 'environment' can refer to anything that is non-genetic can assist social workers' efforts at imagining the full range of factors that pose risks for their clients. Cooper (1987) offers a categorization of environmental hazards (based on a typology by McDowall) that has particular utility for social work. In recognition of the different pathways through which environmental factors affect individuals, it encompasses both biological and sociological conceptualizations of environment. It refers to natural physico-chemical, man-made physico-chemical, biological/organic, macrosocial, and micro- or psychosocial (in Cooper 2001: 97) hazards. Cooper puts forward another model that emphasizes factors hazardous to *psychological* health and that also takes time into consideration. On one axis he places biological and chemical noxae, physical hazards, and political and social mass phenomena and on the other: sudden increases (in hazard), rapid environmental change, and slow (environmental) change, to reflect the differential impact hazards have depending upon the time frame in which they occur. Examples of chemical noxae that may occur suddenly are chemical spills. An example of a rapidly occurring physical hazard is military service, and an example of a slowly changing social situation is long-stay psychiatric care (Cooper 2001: 98).

Given that such conceptual models have been structured around considerations of *how* different environmental hazards affect humans, such models also help social workers establish at what points they can and need to intervene. In the next chapter, we propose our own framework for conceptualizing environment.

If thinking about environments from the point-of-view of biology has utility for social work, what is it that biology can inform us about the persons who dwell within them, and those things most important to them: their emotions, ways of seeing the world, and relationships with those around them?

What is emotion?

Emotions are central to social work, most obviously at the level of practice with individuals but at every level of intervention. Were social workers *not* concerned with emotions, addressing injustice or inequality (through community work and policy development) would be an abstract or merely intellectual endeavour. It is curious then, that social workers on the whole know little about what emotions *are* or, at least, are yet to really consider the ramifications of recent discoveries about emotion within neuroscience.

Past theories posited that the experience of emotion was anything but inherent, that we were socialized to feel emotions. Other theories suggested that whilst emotions were more or less 'natural', they were essentially a product of conscious thought. Social psychologists such as Paul Ekman (1993) established earlier last century that there is a universal set of emotions and that, whilst their expression may differ slightly from place to place, the same emotions are experienced by humans in every culture. Neuroscientists have clarified the 'naturalness' of emotion. From the perspective of neuroscience, emotions are physiological processes that initiate human action (Schulkin, Thompson and Rosen 2003: 16); without emotional investment in outcomes there is little we would be motivated to do. Emotions are governed by separate, though overlapping, neural circuits, each of which has served a distinct purpose throughout evolution; anger, for example, motivates an organism to fight (thus increasing its chances of survival when threatened).

Neuroscience has established several other significant matters about emotion. A number of neuroscientists have helped determine, first, that much of our emotional processing is unconscious; that is, we can make 'emotional judgments' about, and respond emotionally to, stimuli without our conscious mind being engaged. This is possible because, as explored most fully by Le Doux (1999), there are two neural routes through which we process emotionally salient information. One slower route involves the neocortex which, as discussed, is the seat of conscious thought. The other circuit, the so-called quick and dirty route, can allow us to make rapid but imprecise appraisals of stimuli without conscious awareness. This is important for generating an immediate response to threat. We have all jumped away from a fast approaching vehicle or put our hands out in front of us when we have fallen split seconds before we registered we were in danger. This is made possible by the existence of this latter emotional appraisal circuit. Central to this circuit, at least in relation to fear, are connections between the amygdala and thalamus.

Second, as researched by Damasio and colleagues, emotions per se are not merely a product of cognition but require the whole body for generation. In fact, considered from one perspective, emotions are *representations* of body states, meaning that emotions arise as a consequence of our brain's ability to receive messages about body state changes in response to stimuli (Damasio 1996). To expand, in its role of maintaining homeostasis, the brain is constantly receiving feedback from a range of bodily systems. Different body states are represented in the brain in the form of specific kinds of neural patterns. When an individual faces challenge – positive or negative – the body responds in particular ways. Heart rate and blood flow, for example, will increase or decrease as will the activity of certain hormones. Evidence suggests that emotions are the neural patterns created by these kind of changes or that the brain, in other words, is informed about *outside* environmental by changes in the *internal* environment.

And third, rather than rationalization or logic being distinct from emotion, much logical decision-making is likely *dependent* upon our capacity to experience emotion. The development of this hypothesis has relied largely upon research with individuals who have certain kinds of brain lesions. Typically, individuals who have sustained particular kinds of damage to the ventromedial prefrontal region retain normal general intelligence but are neither able to experience normal emotion nor make rational decisions about matters with personal and social ramifications (Bechara 2004: 30). Such individuals may, for example, take considerable financial risks or spend inordinate amounts of time on single tasks at work. Damasio argues that one reason why damage to this area has such an impact is that, under normal circumstances, it receives feedback about the body state. This is important because humans are reliant upon such feedback in daily decision-making. Indeed, there is much evidence to suggest that making decisions about a matter that will have an emotionally significant outcome causes an individual's body state to change, in most cases only fleetingly. When considering bad outcomes, for example, an individual will experience unpleasant gut reactions, an experience that 'marks' an image, hence being described as a 'somatic marker'. This signal will lead him to reject immediately the negative course of action and thus make him choose among fewer alternatives. 'There is still room for cost/benefit analysis and proper deductive competence, but only after the automated step drastically reduces the number of options.' (Damasio 1996: 173). Somatic markers, Damasio argues, may not accompany all decisions, but they make decision-making more efficient. A number of recent studies have provided support for the 'somatic marker hypothesis'. (See e.g. Batson, Engel and Fridell 1999; Suzuki, Hirota, Takasawa and Shigemasu 2003; and Carter and Pasqualini 2004.)

To make things more complicated, Damasio also has strong reason to believe that there is also an 'as-if' loop that operates in the brain (1996: 184). That is, the *somatosensory cortex* – that part of the brain that maps certain physical sensations – is, in certain circumstances, able to behave as if it were receiving signals about body state and thus influence decision-making as if a *real* body state change had occurred.

Negative and positive dispositions

Whilst many generalizations can be made about the functions emotions serve and *how* individuals experience different emotions, there are considerable differences amongst individuals in terms of general disposition: whilst some individuals experience many moments of joy each day or drift through life being comfortably content, others of us have a gloomy outlook and seem permanently on the edge of depression or anxiety. Neuroscience sheds some light on the reasons why this is so.

Whilst social relationships and life experiences help *shape* attitude and disposition, our chances of developing certain kinds of dispositions are determined very early. Positive affect is associated with 'approach' or proactive behaviour, whereas negative affect is associated with withdrawal and inhibition. Kagan and colleagues have found that infants who responded with particular fear (with sudden jerky movements or crying) to a range of novel stimuli at four months were likely to react fearfully to at least one follow-up test at fourteen and twenty-one months. They were also more likely than other children, at four and a half years old, to be inhibited around a stranger. The researchers hypothesize that this is due to a particularly high level of activity in the amygdala (Kagan, Snidman and Arcus 1998).

The amygdala has a number of functions but, of relevance here, is that it is central to both emotional appraisal and the fear response. All sensory information travels to the amygdala. Where threat is detected it signals the sympathetic nervous system (SNS). The SNS is a component of the autonomic nervous system and has, as its counterpart, the parasympathetic nervous system (PNS). Whereas the PNS produces 'calm' throughout the body, the SNS readies the body for 'fight or flight'. Activation of the SNS is associated with a range of automatic responses including increases in blood pressure and skin temperature. Since it is through the amygdala that the SNS is able to control heart rate, Kagan measured the heart rate of his subjects whilst they were still in the womb. Individuals who, in utero, had a heart rate of 140 beats per minute or more had a particularly high chance of being later tested as reactive (Kagan 1999).

Other physiological tests are able to predict temperament. Davidson and colleagues have discovered that a major predictor of positivity, or approach-related behaviours, versus negativity and a tendency towards withdrawal is the level of activity in the prefrontal cortex (PFC). In most individuals, activity in the left and right sides of the PFC is asymmetrical. Children through to adults who have greater activation in the left side are more likely to have a positive disposition (Davidson 2001). In fact, activation levels in the PFC is a better predictor of how subjects will respond to emotionally provocative tests than are subjects' own reports of their dispositions. A greater level of activation in the left-PFC is also associated with higher reactivity to positively valenced stimuli, a faster or fuller recovery from exposure to negative stimuli, and a greater ability to suppress negative affect (Davidson 2004). Whereas the left side of the brain is generally associated with positive emotion, the right side is associated with negative emotion.

Normal individuals show greater right-sided activity in response to negative stimuli, and anxious individuals frequently show an abnormal amount of activity on this side in resting (2004: 1398). Generally speaking, individuals who enjoy the greatest sense of well-being are those who show the greatest ability to reduce right-sided activity (Davidson 2004: 1406).

The above does not indicate that individuals' emotional destinies are entirely predetermined. As discussed further below, factors such as the amount of social support received throughout life influence the temperaments that individuals develop. Individuals particularly stand to benefit from attentive and compassionate caregiving in their early years. Urry and colleagues (2004) hypothesize that activities individuals undertake and perspectives they adopt may also influence temperament or the tendency to feel happy. Urry and colleagues define 'hedonic well-being' as the subjective sense that 'life is satisfying', and 'eudaimonic well-being', as informed by possession of a sense of purpose, mastery and self-acceptance. They found that greater left-sided activation correlates with both hedonic and eudaimonic well-being. They interpreted this to mean that being 'active' in life – taking up challenges, initiating relationships, and so on – may lead to greater happiness (Urry, Nitschke, Dolski, Jackson, Dalton, Mueller, Rosenkranz, Ryff, Singer and Davidson 2004).

Interpretation in emotion

Whilst, as explained above, emotion is an automatic process, central to human cognition, there is still much room for interpretation of emotions, of their source and what they mean. Many things can impact our emotional state, both internal and external: being hungry, for example, can make us irritable or seeing someone we love across a room can make us happy. But, as neuroscience has clarified, there are a number of other things that have no *conscious* component that affect us emotionally. This situation can have negative consequences for individuals with poor self-esteem. Kagan suggests that children with low self-esteem will be more inclined than others to interpret 'unexpected bursts of activity in autonomic targets' (2001: 196) that result in feelings of stress as indications of their own wrongdoing.

Adults, too, frequently misidentify the source of sudden changes in mood. If, on the way to work, an individual feels irritable she may infer she is starting to dislike her job. In fact, the cause of her irritability may be the tightness of a new pair of shoes she has ceased to consciously notice. Below we discuss other determinants of emotion or mood which will not, in every instance, be given conscious representation.

Amongst those things that can affect mood are exercise and diet. Randomized controlled trials with both younger adults and the elderly have almost invariably found that modest daily or weekly amounts of aerobic or anaerobic exercise benefits affect and that, conversely, inactivity can lead to poor mood. The foods we choose to eat can also have a significant impact upon our feelings of well-being. Biological investigation has helped us understand the reasons for this. An excess of sugar, for example, can contribute to temporary feelings of euphoria or high energy in some individuals due to its impact on insulin levels. (Exercise and diet are discussed further in Chapter 6.) The amount of oxygen the brain receives can also affect emotion. Those who take in abnormal amounts as a result of poor breathing habits often experience strong feelings of anxiety (see e.g. Meuret, Ritz, Wilhelm and Roth 2005).

Kosslyn and colleagues argue that dispositions, more so than circumstances, are crucial determinants of how we feel (Cacioppo, Davidson, Hugdahl, Lovallo, Spiegel and Rose 2002: 345). This is an important assertion in light of social work's emphasis upon *circumstances* for individual's well-being. The evidence suggests that in order to ameliorate *individual* suffering, as much needs be done to change clients' emotional responses and ways of thinking as to address their situations or environments.

Emotions across the life span

Whilst the assumption is often made, it is anything but clear whether emotion in children and emotions in adults can be considered to be the same phenomena. Indeed the circuitry involved in the production (and regulation) of different emotions undergo significant (general and experience-based) changes between individuals' infant and adult years. Connections between the cortex and the lower parts of the brain involved in emotion remain immature for some years (Schore 2003). The implication of this is that interventions or remedies designed to improve disposition that work for one age group may not necessarily work with another. The emotional brain in both childhood and aging is explored further in the second part of this book.

Preliminary evidence suggests that suppression of negative emotion, although necessary in many social situations, may be injurious to health. Gross (2002) has found that psychological reframing or *reappraisal* of situations to avoid experiencing may be beneficial for health, but that attempts to dampen negative emotion after its onset may increase heart rate. Increased heart rate over time can lead to cardiovascular disease. It has also been shown that individuals' ability to recall information about a situation in which they employed emotional suppression will be compromised (see Richards 2004). A significant psychological consequence of suppressing negative emotion is decreased ability to experience positive emotion. Research is needed to clarify the long-term effects of this strategy upon neural mechanisms associated with the experience of various emotions. These early findings on reappraisal versus suppression, nevertheless, highlight the importance of philosophical outlook for health; the better developed and more positive an individual's world view, the more easily he will be able to see situations in a new light.

Social structures

The way in which our societies are structured – whether there is a high or low level of social stratification, and whether there are significant differences in terms of the opportunities that are offered to different social groups – has significant impact upon the health of the members of a society. Kagan refers to findings that individuals living in poverty are especially affected by their material circumstances – emotionally and otherwise – when they live side by side with individuals who are better off (2001: 180). Status, this is to say, is a more powerful determinant of well-being than poverty per se. Humans are inherently social; they prefer to be with others than to live alone and develop identities in relation to others. Evolutionary theorists such as Massey (2002) argue that the desire to belong to groups evolved because co-habitation increases chances of survival. And, indeed, countless social psychologists and researchers have found evidence that social isolation and exclusion, as well as neglect and abuse, have a range of negative consequences for health.

As discussed above, one of social work's main arguments has been that social support – as provided by friends, family members, and members of working and local communities – is central to individuals' well-being. Several kinds of findings from social neuroscience support this claim as well as findings on attachment. Social researchers, from Bowlby and Winnicott on, have focused on the importance of infants' attachment – the emotional bond of infants to their mothers or main caregivers – to infants' intellectual and emotional development. 'Secure' attachment – where an infant holds positive affection for his or her mother whilst showing an age-appropriate level of independence – has been identified as a predictor of individuals' later emotional, cognitive and behavioural functioning.

Neuroscientists such as Schore have explored attachment from a physiological perspective. Schore claims that visual and auditory affective transmissions between mothers' and infants' 'emotionally expressive faces' can 'act as signals that coregulate their internal states' (2003: 214). The right-hemisphere of the brain is dominant in the processing of facial expressions and emotional information, as well as the expression of emotional states. In all humans, detection and reflection of others' facial expressions occurs automatically and unconsciously; a phenomenon described by Hatfield, Cacioppo, and Rapson as 'primitive emotional catagion' (Schore 2003: 224). In most cases, facial expressions are coupled with physiological activity associated with particular emotions. That connections to the autonomic nervous system are also highly lateralized to the right-brain means eye contact with others can trigger negative or positive arousal instantly. Repeated synchronization of emotional states, especially between mothers and infants, facilitates bonding.

The more frequently particular psychological states – including emotional states – are experienced the more likely they are to re-emerge. Infants' healthy emotional development and normal autonomic functioning are, thus, greatly dependent upon infants having frequent eye contact with their mothers whilst they are experiencing positive mood states. (See Chapter 6 for further discussion.)

Assistance with emotional regulation is not only provided by mothers to their children. Schore (2003) suggests one of the main functions performed by therapists is to assist clients to gain control over their own emotions. Therapists can help clients experience negative emotions in a 'controlled' environment, teaching them ways to 'come back' or recover from strong emotion. This is also achieved through what Schore refers to as 'right-brain to right-brain' communication, that which occurs through sustained eye contact.

Positive social relationships continue to offer protection throughout life, and an absence of these, or poor relationships, can provide harm through changes within our nervous, endocrine and immune systems. Discussed above is one component of the stress or 'fight or flight' response – the SNS – which, amongst other things, increases heart rate and blood pressure. The SNS also releases adrenaline and norepinephrine (or noradrenaline) from the adrenal glands. As a category of psychological stressor, adverse social circumstances are particularly likely to trigger sustained SNS activity. Uchino and colleagues (2001) found, in one study, that both older and younger subjects who reported a high number of 'ambivalent' social relationships showed greater sympathetic control of heart rate during stress. Sustained SNS activity is associated with a range of negative outcomes. Cacioppo, Berntson, Sheridan and McClintock refer, for example, to a study that sought to establish the relative risk of increased blood pressure for 103 young men who had either a positive or negative family history of hypertension (2000: 833). The researchers in this study found after 10 years that individuals who were at most risk were those with a family history of the illness who had also been, at the first test, in the top quartile of cardiovascular reactivity. Social stressors were identified as the most important determinants of individuals' cardiovascular reactions.

The other major component of the stress system is the hypothalamic-pituitary-adrenal (or HPA) circuit. The HPA axis triggers a chain of events that involves the release of corticotropin-releasing hormone (CRH) and results in the secretion of hormones called glucocorticoids, the most important of which, here, is cortisol. A small amount of cortisol is necessary to our healthy functioning – it motivates us into action – but constant stress over an extended period of time can lead to an over-abundance of cortisol circulating in the system, a condition called hypercortisolemia. An excess of cortisol is responsible for a range of problems including fat deposition and insulin resistance as well as suppression of the immune system (see below). A number of studies have found that individuals who endure social strain have elevated levels of cortisol. Loving, Heffner, Kiecolt-Glaser, Glaser and Malarkey (2004), for example, found that newly wed women who had less power in their relationships than their partners had elevated levels of cortisol both during and for a long period after resolving conflicts with their spouses.

Along with the recent discovery that the immune, endocrine and nervous systems have mutual modulatory effects is that prolonged activity of the HPA system, or prolonged supply of cortisol, may also adversely impact the immune system. There are several ways in which the HPA system is suspected to impact immune functioning. The following is amongst the best under-stood. Under normal circumstances, by inhibiting the production of interleukin-1, a kind of protein that helps activate T helper cells – a class of lymphocytes or cells that regulate the immune system – cortisol prevents the immune system from becoming over-active. Cortisol inhibits the activity of CRH (which, as men-tioned above, helps stimulate release of cortisol), thus creating a feedback loop. When too much cortisol floods the system, how-ever, the immune system shuts down prematurely leaving a body susceptible to infection (Sternberg 1999: 116). Social stress – as the most significant category of psychological stress – thus has significant implications for our general health.

There have been a number of findings regarding the impact of social factors upon immune function. For example, Kiecolt-Glaser and colleagues have found that marital conflict leads to decreased immune functioning in spouses for many hours following argu-ment. (For an overview, see Kiecolt-Glaser and Newton 2001.) In earlier studies, Kiecolt-Glaser and others (1987) found a large proportion of women who had been separated or divorced had deficient immune systems compared with married women to whom they were socio-demographically matched. Women who were tested within a year of separation or divorce had the least robust immune systems, having lower percentages of T helper cells as well as another class of lymphocyte, natural killer (NK) cells (in Kosslyn et al. 2002). (Another study that confirmed medical students had altered immune system functioning following their final exams found that students showing the biggest effects for NK activity were those who had reported being lonely (Davidson, Coe, Dolski and Donzella 1999 in Kosslyn et al. 2002: 348).)

As mentioned above, a range of things can determine whether particular genes get expressed. Recent findings suggest that social stress can affect transcription processes. Transcription is the first part of gene expression where deoxyribonucleic acid (DNA), a nucleic acid that contains all information about an organism, is copied to ribonucleic acid (RNA). Wu, Devi and Malarkey have found that stress endured by caregivers altered genetic processes related to the immune system. Lymphocyte growth hormone (L-GH) influences cellular immunity by increasing the efficacy of lymphocytes, a kind of white blood cell, in responding to antigens they are designed to attack. Whilst the genetic transcriptions responsible for the production of L-GH are to some extent predetermined, Wu, Devi and Malarkey found that the caregivers of spouses with Alzheimers disease had significantly suppressed concentrations of L-GH compared with other individuals of their age (in Cacioppo, Berntson, Sheridan and McClintock 2000: 833).

A concept of particular use for social work is that of *allostatic load*, as described by McEwen. Allostasis refers to homeostasis – or physiological balance – achieved through adaptation to challenge or stress. How well individuals adjust to given psychological challenges depends on their prior experiences, current state of health, and many other factors. Allostatic load occurs where an individual has been over-exposed to various stress mediators such as cortisol, as discussed above, and adrenalin. Allostatic load, in McEwen's words, 'reflects "wear and tear" on the body that is produced almost inevitably by the need to adapt to an ever-changing world' (1998: 44). In addition to psychological stress, the secretion and levels of such hormones are affected by such things as diet, exercise and sleep. Different individuals will accumulate different allostatic loads throughout their lives, as determined by their experiences and the coping mechanisms they employ together with hereditary and lifestyle factors. The concept of allostatic load provides social workers with a way of conceptualizing vulnerability from a physiological perspective that is complementary to Kuh and Ben-Shlomos's notion of 'chains of risk', discussed in Chapter 9. It helps to remind social workers that all psychological events have both short-term and long-term *physical* impact and that individuals are dealing, in their everyday lives, with the accumulated effects of prior stressors.

As mentioned, positive social support offers both short-term and long-term benefits for emotional and general health throughout individuals' lives. High levels of social support are associated with a lower risk of various diseases and conditions such as heart disease and depression. Researchers such as McEwen and Seeman (1999) have found that social support has specific effects on neuroendocrine activity, attenuating patterns of HPA and SNS activity. Grewen, Anderson, Girdler and Light (2004) found, in a controlled experiment, that subjects who received affectionate physical contact with spouses prior to undergoing a psychological stressor had reduced cardiovascular activity. Community-based population studies that have high levels of social support are associated with lower heart rate and systolic blood pressure, lower serum cholesterol, uric acid and lower urinary norepinephrine (Seeman 2000: 201).

One means through which social support provides protective effects may be by aiding the expression of the hormone oxytocin. Oxytocin is involved in a number of physiological functions including promotion of lactation in mammal and is central to bonding and a range of prosocial behaviours. In animals, oxytocin has also been shown to have anxiolytic or anxiety-reducing effects. This effect has been less well studied in humans. Heinrichs and colleagues (2003) have shown that humans provided with either social support during, or direct administration of oxytocin (intranasally) just prior to, undergoing a public-speaking task showed reduced cortisol levels compared to other subjects who completed the challenge. Subjects who were both administered oxytocin and received social support showed the lowest levels of cortisol concentrations during stress exposure.

There are other less direct ways in which our social relationships may assist our health. Seeman notes, for example, that positive social relationships may encourage healthful lifestyles (2000: 207).

Our social structures determine not only the quality of our social relationships but much else relevant to the general well-being of different groups. Lupien and colleagues have noted that those in Western societies who are in the lowest socio-economic groups suffer disproportionately from a range of health problems, including mental health problems (Lupien, King, Meaney and McEwen 2001. See also Baum, Garofalo and Yali 1999). A number of theories have been put forward for the greater prevalence of illness and risk of mortality amongst those poorer. Different hypotheses refer to health 'behaviours' and personality traits. Lupien and colleagues, however, claim that stress may be a significant determinant of the association between Socio Economic Status (SES) and health. Stress, or high allostatic load, can cause a number of health problems (also referred to above), including cardiovascular disease and alteration of immune function. Stress has also been shown to affect mood and cognitive processing (Lupien and McEwen 1997). Apart from concerns about money, there are a great number of stresses to which those from lower SES are made subject. Many of those poorer are required, for example, to live in high density accommodation which affords minimal privacy, and/or in areas with high levels of incidental noise. Research also suggests those of lower SES are more likely to be exposed to, or fear encountering, social aggression (Evans and Kantrowitz 2002).

Whilst we have mostly focused, in this discussion of social factors, on the ability of social relationships to impact individuals negatively or positively, there are other neuroscientific discoveries relating to social decision-making and so forth of potential interest for social work. Neuroscientists have begun to identify, for example, those brain areas involved in social recognition and appraisal. Interesting research on the neurobiology of morality has also commenced. Moll and colleagues have identified neural circuitry that appear to underlie moral appraisal or moral emotion – that set of emotions experienced by individuals that are 'intrinsically linked to the interests or welfare' of others (Moll et al. 2002). The medial and orbital PFC and the superior temporal sulcus region, known to be involved in social behaviour and perception, appear to be central to this circuit. Individuals with damage in the orbitofrontal cortex are often able to select, in laboratory settings, appropriate responses to given moral quandaries even where, in everyday life, they routinely behave in particularly 'unethical' or selfish ways. Moll and colleagues believe that this suggests an impairment in the ability to 'rapidly process moral emotions in response to signs of moral violations' (p. 2736).

A range of theories prescribe how humans should behave towards one another, each of which calls for a specific kind of moral psychology or kinds of reasoning strategies. Casebeer (2003) suggests that early findings on brain regions used for moral appraisal indicate humans' 'natural' sense of morality is more akin to that outlined in Aristotelean 'virtue theory' than, for example, a utilitarian model. Virtue theory specifies that the 'good' person tries to be the best they can by cultivating virtues such as honesty and refraining from behaviours that are upsetting to others. Utilitarianism is the belief that right actions are those which maximise happiness for the greatest number of individuals. Whilst such assertions are highly speculative, it is possible that neuroscience will, in the future, help us understand a little more about such matters as the bases on which we decide to assist others.

Humans as active agents

Central to the social work paradigm is the notion of 'fit' between individuals and their environments. Germain and Gitterman state, 'where there is a good fit, person and environment both flourish' (p. 52). They claim that poor fit may be corrected through changes in either the environment – environment, in this context, referring to immediate or broader social environments – or the individual. It is often the social worker's role to facilitate such changes. In many cases – such as when an individual lives with hostile parents or in a neighbourhood with a high crime rate – changes within the individual's milieu are most desirable. Where changing the environment is not possible, however, or where an individual's own characteristics have been identified as a main source of suffering, perceptions, attitudes or behaviour may be the target of change efforts. Social workers place considerable faith in individuals' ability to change themselves. Neuroscientific research adds to our understanding of which things are amenable to conscious control and effortful change and which, despite all best efforts, are beyond conscious management.

Whether we conclude that individuals are the masters of their own destinies depends on the perspective from which this question is approached. On the one hand, many individuals are capable of expanding their skill base and adopting traits beyond limits previously thought of as possible. On the other hand, as confirmed recently by social psychology together with neuroscience, the range of stimuli capable of unconsciously impacting individuals' emotions, judgments and behaviours is extensive.

Discussed above is the fact that humans can emotionally evaluate and react to stimuli before their conscious mind has been engaged. Just as significant is that (outside) stimuli that *have* been consciously detected can trigger emotional reactions for reasons unknown to the individual. This occurs, firstly, because emotional associations can be formed unconsciously.

There are different circuits in the brain involved in different components of what is collectively referred to as memory. The main categories of memory are implicit (or unconscious) and explicit (or conscious). The explicit memory system – to which the temporal lobe and the hippocampus are central – allows individuals to store and recall events and facts. Implicit memory systems, of which there are many kinds, are involved in tasks such as skill learning and (classical) conditioning. What Le Doux (1999) refers to as 'emotional memory' is a type of implicit memory system, or neural circuit, and is involved in the creation of fear-related memories. Similar neural circuits are likely involved in implicit learning involving other emotions, but these have been less well studied. It is possible for a stimulus to impact our 'emotional' memory without an episodic or clear conscious memory being formed. Memories *about* emotional situations and emotional memories (in other words, the explicit and implicit memories we have formed about a particular event) usually arise together giving the impression that they are one and the same. The 'emotional' memory system, which involves the amygdala and related areas, causes muscles to tense, blood pressure to rise and other physiological changes, when particular events are recalled. The explicit memory system, on the other hand, allows an individual to recall facts about an incident.

That stimuli can impact one kind of memory and not the other has been established through a range of means including research with individuals who have memory problems and/or specific kinds of brain damage. (An early subject in research on amnesia was a woman who was unable to create any new (conscious) memories, including memories of people she had met before. Each time she met with a particular doctor, Edouard Claparede, whom she saw frequently, she had to be reintroduced. Ordinarily, upon meeting Claparede, the woman would shake hands with him, but on one particular day, although she was at a loss to explain why, she refused to do so. In fact, on the previous occasion she had met with Claparede he had hidden a pin in his hand which had pricked her when they made contact. Thus, she had learnt subconsciously to associate Claparede with danger.) It has been found, for example, that individuals with particular kinds of damage to the amygdala can recall frightening events in great clarity whilst showing none of the behaviour or physiological reactions consistent with fear. Ordinarily, individuals exhibit such things as skin conductance when recalling frightening occasions in detail (see Le Doux 1998, chapter 7 and also Damasio 1996, chapter 9). Skin conductance is a function of sweat gland activity and skin pore size, which are controlled by the sympathetic nervous system. Sweat glands become active during stress. When sweat is produced, the skin is better able to conduct current.

Another matter is that it is possible for the human brain to *perceive* objects, including those to which emotional significance has been attached, unconsciously. This is evident through the existence of such phenomena as blindsight and the ability for humans to be subliminally primed. Blindsight is a condition where individuals with damage to their visual cortices (groups of cells specialized for vision), whilst being unable to detect any objects in their visual field, can correctly guess at the location of objects in a room. Subliminal priming is a process by which aural or visual stimuli presented at levels undetectable by the conscious mind are used to bias responses or reactions. Zajonc and others have found that subjects are more or less likely to report liking certain stimuli they are shown – Chinese ideograms, for example – depending on whether images are preceded by positive or negative images (such as happy or sad faces), despite the former being shown at a rate too fast for conscious processing (see Zajonc 2001 for an overview).

Subliminal priming can influence not only preferences but also behaviour. Its influence on behaviour can be explained by the manner in which neural circuits responsible for perception and behaviour are connected. The mere (conscious or unconscious) perception of a particular behaviour by an individual makes likely that she will imitate it. Interestingly, specific types of action may also be suggested to, and thus implemented by, individuals through exposure to action-suggestive words as well as such things as stereotypes. In one study, Bargh, Chen and Burrows (1996) (subliminally) presented images of African Americans to subjects who, subsequently, reacted with more hostility to a mild provocation compared to those who were not exposed to such primes. This speaks not only of humans' strong tendency towards action but also the dangerous and pervasive effects of exposure to negative stereotypes (in Bargh and Chartrand 1999: 466).

Mood may also be affected by stimuli presented to the unconscious. In another experiment, subjects were (subliminally) presented words that described objects with either negative, very negative, positive or very positive connotations. After this task, they were asked to report their mood. The researchers, Bargh and Chartrand found a correlation between subjects' moods and the stimuli they had been subjected to; those who had been exposed to the most negative stimuli reported feeling most negative (Bargh and Chartrand 1999: 474).

It is also the case that behaviour can be directed non-consciously. In other words, stimuli, whether consciously processed or not, can trigger behaviour of which the exhibitor is unaware. In one experiment, Bargh, Chen and Burrows, for example, showed that whether individuals were willing to interrupt someone to ask a question was influenced by the words they had been exposed to (consciously) during an ostensible language test. Considerably fewer of those who were exposed to words relating to politeness, for example, 'respect', 'considerate', interrupted compared to those who had been shown words relating to rudeness (Bargh, Chen and Burrows 1996 in Bargh and Chartrand 1999: 466). Consciously perceived stimuli can also have effects on mood, as well as the development of cognitive and behavioural goals, that go unrecognized by the relevant individuals.

Research by Bargh, Gollwitzer, Lee-Chai Barndollar and Trotschel (2001) supports the theory that even behavioural goals may be formed unconsciously. (In one experiment, researchers asked subjects to unscramble words related to the concept of evaluation. Subsequent to this, they were presented a series of stimuli to listen to. Neuroimaging results indicated that although they had neither been instructed to nor were aware they were doing so, subjects evaluated the items as they heard them. This was clear because the subjects showed neural patterning (involving a rapid shift in right-lateralized processing) that normally occurs when individuals are consciously evaluating something but not when they are undertaking any other kinds of mental activity (Cacioppo, Crites and Gardner 1996 in Bargh and Chartrand 1999: 471).) But, whereas *particular* mental tasks and behaviours are *automatically* or necessarily performed unconsciously, formation of specific goals in familiar situations (as for the formulation of stereotypes and development of various kinds of associations) become automatic only with repetition. Bargh and Chartrand (1999) hypothesize that the unconscious performance of so many tasks (including those which are only activated automatically over time) occurs because the brain has limited energy for conscious self-regulation of behaviour. Even simple tasks such as concentrating, over minutes, on *not* eating a biscuit depletes individuals' ability to perform tasks for some time afterwards (Baumeister, Bratslavsky, Muraven and Tice 2000).

The above evidence would seem to strike a blow for the ideas of free will and self-determination. And, indeed, it is difficult to determine just how much control our unconscious mind has. But, intuitively, we understand there is a great deal we accomplish only *because* we have willed ourselves to act. All the same, where does this leave our capacity to change problematic behaviour and avoid unwanted emotions?

A note about 'Self'

That some of our actions and mental processes are conscious and others are unconscious explains, in part, our ability to view mind and body as separate objects, or our 'selves' as one thing and bodies another. That our heart beats without our willing it to do so or that we can feel sad for reasons unknown to us can lead us to make statements beginning, 'my body is doing' or 'my body is feeling', as though our bodies were distinct from who 'we' are. And yet, as we have established, our emotions, our decision-making and consciousness itself requires input from our neural and endocrine systems.

Adding to our feeling of separateness from our bodies is that the number of our own actions that we are able to perceive is limited. Whilst we can observe the movements of our limbs, or feel our throats contract, for example, we can neither see nor feel the electrical and chemical activity that gives rise to our conscious thoughts. It is easy, then, to believe that our thoughts pre-exist or are independent of these other body parts that, we can see, must work so hard to produce their effects.

As we discuss in more detail in the next chapter, what we notice about our bodies – whether it is merely those aspects that add to our aesthetic appeal, or provide us with athletic ability, for example – has significant implications for our sense of identity as well as self-esteem. The design of the human brain, however, means that our relationship to our own bodies is malleable. Whilst we cannot learn to perceive all parts and actions of our bodies in the same way, we can change the way we attend to information about it.

Social workers are frequently exhorted to undertake 'self-reflexive' practice. A consideration of the (biological) conscious and unconscious forces us to rethink the extent to which such practice is possible. 'Self-reflexive', as used in social work literature, has two main meanings. It refers, in some contexts, to a worker's willingness to consider how aspects of her identity or experience – cultural background, belief systems and gender, for example – inform her decision-making and other elements of her work at any give time. In other contexts, 'self-reflexive practice' refers to the engagement in the post-hoc analysis of practice. More specifically, it refers to the capacity to reflect on what was done and why, and whether, on a range of measures, an intervention was successful. As discussed above, we cannot be sure either of the full range of ways in which our experiences influence the ways we think, nor which of those things in our immediate environment are influencing our decision-making. Another problem associated with the appraisal of earlier instances of practice is that how we remember something – whether as good or bad, for example – depends, to a large extent, on our current mood state. There is little room, in other words, for the objective evaluation of one's own professional performance. The capacity to come to know one's professional self is, thus, limited.

A thornier issue still is that use of terms such as 'professional self' – that which we ostensibly come to know through 'self-reflexive practice' – implies the existence of consistent or true selves. As we discuss in more detail in the next chapter, post-modern theory has challenged the concept of stable identities that was central to enlightenment thinking. Recent neuroscientific findings on memory, emotion and reasoning help us further challenge this construction. Identities are based on such things as experience (and, thus, memories), temperament and predilections. The unpredictability of which memories – conscious and unconscious – we have access at any given moment and the dependency of our perceptions, reasoning and actions upon our current emotional states (which, in turn, are somewhat reliant upon environment) suggests we produce different selves at different moments.

Human capacity for change

For reasons discussed above, humans cannot know all the objects with which they have developed (and are in the process of developing!) strong emotional associations. Attempts to reduce negative emotion through avoidance of provocative stimuli will, thus, rarely be successful. Individuals have a greater chance of reducing negative affect through learning new thought patterns and behaviours.

Emotional self-regulation refers to psychological strategies with the purpose of either making emergence of negative emotion less likely, the experience of negative emotion less intense and/or its offset quicker. It might also be described as a collection of strategies aimed at sustaining or increasing positive emotion. In simple neurobiological terms, emotional regulation is achieved through control of the amygdala by the PFC. As connections from the amygdala to the higher or conscious parts of our brains are weaker than the connections from the cortex to the amygdala, unwanted emotions are particularly hard to control (Zhu and Thagard 2002: 25). The brain, however, as discussed, is relatively plastic. Where there is dysregulation but not severe damage, individuals are able to strengthen downward connections.

The concept of Hebbian learning or plasticity identified by the motto, 'neurons that fire together wire together' refers to the theory that neurons activated at the same time over many occasions need less and less stimulation to trigger each other. The increased 'potentiation' occurs through alteration to the synaptic connections between neurons. There is much evidence that most kinds of learning – whether intentional or unintentional, implicit or explicit – alter synaptic function in this way (see Kandel 2001 for overview of memory). Activation of those pathways involved in emotional control leads to at least temporary changes in the relationship between neurons and, new findings suggest, perhaps even permanent changes.

Psychotherapy offers several techniques for addressing emotional issues. Le Doux hypothesizes that the efficacy of a given treatment may be, in part, predicted by its physical mode of action or, in other words, its function. Some types of psychotherapy assist clients to recall events to which their current problems may be attributed. Le Doux argues that this form of therapy and others that rely on clients' use of insight are likely to be less efficient than other therapeutic models. This is because the lateral PFC, which is involved in bringing past events and so on 'to mind' (or to 'working memory' – that mental 'space' in which everything that is currently thought about exists) has no direct connection to the amygdala. Behavioural therapy, by contrast, attempts to help clients to deal with negative emotion through learning new associations, skills and habits – tasks that rely largely on implicit memory. Central to some of these tasks is the medial PFC which is directly connected to the amygdala (2002: 292).

Meditation, referring here to the activity of sitting calmly and focusing attention on a selected physical or mental object, is another means by which individuals can attempt to regulate their emotions. Neuroscientist Richard Davidson has developed research designs allowing study of the impact of meditation on the brain. Whilst the benefits of meditation can be inferred through self-report and social observation methods, Davidson's findings provide hope that the human capacity for dispositional change can be quantified. Davidson has studied the impact of meditation on both beginning practitioners and Tibetan Buddhist monks. In one study conducted by Davidson and colleagues (Davidson 2004: 1407), individuals who had undergone an eight–week training course in meditation showed significantly increased activity in the left side of their brains compared with controls. Interestingly, the amount of left-sided activation correlated with increases in immune functioning (Davidson et al. 2003).

Until recently, there was scant evidence that activities aimed at emotional regulation, or increasing positive affect, produce anything other than short-term changes in the brain, but recent research suggests permanent changes may indeed be induced. Lutz and colleagues have found that Tibetan Buddhist monks with between 10,000 and 50,000 hours of meditation practice have very different brain activity during meditation compared to individuals who have undertaken only a small amount of meditation. The monks studied showed unusually high levels of gamma (brain) wave activity where the novices showed only a small amount of gamma activity. Brain waves are the electrical signals that can be recorded from the brain (through EEG; see above) and different frequencies are associated with different kinds of mental activities. Gamma activity appears to be associated with higher thinking and consciousness. That, even at *resting state* (i.e. when the monks were neither moving nor focusing on any particular mental task) their brains showed higher than normal levels of gamma activity suggests that meditation had effected structural changes; that is, changes to neural connections (Lutz, Greischar, Rawlings, Ricard and Davidson 2004). Structural change translates, at the behavioural level, into tendencies towards new behaviour becoming stronger than those towards old behaviour. Thus, whilst previous research has established that individuals are born with greater and lesser capacities for happiness or other positive emotion, it seems that, with considerable conscious effort, one's capacity for such may be expanded.

But what of those things outside of emotion, other kinds of thought patterns and behaviour that individuals desire to change? Much problematic behaviour is the result of poor emotional self-regulation; as discussed above, the onset of strong emotion is often a sufficient catalyst to action. Thus, the best means of reducing certain kinds of behaviours is the development of better emotional regulation. The number of instances in which an individual physically aggresses, for example, may decrease as she learns to gain greater control over her feelings of anger. Other behaviour can be changed through rehearsal of alternative actions. What needs constant willing at first may eventually become automatic as the synaptic connections making the new behaviour possible strengthen. Which is not to say that all problematic behaviour, thought patterns, or even emotions, are amenable to change. For example, as Le Doux discusses, particular phobias may be immune to extinction (1999: 238).

Another argument to which neuroscience lends support is that the success of individuals' change efforts will be, in part, dependent upon the strategies they adopt, or that different interventions are more or less suitable for different individuals. Investigations by Kosslyn and colleagues have revealed that the ability to perform tasks associated with mental image generation – image scanning and rotation, for example – is anything but uniform across the species. Participants in one experiment who found it hardest to generate mental images showed reduced activity in particular areas of the brain (in particular Brodmann Area 17) (Kosslyn et al. 2002: 342.) Amongst the many things this suggests is that slight through to significant neuroanatomical deficits may prevent some individuals from benefiting from psychotherapeutic interventions that rely on clients' use of visualization. Depending upon other inherited or experience-related deficits, individuals' success with other kinds of change strategies will also be highly variable.

A biological perspective on human consciousness, learning and self-determination helps clarify that whilst humans are not entirely self-determining, nor are they without the capacity to change the contents of their thoughts and aspects of their behaviour. More difficult to determine is the extent to which individuals may change those things within their *environments* that encourage violence, depression and other unwanted social and psychological phenomena. Most Western societies have the technological and organizational capacities to make particular kinds of changes that will benefit the majority, but effecting them requires will. Whilst neuroscientific findings indicate humans are capable of developing the greater empathy required to, say, make social systems more socially and economically egalitarian, whether all individuals are motivated to do so is another matter. Encouraging humanitarian vision and social change, as well as individual change is, of course, the ultimate task of social work.

Working with the marginalized and vulnerable

What utility then neuroscience and thinking have about the body for work with the marginalized and vulnerable? In fact, the consideration of the human subject from a physiological perspective delivers a number of benefits. They can be summarized as follows:

• **Individuals in their psychosocial world:** A biological or, more specifically, neuroscientific focus assists our understanding of individuals as highly varied creatures whose interpretations of, and ability to negotiate, different situations depends upon hereditary *and* experiential factors. More than this, it helps us understand the interdependence of environments and persons. It encourages social workers to consider the range of things that comprise 'environment' that may be harmful or supportive. A biological perspective also establishes the primacy of emotion as a determinant of psychological and non-psychological well-being, appraisal and action. It thus suggests that there is a special role for social workers in helping clients to achieve better emotional regulation.

• **Human beings as active agents:** Whilst revealing the limits of self-determination, a neuroscientific or biological perspective confirms humans indeed have the capacity to change aspects/ elements of their behaviour, cognition and affect. More importantly, in identifying some of the physical changes required to effect behavioural, cognitive and affective change, a biological perspective helps identify best strategies for adoption. Reduction of fearful emotion, for example, is best achieved through activities that draw upon implicit, as opposed to explicit, memory systems.

• The suitability of a cognitive or behavioural intervention for a given individual is, in part, determined by her level of interest or faith in the technique. As neuroscience has established, its applicability is also determined by the individual's particular abilities. Individuals vary in their aptitude for such things as visualization, (explicit) memory formation and recall, and/or reasoning, each of which is central to different interventions. Deficiencies may only be obvious at the neural level. Social workers will be increasingly able to rely on neuroscientific information to guide selection of interventions for given problems and individuals.

- **Influence of social structures on human life:** A biological perspective reveals that social environment and specific instances of social interaction impact emotional state and, in the long term, emotional regulation. It also clarifies that social relationships, through their effect upon the nervous system, also influence immune functioning and, thus, resistance to illness. This justifies social work's long-time focus on helping clients achieve 'social integration' and provides evidence of the importance of the specific relationship between social worker and client. It also suggests that those socially marginalized are amongst the most susceptible to illness and depression.

- **Conceptualizing vulnerability:** Concepts such as McEwen's 'allostatic load' provide a means for understanding the differential nature with which psychological and non-psychological stressors impact individuals. It also makes plain the accumulative impact of stress upon an individual's coping mechanisms or personal resources. An individual's emotional, cognitive and 'physical' vulnerability, thus, is not merely determined by his current circumstances and mental state but rather by his genetic heritage in combination with all previous experiences, and past and current lifestyle factors. Such a perspective suggests the importance of social workers continuing to provide particularly emotional support for individuals even once their material and social circumstances appear to have stabilized.

At the beginning of this chapter, we stated that neglect of the biological body by social work may be related to a perception that it has little relevance for social work. We earlier speculated that this neglect might also be associated with the belief that physiological perspectives are reductionistic. In the above, we hope we have made clear both the genuine importance of the body for social work and the fact that examining something from one perspective does not preclude the ability for it to be seen from others. Contemplating the neural circuitry and hormonal activity that enables a human to experience love neither denies that biological perspectives can only reveal so much about the phenomenon nor the richness of sociological perspectives on love. It may perhaps, however, in time, help us find new ways to enhance it.

3   Social Bodies

We began this book with an exploration of how the human body has been understood within social work theory, arguing that the focus has been 'all around' rather than centred on the body. We argued that social work theory and practice can be seen as underpinned by four preoccupations or themes: (1) a view of human beings as individuals, active agents in their own lives; (2) a recognition of the influence of social structures in constraining and enabling human action; (3) an awareness of inequalities which characterize social life; and (4) an interest in and focus on working to ameliorate the situation of those who are marginalized, excluded and vulnerable. However, in the ways in which these themes have been analysed, the body remains hard to find, assumed and taken-for-granted with emphasis on understanding the nature of 'being human' rather than on the flesh and blood material body. We noted that recognition is given to the necessity of understanding human beings within their environmental context, but the nature of this relationship with the environment remains relatively unconsidered, and definitions of what constitutes environment are somewhat unclear, except in so far as person and environment are considered separate, although interacting, entities. Social work theory, we argued, does place emphasis on the effect of stressors impacting persons as they grow and develop and the importance of resilience in enabling the best adaptation to life's challenges, but this is largely in relation to social constructionist and critical theory perspectives.

Then, in Chapter 2, we turned to discussing the biological body, relating this where relevant to the four themes. We described the structure and function of the brain and placed particular emphasis on the generalized and individualized ways in which it changes throughout the life course. Our discussion of environment highlighted the constant dialogue that takes place between the 'inside' and the 'outside' of the body, arguing that recent findings from biology and neuroscience have concluded that environment might be defined as referring to all matter and phenomena that are non-genetic, and that there is constant exchange (interdependence) between the body and the environment. Instead of emphasizing concepts of stress and resilience, we introduced the notion of allostatic load. This refers to the long-term and short-term physical impacts that individuals encounter in their everyday lives which build upon previous stressors, accumulating over the life course.

These two chapters then, provide us with perspectives on the body which are not necessarily parallel. Indeed it is apparent that, as the material body is 'side-stepped' within social work theory, we encounter various contradictions. On the one hand, we acknowledge and indeed foreground a concern with recognizing the role of social structures in creating differences in life chances and opportunities, personality traits and abilities, while still proposing that the body is a universal and undifferentiated entity which, by and large, evolves in a uniform way over the life course.

Thus, if we are to place the body at the centre of social work theory and practice, it is a different theoretical perspective that is required. However, most important, this perspective must be one that remains with social work's particular contribution to the human sciences, that is, its active and practical commitment to the betterment of human lives. One way of moving towards this is to suggest that the very title of this book is inaccurate: there is no one body which should be at the centre of our attention, but rather 'bodies'. Neither biology, nor sociology, nor social work alone can adequately deal with 'the body' as a single, coherent conceptual entity. As Fraser and Greco (2005: 3) highlight, 'there is no body as such which is given and fixed for all time and (it is better) to recognize that experiences rooted in different forms of embodiment may be radically incommensurable'.

In Chapter 2 we noted the continuing influence of Cartesian thought in dualistic mind – body conceptualizations to which social work theory remains heir. In contemporary thought in the social sciences as Elizabeth Grosz (1994) proposes, three lines of consideration of the body continue in this vein. In the first, the body is seen as an object of investigation by the natural sciences, as well as by those human and social sciences which separate its functions (emotions, attitudes, experiences etc) for analysis, as, for example, in experimental psychology. In the second, the body is considered as a tool or instrument which is to be acted upon, either by the one who possesses it, or by external constraining forces, as for example, in some feminist analyses which consider women's bodies as objects to be controlled either by women themselves or by men under systems of patriarchy. In the third, the body is considered a vehicle of expression, the means through which information about the exterior world apprehended through the senses is conveyed, and through which information from the interior of the psyche – private thoughts, ideas, beliefs, feelings – are communicated, as for example, in perspectives deriving from psychoanalytic theory. The key point Grosz is making is that these perspectives, despite their very real contributions, fail to do justice to the complexity of the body in terms of its corporeality and agency. Indeed, the ideas that underpin this book as we discussed in Chapter 1, are premised upon recognition of both the materiality of our bodies and our capacities as actors, shaping and being shaped by environment. The complexity synonymous with person-in-environment and social work's espoused mission of social change demand that we at least recognize the magnitude of the task we as social workers have set ourselves.

Despite Grosz's critique, it is also the case that sociology – a frequent source of insight for social work – has shown an increasing interest in 'bringing the body back' into theory, with a large contingent of sociologists working to conceptualize and develop sociology of the body as a distinct stream within their discipline (see Howson 2004; Fraser and Greco 2005). These more complex and nuanced analyses provide valuable contributions to social work's understanding of person-in-environment.

Bodies, selves and identities

A continuing interest of sociology is the relationship between body, self and identity, and the extent to which body and self are synonymous, or indeed whether it is accurate to think of ourselves as having stable identities (Howson 2004; Coupland and Gwyn 2003; Fraser and Greco 2005). As we saw in our earlier discussion of use of self in social work, self and identity have also been of interest to social work but largely kept as background to a practice and practical interest in developing skills of impression management and use of self.

Symbolic Interactionism and especially the work of Erving Goffman (1959; 1963) has drawn attention to the place of the human body in the development and presentation of the self (Howson 2004; Coupland and Gwyn 2003). In this work, we can recognize the central significance we, at least in the West, place on our bodies. The physical appearance of our body, the efforts we put into managing, presenting and controlling it, demonstrate the vital importance we accord visual appearance as marker of both social value and expression of self, communicated through our face, expressions and gestures. This requires that we know what social norms exist for determining the acceptability of our bodies and hence of our selves. Reflections and analyses of the social construction of disabled bodies have also emphasized the important role of physically different bodies in defining 'normal' bodies (Wendell 1996; Davis 1997; Freund 2001). For it is through interaction with others that we learn how they see us, which, like the mirror, enables us to see ourselves, incorporating this interplay between self and other into the formation of our own sense of identity. In the previous chapter, this was discussed especially in relation to the importance for an infant's healthy emotional and neuronal development of the availability of frequent eye-contact with their mothers.

We can see social work education's debt to Goffman and the Symbolic Interactionist school in noting the use of videos in skills training. The learning tasks assigned to students are designed to replicate this process of learning about one's self by seeing, being seen by others, observing and acting how to become a social worker and to absorb this learning into one's professional identity.

In the laboratory or skills training setting, social work students study the 'theatre' of practice, learning through visual and non-verbal as well as verbal means how to perform the role of social worker. This requires that they understand how to communicate and manage the expressive and gestural information they want to convey about who they are through eyes, mouth, face and limbs. It is a reciprocal process, just as it is in everyday life, where the facial expressions and gestures of others (clients or social workers) require de-coding and interpretation if useful mutually understood communication is to occur. This reciprocal communicating and de-coding requires that both social worker and client have a shared understanding of body idioms, of the 'vocabulary' of bodily gestures and expressions characteristic of a particular culture or context.

The importance we place especially on the face – in everyday life and in teaching communication skills – underpins our recognition of the face as one of the most significant surfaces on which emotion is displayed. Such recognition is well-placed. As we noted in the previous chapter, it is the right-hemisphere of the brain which is dominant in processing facial expressions, emotional information and the expression of emotional states, a process which occurs automatically and without conscious awareness. Thus, as Goffman and like-minded Symbolic Interactionists remind us, we pay careful attention to the ways in which we use our faces. It is through our faces and facial expressions that social workers in interaction with service users require effort to manage the impression that they are attending, listening, empathizing, alert and concerned, where other emotions (which may equally be present) such as indifference, anger or frustration are concealed. Howson (2003: 31–32) reflects that the emotions which are often most readily communicated through the face and facial expressions, can be considered as 'emergent properties of the interactions between the body, environment and social relations', highlighting the unconscious as well as conscious responses that we make, evidenced through changes in our bodies (e.g. a flushed face) as we interact with other bodies in varying contexts.

The management of emotions in everyday life – and perhaps very importantly for social workers, in professional life – might be understood as demonstrating sophisticated 'feeling rules' for communicating, understanding and facilitating interaction with others which may change external appearance, or even change emotions, in order to perform a role. For example, a social worker may turn her irritation into empathizing with a client's situation. To do this effectively means developing the capacity to let the client see 'who one is', that is, for the body to communicate a sense of oneself as a person performing a constructive helping role within the encounter. However, what we also know from research on the brain (discussed in the previous chapter) is the capacity the brain has for registering emotions unconsciously, suggesting that we may not in fact be as capable of managing or even recognizing the emergence of some emotions, especially unwanted or negative ones, yet they continue to impact on our behaviour.

Very importantly, from a Symbolic Interactionist perspective, the presentation of the self needs to be a coherent one in which what happens in interactions (e.g. between social worker and client) reflects the roles adopted. These roles are, in effect, organized frameworks or performances in which both parties know how to 'go on' in a particular context or circumstance. There is a predictability or perhaps an expectation about what is taking place which facilitates both parties in making sense of it, interpreting the meaning of bodily gestures and emotional expressions with accuracy.

Giddens (1991: 57) argues that it is the *relationship* between agency and the body which requires analysis. From his perspective, bodily discipline and self-regulation are essential to the competent social actor and a defining feature of daily life. The body has a dual significance, both in relation to self control and social acceptance, and it is from this basis of confidence that our body will not perform in unwanted ways, that, for example, excretory functions are under control, that agency is possible. Humans 'bracket out' their awareness of body functioning in order to carry on what they are doing in everyday life (1991: 58). 'To learn to become a competent agent – able to join with others on an equal basis in the production and reproduction of social relations – is to be able to exert a continuous, and successful, monitoring of face and body' (1991: 56).

For many, the definition of "disabled" is synonymous with a body which is not 'under control'. Such is the importance of bodily control that the 'uncontrolled' or 'disabled' body may also become the rejected and stigmatized body. Thus, the importance of achieving a 'normal appearance' resonates both with our presentation of ourselves and maintenance of our sense of self worth and acceptance within the collectivity. The gap between what is normal and acceptable and what is socially unacceptable attracts the label of stigma. Stigma excludes people from participating in social relationships in ways both profound and damaging to the sense of self, marking someone as 'less than human' (Howson 2004: 24). As Wendell (1996) powerfully argues in relation to disability, distinctions which are social and political rather than biological are made between those with acceptable bodies and those with rejected bodies. What is defined as 'disability' will differ according to social, cultural and political contexts. Indeed, the extent to which being categorized as disabled determines particular life chances and opportunities relies on socio-cultural rather than biological criteria.

For social workers, an understanding not only of the social consequences of stigma but also of its origins in interpretations made of material bodies and their meanings are important. Many service users belong to stigmatized groups and the concept of person-in-environment has special resonance when we consider the implications of a stigmatized status for access to goods and services, its implications for human well-being, its impact on an individual's sense of self-worth, and the exclusion, isolation and marginalization which accompanies it.

Bodies, meanings, lived experience

Our gestures and expressions are thus imbued with and the means whereby we communicate meanings, for ourselves and for others. But it is also the case that our bodies themselves are highly significant generators and sources of meaning.

The phenomenologist Merleau-Ponty (2002) placed focus on the 'lived body' and the centrality to people of the capacity to interpret or make sense of their bodily experiences. This approach perhaps shares greater ground with existing social work theorizations and, while implicit in notions of 'use of self' (see earlier discussion), takes them further.

Phenomenologists assert that the body provides a material and ontological basis for the self. Bodies are not separate from minds but rather the body is the basis for our being-in-the-world (Nettleton and Watson 1998; Howson 2004: 36). The body equipped with senses enables us to develop our sense of ourselves as we actively engage with the world and with others. While we may, in every day life, take our body for granted, when we are ill or in pain or disabled, our consciousness of our body comes to the fore (Fraser and Greco 2005: 20). In particular, we may become aware of our physiological or mechanical functions, perhaps our digestive or cardiovascular system intruding on our thoughts and capacity for action. At other times we may be alerted to bodily and physical sensations, such as increased heart rate, when emotional responses are triggered. As the interpretations we make of our bodies – our body image – are mediated by the social and cultural contexts in which we live, how we handle our bodies in social situations, when, for example we are sick or angry, our perception of others' responses when our bodies are exhibiting these changes, is very important to our sense of self and identity.

Phenomenological approaches to the body thus stress the socially constructed nature of our sense of self, synonymous with the 'lived experience' of our own biological body (Nettleton and Watson 1998). For some sociologists of the body, the notion of health itself is defined by a lack of body awareness, a 'silence of the organs' (Fraser and Greco 2005: 20). Thus, in contrast to biomedical approaches, meaning is attributed or sought when illness strikes, and disease itself is seen as a communication which requires interpretation (Fraser and Greco 2005: 21; Frank 1995; Kleinman 1986). Many social workers, especially those in the health field, work with patients struggling not only with the symptoms of their illness, but with the guilt and self-questioning about what their illness communicates to themselves and others, arguably more painful than the ailment itself.

In reviewing sociological perspectives on the life course, images of the body figure prominently, foregrounding their impact on the experiences of embodiment and the relationship between the body and the self (Howson 2004: 162). Sociological accounts of the life course thus draw on both the phenomenological and social constructionist approaches, emphasizing the meaning or 'lived experience' of various life stages as well as the images which are generated. So, at different periods in the life course – adolescence, mid-life, late life in particular – we are more aware of our corporeality than at other times. As we saw in the previous chapter, the brain too is changing throughout the life course, responding to environmental and social environmental stimuli. Our awareness of bodily changes in appearance, cognition, ability, emotionality at puberty, menopause, late life, may mean that we need to construct new identities to coincide with biological ageing (Nettleton and Watson 1998: 13), and we are equipped with a brain that is capable of making such changes. Our view of ourselves as persons-in-environment can (and does) change as our bodies change.

Interest in the images of childhood (Howson 2004) and of old age (Turner 1995; Featherstone and Hepworth 1991; Featherstone and Wernick 1995; Gilleard and Higgs 2000; Heikkinen 2003) provide very rich accounts of both the 'outside' image that is associated with these stages in the life course and the 'inside' or lived experience. The frequent 'lack of fit' between the lived experience and the external image can be a source of tension as we struggle to accommodate our knowledge of our changing bodies to 'outside' societal or cultural images of what 'we ought to be'. For example, Howson (2004: 147) refers to the image of childhood as carefree, innocent and dependent while the experience for children is more often of anxiety, insecurity and restriction. Similarly, Featherstone and Hepworth (1991) describe the 'mask of ageing' in which the external image of bodily decline may not relate to the lived experience of vitality and optimistic engagement with life. Very often it is elements of these kinds of conflicts which social workers encounter when working with people at these transition points in their lives, for example, older people with enduring mental capacities but failing bodies.

Within the sociological literature on the life course, consideration is also given to death. But it is death as 'problematic', an event which seems 'unnatural' in a contemporary world which celebrates the body as unendingly repairable (Howson 2004: 156–162; Shilling 2003: 162–169). Developments in medical technology offer the possibility of prolonging life even when brain stem death has occurred. Complex ethical, social and theoretical problems arise in relation to the practice of organ donation and transplantation (Scheper-Hughes 2000; Lock 2002). And we also confront the impact of degenerative brain diseases which may result in 'social death' whilst the body remains functioning. Debating these issues in relation to the life course takes sociological theorizing in directions which exemplify its contribution to a social analysis which problematizes the materiality and meaning of the body itself (Haraway 1991; Waldby 1999). In all this of course, social workers frequently have key roles to play as members of multidisciplinary health teams, or as patient and family advocates. As such they cannot avoid entering the debates and making decisions which challenge and subvert the taken-for-grantedness of linear theories of the life course which describe a universal, generally straight-forward, trajectory from birth to death. They might also work with patients who have received organ transplants for whom the very meaning of their body may radically change.

Bodies, discourses, texts

A further rich vein of sociological theorizing about the body leads us away from notions of the body as a source of meaning in lived experience towards more abstract conceptualizations, challenging the very materiality of the body and asking us to question what bodies *are*. Foucault (1977; 1978) in particular, has questioned this 'facticity' of the body, proposing rather a malleable and endlessly flexible body defined and thus able to be redefined through discourses. Discourses – those structures of knowledge that influence systems of practice (Chambon 1999: 57) – emanate from specialist disciplines, such as medicine and the law, and establish their definitions of the body by means of measuring, categorizing and comparing in order to label bodies as normal or deviant in relation to socially constructed and culturally specific standards of normality.

The work of post-structuralists, in particular Goffman and Foucault are key contributors to an approach which Grosz (1995: 34–36) refers to as the inscriptive model of corporeal subjectivity. Rather than being 'natural' and thus immutable, sociologists approaching from the inscriptive model argue that the body is constructed by discourses that constitute the social world. Such a view stands in clear contrast to naturalistic approaches which consider the body as essentially biological, stable, uniform and universal in its structure and function.

Foucault's preoccupation (Coupland and Gwyn 2003: 3) has been with both the 'epistemological view of the body', that is, with the theoretical bases for knowing what bodies are and with the institutions that govern and regulate bodies – prisons, hospitals, asylums. It is, as Chambon, Irving and Epstein note (1999: 76), a perspective which looks at the body as both social and personal. While institutions actively make 'multiple imprints' (Chambon, Irving and Epstein 1999: 59) on the body, social institutions (the social body) in which humans participate are themselves generators of social identities and practices, many of which are directly concerned with the care and regulation of the body and hence the self. In the mental health field, many practices demonstrate this dual focus on the body as both social and personal. For example, the compulsory (often involuntary) containment of acutely mentally ill people in institutions or through administration of medication, are practices which aim to minimize disruption to the social body through interventions on the personal body of those identified as mentally ill and socially risky. Social workers frequently work in such situations, not only confronted by the potentially oppressive nature of their role in a profession which asserts principles of citizenship and social justice, but also at the same time aware of the importance to the person themselves, family members and the community of ensuring safety.

Sociologists have long been concerned with the problem of social order and the perceived antagonism between the individual biological body and the social body, between self and society, and between society and nature which social workers in the mental health and criminal justice systems daily encounter. As Fraser and Greco (2005: 10) remark, bodies are 'theoretically conspicuous for their capacity to exceed, escape, defy or threaten social order, and for requiring training or discipline as a precondition of social life'.

Foucault (1977) analysed the body as the focus of power. His 'docile body' is one which is not only subject to internal self-discipline (as distinct from being the object of discipline as in the pre-modern period), but this very self-mastery requires a loss of power as it is the result of subjugation to prevailing hegemonic discourses and disciplinary mechanisms produced in post-modern societies. Here we might think for example, of practices of self starvation in order for the person (usually a young woman) to achieve what are purportedly contemporary ideals of the perfect body.

Since Foucault's original work there have been multiple and fragmented approaches to bodies, identifying a range of different ways in which bodies has been conceptualized – the discursive body, the medicalized body, the talking body, the commodified body, the docile body, the regulated body – to name but a few (Howson 2004:8). This perspective presents a profound challenge to notions of the body as material and factual, arguing instead that the body is a biophysical entity only prior to its entry into discourse, at birth or perhaps earlier. Once the body enters the social realm it becomes both a sociobiophysical entity and simultaneously, the target of and a potential site of resistance to power (Schatzki 1996: 52).

Elizabeth Grosz (1995) proposes that the body is inscribed as a text: 'Bodies speak social codes. They become intertextuated; simultaneously, social codes, laws, norms and ideals become incarnated' (1995: 35). This is a multidimensional understanding of the body which theorizes it as simultaneously material, symbolic, corporeal and psychic. It is a body located within a culture and a history which is incorporated, reflected in bodily styles, habits and practices. As an inscribed text a conceptualization of the body as natural is refuted. The body becomes a bearer of a range of very different kinds of meanings, both for the one whose body it is and for the social group. Drawing on psychoanalytic theory, she argues that one's sense of one's body is both imaginary and object- ive, deriving initially from an image of the body patterned along the libidinal and organic elements characterizing bodily processes. These material and symbolic 'sites', for example, the mouth, eyes, breasts, genitals, construct what is simultaneously a corporeal and psychic entity. The body then, is a set of potentialities which may be developed into a range of dispositions (Burkitt 1999: 98). In this theorization, the materiality of the body is retained and recognized as holding the potential to generate change within the social order. For example, while sexuality and gender reflect the macro dimensions of power which in turn influence body prac- tices, different bodily performances which blur gender differences (such as drag queens) present challenges to established power relations. No longer is it possible to discern gender differences and, as a consequence, the allocation of power on the basis of gender is subverted.

Judith Butler presents a theorization of the body as a cultural product, formed through social and political signification and dis- course. For her, the materiality of the body is better understood as a process occurring over time, and constrained and limited by regulatory norms, evident for example, in expectations about what is 'appropriate' behaviour for men and women (Butler 1993; Kontos 1999: 683; Salih 2004). Drawing on the work of Foucault and Freud amongst other 'multiple theoretical provenances' (Salih 2004: 5), Butler conceptualizes of gender as a sequence of performative acts. The sexed, gendered and raced body is constructed, the effects of discourses and interpellations (2004: 142). For Butler, one is not 'born a girl'; rather one is hailed or called a woman through discourse (2004: 139). Thus in naming a new born a girl, the body is brought into language, discourse and kinship. During life, what Butler refers to as 'this founding interpellation', is repeated and reinforced by the various institutions though which we pass – family, school, church – so that over time this 'naturalised effect' (2004: 7) of sex and gender is either reinforced or contested. Thus, for Butler, the gendered body is primarily performative, constituted in the process of being and doing (Schatzki 1996: 60).

Bodies and social work

This brief and far from comprehensive excursion into sociological work on the body highlights the theoretical and conceptual richness within social constructionist and post structural perspectives available for social work to mine. While the body almost disappears as a material entity in the work of Grosz and Butler, their emphasis on the body as socially constructed offers a challenge to views of the body as static and universal. At the very least, such perspectives confront social work's tendency to take the body for granted as fixed and universal, encouraging us to question what bodies are or might become, to pose questions about the relationship between the physical body and the sense of self and identity.

The insights from contemporary sociology and neuroscientific advances in understanding brain and behaviour cause us to question social work's individualized view of human beings as active agents in their own lives. The instability of identity and changing understanding of our sense of self as we age, the limitations on our capacity to fully control our bodies and our emotions challenge notions of the apparently limitless abilities of humans to actively shape their own lives. This is not to downplay the value and importance of human agency but rather to seek understanding of the limitations and scope for human agency. Such knowledge is an invitation to enter debates about how we are to understand the impact of culture and social context on the materiality and physicality of the body, and to question the contemporary focus in

Western liberal democracies on the control, discipline and regulation of bodies.

Within social work we have had extensive engagement with analyzing social structures and their impact on creating and maintaining social inequalities. There has long been recognition of the ways in which social policies and practices have led to differential access to resources such as health services and education and the impact of these structural inequalities on individual human bodies. The complexity of this relationship between the social and the individual has as we have noted, been a primary concern of some sociologists. For social workers, Foucaultian analysis in particular is far from abstract, enabling those working in the mental health, criminal justice and disabilities fields to witness first hand the consequences on individual human bodies of stigma, institutionalization and deviance.

Very importantly, the debates and questions addressed by sociologists of the body directly pertain to issues which social workers encounter in their everyday practice but which have largely remained in obscurity. While social workers' concerns and preoccupations differ significantly from sociologists – in particular with respect to the interventionist focus of social work – sociology nevertheless offers very useful conceptual contributions. The theoretical understanding that social workers draw on for their practice can only be enhanced by explorations of the tensions between discourses and lived experience in relation to theorizations of the life course, integrating sociological perspectives into our understanding of self and identity, analyzing the impact of discourses in shaping, defining and re-defining what a body is. These are all issues of concern to social workers practicing in many, if not all, domains – health, mental health, child and family welfare – where the human body is – and we argue should retain – central concern. Indeed, the four themes or preoccupations which we argued in Chapter 1 underpin social work theory and practice, are neither undercut nor derogated by the sociological theories we have touched on in this chapter. Quite the contrary: as an applied profession, social work has and does offer a unique contribution in intervening in the lives of others – often those who are the most vulnerable and marginalized. There is thus an ethical and moral responsibility to do such work from a basis of the best available knowledge and scholarship which is wide in scope and comprehensive in recognizing and analyzing the complexity synonymous with human (embodied) action.

In drawing together our discussions in this and the previous chapter, we see that concepts and understandings of the human body become increasingly complex and multifaceted. Our purpose however, is not to move into abstract realms, distant from the world of practice but rather to stay 'true' to social work's primary concern with person-in-environment and with knowledge that can assist social work in its commitment to working with those who are marginalized, vulnerable and oppressed. To this end, we explore in the next chapter a way of bringing together knowledge and insights from biology, neuroscience and sociology which enable us to place the human body at the centre of social work attention, and in so doing advance a theoretical perspective guiding what we have termed 'body-cognizant' social work practice.

4 Social Work and the Body: Towards a Theoretical Framework

In the previous three chapters we have discussed the human body as theorized within contemporary sociology/social theory and biology. Our argument has been that the body, and in particular the biological body as studied within the neurosciences, is largely absent within social work theory. At the same time, there is continuing emphasis within social work on person-in-environment or person-in-psychosocial situation which struggles to account for the lived bodily implications of such a concept.

What we have proposed, however, in particular in Chapter 2, is that a considerable amount of what determines our lives is outside our control and outside our awareness. Indeed, some elements of which we are only dimly aware have been consigned to the spiritual realm of existence (Germain and Gitterman 1996; Harms 2004), which, although naming such experiences as spiritual may alienate some people, does at the least provide recognition of forces or elements which appear to influence outcomes for ourselves and others, the provenance of which cannot be specified. However, even to acknowledge that we are only partially aware of the determinants of our actions and thoughts places us in a stronger position to want to know more and to want to act as consciously as possible in regard to what we do – particularly as it might involve interventions into the lives of the vulnerable and disempowered.

Chapter 2 provided an account of the way in which the brain works and its primary role in transmitting messages and information from internal and external environments. How we process that information and make sense of it – the meaning we give to it – is where sociological insights are of especial relevance and aspects of which we sketched in Chapter 3. While biological and social forms of explanation are different (Lyons 2003: 84), taken in

79

tandem and interwoven with a life course focus and a concept of environment that emphasizes its temporal and processual elements (Cooper 2001), we begin to identify some of the factors that play a role in determining our experience of ourselves.

In this chapter, we make the argument that biological and social constructionist perspectives, whilst appearing in some respects conflictual, can be incorporated into a more developed understanding of psychosocial situation which has at its centre the flesh and blood human body. Central to our position is a belief that biological and sociological theories are informative, not only about the body, but also about each other.

Sociological perspectives remind us that the kinds of inferences we draw from the study of biological processes will be dependent upon observer expectation or bias, and context – the amount of information we have available to us at a given time. For example, each of a group of neuroscientists may draw different conclusions from the same experiment. This outcome, from a social constructionist point of view, might be explained in terms of their social, political and economic location, or with reference to the organizational culture characterizing their laboratory (Latour and Woolgar 1979; Charlesworth, Farrell, Stokes and Turnbull 1989).

All the same, findings on particular phenomena have been remarkably consistent across laboratories. This may indicate the prevalence of particular kinds of biases or false beliefs; what biological scientists now believe about how memory functions, for example, may be revised as more is discovered about other functions or areas of the brain. Significantly, however, many neuroscientific findings have informed development of successful treatments for a wide range of disorders. There is, in other words, strong argument for at least *provisional* acceptance of many findings from biology (whether as fact or, *useful* constructs.)

If we accept that particular biological findings on memory, affect and information processing have some validity, we can argue biology sheds as much light on how the body is constructed by sociologists (or others) as does sociology upon the fallibility of the scientific method. Neuroscience helps us to understand that the range of interpretations we can make of various phenomena is finite and constrained by our genetic design. Damasio states, 'There is a remarkable consistency in the constructions different individuals make of the essential aspects of the environment. ... If our organisms were designed differently, the constructions we make of the world around us would be different as well.' (Damasio 1996: 87). The way we perceive other human beings, their bodies and our own bodies is reliant, not only upon their *actual* shape, and so on, but also upon such things as the organization of our visual cortex. Similarly, the range of interpretations we can make of behaviour and forms of bodily communication, through to the possibilities we can imagine for our bodies, is restricted by the limits of our logic or imagination or, in other words, biological design.

This is not to say that there is no variety amongst perceptions and interpretations of the body. There is, in fact, much variety, for which there are a number of explanations. Certain types of brain damage will significantly alter perception. Individuals with damage to specific corticles, for example, will see human bodies, (as all other things) in greyscale. The way human action and forms of bodily communication develop and are interpreted depend greatly upon culture. Culture itself is shaped in part by affect. McEwen (1998) suggests that the traditions which take root in a given society reflects the dominant disposition of those comprising it. It may be argued that cause flows in the opposite direction and that philosophy is in fact a determinant of individuals' diet, interpretation of events, and other things that – as established by neuroscience – impact affect and, over time, disposition. The most likely situation is that philosophy and affect are mutually informing.

Given neuroscientific findings about the influence of emotion upon perception, attention and so on, we argue that emotion impacts aspects of culture aside from philosophy. Affect determines how an individual will behave towards another in a given instance and, thus, how communication norms develop amongst groups of related individuals over time. The norms to which individuals have been exposed in turn influence the interpretations they make about the meaning of bodies, bodies' roles in communication and bodily symbols. The particular experiences that a society offers individuals will also affect how they construct bodies and behaviour. Neuroscience, together with cognitive and social psychology, has shown that our prior experiences affect those features of an object we attend to and how we interpret information. Thus, a sociologist who grew up in a culture where sport was a significant part of life may consider athletic ability central to individuals' identity formation where another sociologist sees only a minor role for athleticism.

Biological and sociological theories thus provide us with complementary ways of viewing and understanding the body. Sociological theories explain how we interpret and respond to our own and each other's bodies, as well as reasons to remain cautious in our acceptance of any scientific findings. From biology we derive an understanding of relationships amongst affect, learning and behaviour, as well as limits to, and influences upon, human interpretation. Particular sociological and biological theories also provide useful ways for understanding environment. Specific findings within these categories have particular utility for social work.

A combined sociological and biological approach to understanding humans emphasizes that they are creative, (within reason) self-determining, emotional and rational creatures. Humans are also highly individual, having distinct interests, fears and ways of seeing the world as well as specific strengths and weaknesses. Individuals are more or less vulnerable depending upon the particular cognitive, emotional and *kinetic* capacities they possess, their overall health and stage of development they have reached.

The life course

Theorizations of the life course have traditionally been invoked in social work theory in order to explain the connection between individual human lives and the environment. Models such as Erikson's eight stages of human development (1968) refer to internal or ontogenetic forces which are considered to be universal, sequential and irreversible, qualitatively rather than quantitatively distinct. Sociogenetic models, in contrast (see Aldwin and Gilmer 2004), place emphasis on the social roles which individuals acquire over the life course. Role transitions occur as the individual moves through life. These transitions are not so much to do with internal psychological processes as with the pressures from the social context and larger structural requirements. The capacity to adapt to biological changes over the life span is understood from a sociogenetic perspective as indicative of our ability to act and to make choices about how we live.

Such life stage models have been subject to critique principally because of their tendency to be reductionist and individualistic with limited capacity to account for structural factors, especially the influence of a stable rather than unstable social environment. There is also little ability to account for important events in later life, for example, sudden loss of income, and a tendency to prioritize the influence of early life events (Hagenstad and Dannefer 2001). While, as we saw in Chapter 1, social work does focus on the concepts of stress and resilience in order to account for individuals' adaptations across the life course, this has been almost exclusively in relation to psychosocial correlates and behaviours which serve to maintain distinctions between nature and nurture, biology and psychology.

Social work is best drawing on life stage models that acknowledge the mutual influence of genes and environment upon individuals' cognitive, emotional and 'physical' development; which give equal emphasis to common and individual determinants of development; and which provide some account of the social institutions impacting development.

Environment

As we have discussed, environment determines more than whether 'programmed changes' should unfold as expected. What we draw from a combined biological/sociological view of the body is that environment also impacts – from moment to moment as well as in the long term – our immune functioning, our emotions, our perception (including self-perception), our learning, our decision-making and our ability to communicate with others, each of which can impact the other. Environment, as discussed in previous chapters has been highly under-theorized within social work. Thus, we offer a new model relevant to social work practice that incorporates biological, psychological and sociological concepts.

Using a camera metaphor, we propose that environment may be examined from three vantage points:

1. a wide view, which takes in macrosocial factors, community-scale biological and chemical changes – with the term 'biological' here referring to such things as alcohol consumption levels through to viral epidemics, and 'chemical' to such things as

toxic disasters and industrial poisoning – and physical factors, where 'physical' refers to such things as earthquakes through to standards of service available at hospitals;
2. a middle range view that incorporates the intersubjective/ interpersonal factors, and small scale biological, chemical or physical changes, that is those affecting a person or her home environment; and
3. a close-up view that refers to intrapersonal/intrapsychic factors.

At any point in time we can (1) look at the whole picture, (2) focus on a wide-screen view, (3) focus on the middle-distance, or (4) take a close-up view.

Each view is of a 'world in itself' and we could 'look at' each 'domain' as if through a lens, illuminating aspects of the social and material world and obscuring other elements. These worlds, however, do not operate independently but are constantly inter-acting, being sometimes in harmony and at other times in ten-sion. Some aspects of each world are protective, and some are adversive.

In observing these domains from within our human (embodied or close-up) domain, we acknowledge that we are aware of elements of parts of each domain and unaware of other elements. Awareness is not a condition of their existence or capacity to affect and be affected by one another. These interacting elements cause effects, some of which are intended and some unintended; some effects of which we are aware, others of which we are not.

We argue that the world is material and real, and humans are real, embodied and corporeal – flesh and blood. This is the position from which our 'photograph' of the whole is taken. As Shilling suggests (2003: ix), 'The body is central to our ability to "make a difference" to, to intervene in, or to exercise agency in the world, and our bodily emotions, preferences, sensory capacities and actions are a fundamental source of social forms'.

Below we expand on the range of things that each domain may contain:

The wide-screen view, or the 'wider' domain: This includes elements and forces in the biosphere, water and gases, climate and weather, as well as plants, organic and inorganic matter, and living creatures who share our world. In addition, nation states, governments and multinational companies and industries, global corporations, political and religious cross-national coalitions are also active in this domain.

The 'wider' domain refers to the ongoing life of people collectively, and to the world in its entirety. It is reflected and actualized in such effects as environmental degradation, green house gas emissions, differential health statuses, wars, famine, dispossession, capital accumulation, commodities pricing. We may not be aware of much of what is happening at this 'wider' domain but nevertheless it is profound in its effects upon us.

Such effects on humans occur through or may be observed in some of the following: extreme weather, climate change; pollutants – produced through industry and war; food production – availability and quality of food. The effects are felt in relation to bodily survival (and survival of human groups), disease, disability, creation of fear, anxiety, threat. The effects on the human immune system have been noted with changes in tolerance levels to 'foreign', non-self micro-organisms, in changes in incidence of different diseases (Wilce 2003).

The middle-distance view, or the intersubjective/interpersonal domain: This comprises families, friends, workplaces, communities. This domain 'carries' both the intrapersonal and the 'wider' domain, that is, it is reflected in culture, artefacts, language, discourse, music, stories, policies, belief systems. It includes the symbols, the sometimes unarticulated areas of shared meaning and understanding which allow us to communicate verbally and nonverbally with one another.

Within this domain, the human necessity for relying on other humans for survival is paramount – as caretakers (infants, frail aged, disabled), as having skills to heal and treat diseases, grow crops, educate and so on, as sources of social support central to cohesion within human groups, for socializing (learning to live together) and for relieving isolation and exclusion from sources of survival.

While we can be aware of why those people around us do things if they tell us or confirm our insights, it is also the case that the reasons for much of what others do remains outside our awareness. Nevertheless, it can profoundly affect us.

The close-up view or the intrapersonal/intrapsychic domain: This refers to the embodied individual. While humans have the capacity to think, to make sense of and to interpret their lived (bodily) reality and experience, much of what happens within us we are unaware of, for example, the functioning of our immune or hormonal or nervous system. Nevertheless, these systems are centrally implicated in affecting what we can do.

While we might be unaware of our immune system's work, we often are aware of the feelings of stress – anxiety, depression, fear, anger. Emotions can be thought of as 'making' the human body semi-permeable. That is, humans might respond with fear and anxiety because of the threat of war, and this will register both in the immune system and in the secretion of cortisol, creating stress on the body which may result in feelings (of which the person is aware) of anxiety and tension, or may result in bodily reactions to that stress, for example, increased blood pressure which the person may not be aware of.

The intrapersonal domain can be understood as 'carrying' these other domains – affected by and affecting the other domains, and 'carrying' the evidence of them within our embodied state, with or without awareness of them. For example, we may be aware that we are starving due to crop failures but unaware of the impact of climate change on levels of food production. Or we may be aware that, because we suffer from schizophrenia we are without friends, but unaware of the way in which stigma and social exclusion refer to patterns of collective behaviour (intersubjective domain) and so on.

In each of these domains social work's four preoccupations – with the individual person in their psychosocial world; with recognition of human beings as active agents; with the influence of social structures on human life; and with the situation of the poor, vulnerable, marginalized, excluded – remain. So, a concern with the individual embodied human actor incorporates recognition of the impact of both the 'wider' and the intersubjective domains. Our understanding of individual action is incomplete without drawing into awareness the influence and reciprocal relations that exist across all three domains. Embodied humans are biologically and materially 'marked' by elements or conditions which 'belong' with these other domains. For example, discursive constructions of the meaning and practice or performance of gender refer to and illustrate, in everyday lived experience, what it means to be a man or a woman in a particular culture or collectivity at a particular moment in time and history.

Our aim is to increase the degree of knowledge about and awareness of the constituents of each 'domain' and to emphasize their interpenetration into the everyday life of human beings. By placing the body at the centre of our attention – the biological and social body, partially 'accessed' through the emotions – we want to show how our lives are both constrained by embodiment at the same time as asserting our capacities as agents, as active beings in relationship with one another and with the material, organic and inorganic world. Seeing ourselves as beings with agency means that we have capacities to be changed by our embodied location (e.g. living under constant stress, developing allergies), to change it (e.g. through pharmacological interventions, group therapy) and to change the conditions in the world in which we live (e.g. through social activism, community development, building social cohesion). We want to expand our level of knowledge and awareness in order to act strategically, knowing the difference between what is malleable and what is not. As social workers we want to pay attention to the nature of and conditions for optimal human development and adaptation across the life span and to the factors which are implicated in health, physical and emotional well-being, including biological, material and political conditions.

By identifying (or theorizing) three 'domains', we retain recognition of the implications of person-in-situation, but 'situation' here is expanded to include the 'wider', global domain, and takes a new look at the intersubjective/interpersonal domain demonstrating a multilayered, multifaceted, reciprocal impact on the corporeal reality of individual human bodies.

We, thus, argue social workers must be aware of the body, must, in effect, be what we will term 'body cognizant'.

Body cognizant social worker

As we have noted earlier, social work has placed particular emphasis on the centrality to practice of social workers' 'use of self' and reflexivity in the helping relationship. The suggestion underlying these ideas is that social workers may, through introspection and theoretical engagement, actively control and monitor their own reactions (visual, verbal and non-verbal), using them strategically to effect the kinds of outcomes they have in mind.

There are two primary sources (as we saw in Chapter 2) from which we construct our sense of ourselves: emotion and memory (or learning). Each of these is centrally implicated in the work of the brain. These elements or capacities – emotion and memory (or learning) – are basic to our sense of identity (Turner 1995: 251) and hence to our experiences of ourselves over time, in place and in our bodies.

From this perspective, reflexivity and use of self take on a different quality. They are practices which require us to first, acknowledge that we do not have access to all the available data influencing our decisions and actions; second, to take a keener interest in observing bodily signs and signals which alert us to our bodily states; and third, to retain a critical appraisal of the meanings which may be given to our reactions and decisions, noting the culturally derived and driven character of interpretation and meaning designation. In this last point, we are referring to the symbolic meanings of behaviour and appearances, and their expression in the face, in gestures and in language.

Thus, we argue that a social worker who is body cognizant will practise in a way that indicates that the social worker is aware of:

- environment and human behaviour affect information processing and learning from a 'biological' perspective, or relevant findings on these from biology, and
- meanings ascribed by the worker, client and wider society to bodies, and the significance of this for client well-being, as well as ways in which the body is used by any of these parties in communication.

Corporeal capacity

In order to move from more abstract theoretical discussion to the world of practice, we propose and elaborate on the concept of 'corporeal capacity', a framework for recognizing our location as environmentally embodied beings, adapting, changing and shaping ourselves and the material and social world as our lives unfold. Corporeal capacity refers to the dynamic relationship between human bodies and the environment, reflecting the plasticity of the human brain which is so central to the possibility of recovery from exposure to trauma or adversity. The notion of corporeal capacity thus offers a different but somewhat allied perspective on resilience to that traditionally understood within social work theory. In fact, corporeal capacity may be in some respects an alternative way of thinking about resilience, one which highlights the bi-directionality of the relationship between organism and environment.

Environmental inputs both external and internal to the individual, such things as the effects of trauma, the actions of hormones, the consequences of development and ageing (Curtis and Cicchetti 2003), comprise an individual's experience. The capacity to adapt to these experiences in ways which minimize disorder or maximize resilience arises from the interaction of biological factors related to an individual's current experiences, the social context, timing of the adverse event or experience, and the individual's developmental history (Curtis and Cicchetti 2003: 774). In other words, the concept of resilience can be usefully elaborated upon in order to encompass elements of what we refer to as an individual's corporeal capacity.

An individual's corporeal capacity is determined by limitations of the species, and her particular *inherited* strengths and weakness in addition to kinds of environments – social, political and natural or chemical – that an individual has been exposed to. Corporeal capacity refers to an individual's developmental stage, psychological and 'medical' health, her skills, self-perception together with her sense of hopefulness/optimism. The opportunities that an individual will have to express her capacity are determined by her *immediate* and *current* environment. 'Immediate environment' refers to the situation that an individual is in at any given moment. Her capacity to deal with a specific situation will be better or less well developed depending upon her prior experiences. An individual's *current* environment, on the other hand, refers to the people and chemical, biological and physical noxae with which she may come into contact on a day-to-day basis. Her ability to change her environment will depend upon the nature of the change desired, the level of resistance the relevant environmental factors offer and her own corporeal capacity. An important part of this aspect of self-identity and interaction is how the body is perceived and how the body is used in interaction with others.

To summarize, in this chapter we have proposed a way of theorizing the relationship (central to social work) of person-in-environment. To this end we have argued that both biological and social constructionist perspectives can operate in synchrony, providing complementary ways of viewing and understanding the body. We argued for the importance of seeing the person's development and bodily well-being over the life course as being influenced both by genes and environment as well as by the impact of culture and social institutions. Our concept of environment was explained through using the camera lens as a metaphor, enabling us to register the simultaneous impact of a range of phenomena discernable at the 'wide-screen', 'middle-range' and 'close-up' viewpoints, but together accounting for the whole context in which humans act and are acted upon. We introduced two concepts – body cognizant social worker and corporeal capacity – in order to locate the social worker as an embodied actor whose practice is informed by biological and sociological perspectives.

In the next chapter, we offer guidelines for practice which emerge out of this theorization of person-in-environment.

5 The Body Cognizant Social Worker in Action

In this chapter, we provide a description of how corporeal capacity can be made use of by social workers in practice. A social worker working from a corporeal capacity framework will see the world through the three 'lenses' we have described in Chapter 4 – wide-screen, middle-range, close-up – recognizing the interpenetration of those broad 'levels' of social and material reality which are simultaneously and continuously 'producing' the immediate situation which we are trying to understand and to work with.

We have earlier (in Chapter 1) been critical of assessment protocols favoured in social work. To address what we perceive as problematic with such assessment schemas we propose what we will call the Body Cognizant Assessment Guide(BCAG). At the centre of the assessment task is the person-in-environment configuration, with the embodied person our target of under-standing. We utilize our knowledge derived from social work's four theoretical 'pillars' – systems theory, ecological theory, critical theory and social constructionism – in order to investigate both protective and adverse elements at the macrosocial (wide-screen), community scale and small scale (middle-range), intersubjective and intrapersonal (close-up) 'levels'. We note the strengths and vulnerabilities present at each 'level', as well as identifying those factors which can be changed or enhanced in order to maximize protective factors and minimize adverse elements. The social worker making the assessment might utilize both information that the client has provided about their circumstances as well as hypotheses or ideas for further investigation. In so doing, our focus is on the embodied person understood both as a biological and a social being. Very importantly, the BCAG alerts the worker to focusing on potentially adverse as well as protective corporeal factors as well as those in the client's milieu which provide targets for amelioration and/or enhancement.

Let us explore this by way of an example:

Client profile: Client is a 36-year-old man who is unemployed, experiencing financial problems, and suffering from low self-esteem and a feeling of general unease and unwellness. He also suffers from respiratory problems. He is seeking help with several things including, finding work – in particular so he can afford to keep paying rent at his current address – feeling better about himself, feeling healthier and with getting back in touch with family members. Because he has a history of violence and has been itinerant for a number of years, he has not spoken to his brother and sister for several years.

The BCAG provides social workers with an assessment protocol which maintains attention on the person and directs us towards exploring how environment may be seen to interconnect and impact on the person, demonstrating and illuminating the bi-directionality of the person/environment configuration.

But placing the body at the centre of social work theory and practice asks us to go further than this, to account for the social worker herself as an embodied actor entering and engaging with the client's world.

The twin ideas of body cognizant social work practice and corporeal capacity have many practical implications for social workers in their day-to-day activities, helping us to answer such questions as: how do we experience ourselves? What does it mean to be a body cognizant social worker? What are its implications for practice? Below we provide a description of the kinds of considerations and ways of working which might typify a social worker practising from this perspective. In the following we describe the strategies of a 'body cognizant' worker. As discussed, 'body cognizant' refers to awareness not only of how bodies are experienced or perceived but also a range of findings relevant to social work practice that has been derived primarily from neuroscience (and as discussed in more detail in Chapter 3).

Environment

The body cognizant social worker will be aware of the importance of immediate environment for the comfort of her clients and herself. Knowing that such stimuli may affect mood or cognition

	Potential sources of client vulnerabilities/strengths		Targets for amelioration/enhancement	
	Adversive	Protective	Adversive	Protective
Macrosocial factors	**What:** e.g. Reduction in unemployment payments; increase in number of work tests for unemployed **How (impact):** e.g. Re payment reduction: stress inducing, provides client less money which has meant poor nutrition which, in turn, has possibly affected mood, health, capacity to think clearly; re work tests: has impacted on self-esteem, and means client has less time to look for work	**What:** e.g. Public support for better training programs for unemployed **How (impact):** e.g. Has reduced client's sense of stigma, has provided hope/opportunity for policy change	**(Address) What:** e.g. Reduction in unemployment benefits **(Address) How:** Advocate with DSS re client's rights to receive adequate payments and adjustment of requirements for work tests.	**(Address) What:** e.g. Public support for better training programmes for unemployed **(Address) How:** e.g. Write a letter/campaign Department of Employment, Education and Training for more funding; attempt to negotiate with administrators with regard to providing funds for client's desired form of training.
Community scale biological/ chemical or physical factors	**What:** e.g. Frequent industrial noise; poor water system	**What:** e.g. Recent movement of rubbish site; improvement in local hospital facilities	**What:** e.g. Industrial noise and water access	**What:** e.g. Improvement in local hospital facilities

Continued

Continued

	Potential sources of client vulnerabilities/ strengths		Targets for amelioration/ enhancement	
	Adversive	Protective	Adversive	Protective
	How (impact): e.g. Re industrial noise: Has been distracting for client and potentially created attentional problems, stress; re poor water system: has potentially caused client cognitive and affective problems	**How (impact):** e.g. Re rubbish site removal: may mean reduction in disease and has decreased client's fear of illness; re better hospital: has meant client can receive faster treatment for illness	**How:** e.g. Re noise: write to council about noise and ask if any new restrictions can be imposed on businesses, see if any cheap sound proofing can be made for client's house; re water available: attempt to acquire water filter for client's personal use	**How:** e.g. Client can ask questions about new facilities or services the hospital may have, such as information sessions on respiratory ailments, dietary issues or other aspects of 'wellness'.
Small scale biological/chemical or physical factors (as afflicting person or home environment)	**What:** e.g. Old, broken furniture; damp house **How (impact):** e.g. Re bad furniture: causing client physical problems, back pain; re damp house: the house has been colder than it should be making client	**What:** e.g. Client's landowner has recently installed better security system; friend bought essential oils as a present **How (impact):** e.g. Re security system: has helped the client feel	**What:** e.g. Poor furniture and damp house **How:** e.g. Re furniture: help, where possible, the client obtain better furniture – from op/second hand shops to reduce muscular pain and thus psychological	**What:** e.g. Client's recent development of a 'sense of place/home' at his current address **How:** Assist the client to think of ways in which he can enhance the pleasantness of his home environment/use

	uncomfortable and gloomy, but only in winter, and could be exacerbating client's respiratory problems	safer in his home; re present: has created a sense of home in current abode, which is a new experience for the client	stress; re damp house: contact the landowner to demand he/she address rising damp issue	his home environment to provide him sense of calm and positive sensory stimulation
Intersubjective / interpersonal factors	**What:** e.g. Client's parents deceased and has poor relationships with siblings **How (impact):** e.g. Client has little instrumental assistance, and feels rejected and a social failure.	**What:** e.g. Client has relationships with two new friends **How (impact):** e.g. Friends have limited loneliness for client, and provided him with different perspectives on life	**What:** e.g. Poor relationship with siblings, and feelings of failure in interpersonal relationships **How:** e.g. Have the client reflect on his capacity for generosity and recent success with making friends to assist him with developing confidence to approach his family members	**What:** Successful relationship with friends **How:** e.g. Encourage client to identify contributions he has made and forms of communication (including verbal and physical) he has used that has allowed him to develop friendships in recent times, to help him widen his friendship circle
Intrapersonal/ intrapsychic factors	**What:** e.g. Client has long since believed he is unable to achieve any of his dreams/aims. He is ashamed because of his past violence.	**What:** e.g. Client has strong ability to persevere with activities that will benefit others	**What:** e.g. Poor nutrition through reduced income; pessimistic outlook	**What:** e.g. Client's ability to undertake activities that will benefit others

Continued

Continued

Potential sources of client vulnerabilities/ strengths		Targets for amelioration/ enhancement	
Adversive	Protective	Adversive	Protective
How (impact): e.g. Client's feelings have caused the client to stop pursuing constructive or psychologically beneficial activity	**How (impact):** e.g. Has allowed client some small sense of pride throughout life	**How:** e.g. Assist the worker to establish healthier and cheaper eating practices; work with client to help him understand faulty thought processes (CBT model) and social beliefs that reinforce negative view of self and future. Work with client in regard to strategies for decreasing feelings of anger and violent behaviour.	**How:** e.g. Assist the client to discover what it is that allows him to work so hard on behalf of others so he might be able to become consistent around this. Also, use this orientation to help client find a position of employment to which he might be more suited than work previously undertaken

consciously and unconsciously, the worker will check such things as the lighting and noise levels in, and temperature of, the room in which she is meeting a client. Where too little light may appear gloomy, too much bright light may force the worker or client to squint; sounds such as those from nearby factories or works, or mechanical noise inside the room, may be subtly distracting; and too cool a temperature may make either the client or the worker tense her muscles. Any of these effects may cause a worsening of mood in either client or worker.

The worker will also be aware of the possibility that she has developed unconscious associations in relation to the room in which she will be meeting a client or that the client herself may have associations – whether negative or positive – with kinds of objects kept in the room. The lighting, smell of the room, or a combination thereof may remind a client of past agency visits, or perhaps another location of which she has either very fond or very negative memories. Aspects of the room might, instead, remind the client of specific moments in her past.

Shortly after the client has arrived for an appointment, the social worker may choose to draw the client's attention to potentially challenging features of the immediate environment or explore the client's feelings about the meeting place. This may make the client less likely to misattribute any sense of discomfort she has derived from the room to other sources. The worker will also want to explore the client's or her own feelings in regard to any off-site locations in which she is required to meet a client.

Client/worker interaction

The 'body cognizant' social worker will be aware of the importance, to the therapeutic endeavour, of how she and her client receive one another. The social worker will also be conscious that how she and the client appraise different objects around them – including each other – will be largely determined by their moods. At the point of meeting, either the social worker or the client may be in a very positive or negative mood due to any of a range of factors (of which they will be more or less conscious). These include what they ate that morning, their experiences immediately prior to coming to the meeting, their general state of health and their levels of comfort in the immediate environment.

The social worker will also be aware that judgements she and the client make of one another will be affected by any conscious or unconscious associations that have been activated by the other's appearance, manner or other characteristic such as vocal tone. Aspects of individuals' identity upon which individuals are especially likely to base preconceptions are gender, ethnicity and class.

There are other reasons the worker may want to reflect upon her mood before meeting with a client and, where both necessary and possible, moderate or improve it. The most important of these is that her mood will have genuine potential to affect the client's sense of well-being. The worker will be aware that even *consciously* undetectable facial expressions she may exhibit will be capable of impacting the client's mood. A client's mood may also impact the worker's mood, but this is less likely where the worker remains aware of, and has a certain level of mastery over, her feelings.

The worker's facial expressions will be significant throughout her relationship with a client. Schore (2003) discusses that a worker's expressions can be used both to convey empathy and as a means to helping the client improve his own emotional regulation skills. As discussed earlier, a client may increase his capacity to regulate his emotions where he is given opportunity, in the practice situation, to experience negative thoughts and feelings before attempting new strategies for recovery; recovery is facilitated where the worker reflects the client's negative feelings before shifting to a more positive state.

The client's capacity to learn new self-regulation strategies will depend upon the 'biological causes' of his distress or, in other words, the condition of those physiological structures governing his emotional responses. The worker will attempt to establish, over time, whether the client has significant ongoing affective problems that may impact his ability to benefit from the rehearsal of such strategies. Certain types of depression, for example, challenge clients' ability to learn new behaviours. Severe depression and, in particular, certain kinds of learning disorders can also impair attention span. The worker may want to keep shorter any meetings with clients who have affective or learning difficulties, for example, or whose learning abilities are temporarily compromised (through use of medication, or other).

The worker will be particularly aware of her posture and body language. The worker should attempt to communicate, as much through her arrangement of the physical environment as her own behaviour, both that she is respectful of and willing to work with the client.

Assessment

Upon first meeting, the body cognizant social worker will want to establish which aspects of a client's circumstances need addressing and by which means. As part of this process, the worker may use, in addition to any other relevant tools, the BCAG, mentioned above. The BCAG will help determine what in a client's environments – including intersubjective environment – requires amelioration or enhancement. The worker may also ask the client about her 'emotional history'. Conducting an 'emotional assessment' may help the worker gain a sense of other cognitive and health issues with which the client may be currently struggling and how the client has arrived at her current circumstances.

The social worker's overall assessment will rely on various sources of information, the most important of which will be that which the client tells her. As the worker will be aware, what the client imparts about his circumstances and other matters will depend on a number of factors, only one of which will be the particular problem for which he is seeking help. Factors such as his mood, level of trust in the worker, sense of comfort in his environment, and things of which his environment has reminded him, will impact what he discloses and emphasizes. The client's ability to recall particular events or other information – which will be facilitated or hampered by his emotional state – will also determine what he tells the worker and the manner in which he expresses it.

The body cognizant worker will be aware of the limitations of the client interview as a source of information about the client's predicament. There are many things about himself – beyond the reasons for his feelings towards the worker, the office and so on – of which the client will be unaware. Intelligent, purposeful questioning by the social worker will help the client arrive at some realizations about his fears, priorities or similar, but other important information will be inherently unknowable by the client. One important aspect of the BCAG is that it allows client and worker to consider factors that may be contributing to the client's predicament that would be difficult for the client to identify merely through self-reflection.

The body cognizant social worker will also be aware that the kinds of verbal and non-verbal information about the client she attends to and kinds of assessments she makes will depend upon her own long-term or mood-dependent biases.

Intervention

As stated above, the BCAG, in combination with worker observation, is used to elicit information about a client's intersubjective environment or, in other words, her corporeal capacity. As a reminder, corporeal capacity refers to an individual's developmental stage, psychological and 'medical' health, skills, and self-perception together with her sense of hopefulness or optimism. A client's corporeal capacity will be a crucial determinant of how her problems are prioritized by the worker. Problems will also be prioritized according to how inherently 'solvable' they are perceived to be and how much time is believed necessary to address them.

Information about the client's strengths and weaknesses will also guide the worker's selection of intervention strategies. Which interventions are chosen will reflect, too, a client's preferences. The worker, however, may feel a client needs more information about the manner in which different interventions are thought to work prior to expressing his preferences. A lack of knowledge about mechanisms of action can lead clients to reject forms of intervention that would in fact be useful. In particular, a poor understanding of the relationship between mind and body has led clients to embrace either 'physical' interventions (such as dietary change or pharmacology) or psychological interventions, and reject the other, where both kinds of intervention would be appropriate. As even basic information about particular kinds of physiological processes can help clients better understand themselves, education of this kind can be considered an intervention in itself.

As we have already stated, another important intervention in its own right is the interaction or relationship between a social worker and her client; it is through empathic and intelligent listening that the worker may strengthen the client's own emotional responses and thus capacity for regulation. The worker, through using a model such as cognitive-behavioural therapy, may also assist a client to identify 'distorted' thinking or unhelpful thinking patterns. Another important task is helping a client elucidate her philosophical perspective. Assisting a client to do this not only helps client and worker establish how problems should be prioritized, but is useful for reducing any anguish or anxiety the client may be experiencing. The more conflict that exists amongst the various values and aims held by a client, the more confusion the client will experience.

Interventions implemented or suggested by the worker may pertain to any of those factors referred to in the BCAG, that is, intra-personal or inter-personal issues; local or larger scale physical, biological or chemical factors, or macrosocial factors. The body cognizant worker will be especially aware of the importance of social integration and support for individuals' well-being and thus, where relevant will focus on social interventions.

Whilst social workers informed by other practice models are also focused on the social lives and well-being of their clients, the body cognizant worker has broader knowledge of those factors that are able to impact social opportunities or functioning. Where other workers might not think to do so, a body cognizant social worker may suggest a client experiencing specific kinds of changes in such as his social behaviour or affect undergo a blood test, for example. Different blood tests can point to deficiencies in diet or allergies and other factors that can affect such.

Intra-personal strategies Clients may seek assistance for any of a range of personal struggles from poor self-esteem, through to behavioural issues. The worker may help the client with these in any of a number of ways. First, she may help the client identify demands in her life or aspects of her environment that exacerbate her behavioural or psychological concerns, and discuss ways to address these.

The worker may also, where appropriate, assist the client to change behaviour or thought patterns by working directly with them. Cognitive behavioural therapy (CBT) is a method that helps individuals identify ways in which their patterns of thinking are flawed and/or contribute to their unhappiness or discomfort, as well as how such problematic behaviours emerge. Neuroscientific research suggests that repeated rehearsal of new behaviours, including new ways of thinking eventually leads to their automatic activation. A worker can help a client practise new behaviours. CBT is considered appropriate for most individuals beyond middle childhood, but the worker will need to remain aware of those things that may hamper the client's ability to learn new thoughts and behaviours (including past drug abuse, and extreme depression.) A worker may also want to emphasize the relationship between negative patterns of thought and other kinds of ill health, (as explored further in Chapter 6).

The body cognizant worker may recommend clients with poor self-esteem, low energy, and affective challenges to undertake more exercise and/or dietary changes. (She may, instead, refer clients to fitness centres or dieticians.) Physical exercise can cause improvements in mood and self-confidence. Increasing or decreasing consumption of particular foods will, in some cases, aid mood, outlook and energy levels. An individual's sleeping patterns can also affect states of mind; thus the worker may discuss the benefits of proper sleep with some clients. (Exercise, diet and sleep are discussed further in Part 2).

A number of things will affect a client's ability to implement strategies away from the therapeutic environment or agency situation. The client may have formed particular associations with her home, for example, that strongly reinforce certain kinds of (unwanted) behaviour. Her home or broader environment may contain other kinds of distractions that make change difficult. The worker and client may, therefore, need to address intra-personal and broader environmental factors in tandem with psychological issues.

Inter-personal strategies The problems a client may experience with members of her family, or those to whom she is, in some respects, close, are countless. So, too, are the ways in which such problems may be addressed by client and worker. Consistent with other models of social work, however, the body cognizant social worker will adopt approaches to interpersonal work that are considerate of all relevant parties and that boost the client's self-confidence and self-efficacy.

Particular interventions will be considered more or less appropriate not only on the basis of the client's desires, interests, developmental stage, addiction status, emotional and general health and so forth, but also those of the other relevant party or parties. The worker will help the client to understand the relevance of each of these factors to interpersonal communication. She will also rehearse, with the client, modes of communication and assistance that are most appropriate to the problems at hand and individuals with which the problems are being experienced.

Local biological, chemical and physical factors In this context, 'physical' factors refers to natural phenomena such as weather patterns, and unnatural or human made structures and phenomena likely to impact an individual's safety. Examples of 'local' physical factors are noise pollution and standards of hospital care. 'Biological' and 'chemical' factors are those things that effect particular kinds of physiological changes within the individual.

The worker may help the client to limit or address particular physical or chemical hazards. She could, for example, help a client who has a poor respiratory system to move from a damp house or discourage a client who is experiencing headaches and dizziness from using strong solvents. It may instead be appropriate for the worker to refer the client to a general or other kind of health practitioner or expert.

Macrosocial factors and large-scale environmental factors The worker will, where possible, attempt to address aspects of the (client and worker's shared) macrosocial environment, or community-scale chemical or physical hazards that have contributed to the client's predicament. 'Macrosocial environment' encompasses political and legal systems, and prevalent beliefs and practices, including economic practices. Means the worker might adopt in challenging these include initiation of information campaigns or other forms of lobbying or social action.

The worker may also encourage a client to become involved in kinds of social action; whether she does so will depend partly on kinds of philosophy the client subscribes to, and partly upon the resilience of a client. Attempting to effect change at a broad social level can easily give rise to feelings of frustration and futility. The sense of discouragement that a more emotionally vulnerable client might feel were change not to be achieved could easily spread to other areas of her life.

The body cognizant worker would bear in mind that a client's levels of faith in suggested interventions at any level, and optimism about outcomes, are likely to wax and wane with her emotional state, as will her ability to implement planned strategies.

A note regarding practice ethics from a 'body cognizant' perspective   Clients will vary in terms of their capacity for self-determination the extent to which they will want to, or be capable of, making decisions about their circumstances. Thus, whilst developing self-mastery is important to clients' well-being, workers would be careful about placing the burden of all decision-making upon clients prematurely. Having to make decisions about significant aspects of life can generate or exacerbate anxiety for many clients, where anxiety itself can, in turn, impact negatively upon the ability to think clearly and make decisions. A worker may decide to be moderately directive early in her working relationship with a client, becoming less so as the client is less overwhelmed by external pressures and emotional strain.

Review and preparation

As discussed in previous chapters, we believe there are limitations to 'reflective practice', that reflection will not *necessarily* allow workers to gain better understanding of the reasons for, or efficacy of, earlier actions. Similarly, no amount of preparation before a meeting with a client will allow a worker to have either complete (conscious) control over her actions during their encounter nor full understanding of her motivations, reactions, and so forth. As intimated above, however, there are a number of questions relating to current mood, sense of comfort and so on that a social worker may ask herself both before and after meeting with a client that will benefit both her relationships with the client and attempts at self-care.

The worker may also wish to take 'process notes' in which would be detailed such things as what was said or not said, or observed or not observed during the course of a meeting, and what feeling states were evoked. This may allow the worker to make associations between her own or the client's thoughts, feelings and behaviours not previously made. A worker may realize upon reviewing her notes, for example, that a client's sudden disinclination to talk closely followed a change in her own mood. The worker could then attempt to fathom whether an unwitting transmission of her feelings had precipitated the clients' withdrawal.

The body cognisant worker in group work

The body cognizant social worker will be aware that issues relevant to work with individuals become more complex where groups are concerned. First, group processes, the set-up of meeting rooms, and others aspects of the therapeutic arrangement that suit some group participants will not suit others. The worker will be required to negotiate with group participants to develop practices, environments, rules and so forth that are at least satisfactory to all members. She will also remain aware of any specific needs of different individuals. Some members may need to leave the room more often, or require specific kinds of chairs, for example.

The body cognizant worker will be particularly attentive to the various verbal and non-verbal exchanges amongst group members to ensure that group members have equal opportunities for learning. The way in which individuals learn in groups differs from how they learn in 'one-on-one' casework settings. Instead of arriving at understandings about self and life through discussions with only the worker, group members learn directly and indirectly from one another. Group members are bombarded by 'talk', or different forms of communication, points of view and ways of thinking. They will register some of these consciously and others, unconsciously. Exchanges occurring in groups, in many instances, lead to shared or enhanced understandings about specific problems and the world. The longer the group runs for the more opportunity individuals have to learn from one another.

The body cognizant worker in community development and policy

The body cognizant worker's *approach* to community development will not differ significantly from that of other social workers'. As for her work with individuals, however, it will be informed by awareness that human well-being is determined by complex relationships amongst intra-personal, inter-personal, (physical) environmental and macrosocial factors. Thus, regardless of the community issue being tackled, the worker will see it as necessary to work with aspects of each of these spheres of influence. In conducting a community project aimed at reducing drug use amongst young people, for example, a body cognizant worker might want to take into account the following broad range of factors: common family or social stresses that young people using substances may have been exposed to as children; values and goals these young people currently hold; the quantity and kinds of positive support and negative reinforcement they receive and have received from others; what they understand their social status to be; their nutritional intake; levels of intellectual activity and physical exercise they undertake; hazardous or potentially hazardous aspects of their physical environment; social perceptions of illicit drug use, and how various of these are interrelated or interact.

The body cognizant worker employed in areas of policy review and development will take a similarly wide view of which factors are relevant to a given community issue. Suggested policy aimed at increasing literacy rates, for example, would consider a range of environmental and intrapersonal issues that are likely to inhibit or discourage learning, in addition to, say, the availability of adult learning services and attitudes towards literacy.

Inter-professional relationships

The range of professionals from whom a body cognizant social worker is likely to seek support or advice is broader than that drawn upon by conventional social workers. Most social workers are likely, at some stages of their practice, to seek advice from, or refer clients to, health and allied health professionals or other community workers. Body cognizant social workers may also consult with environmental auditors, dieticians and exercise professionals, for example.

Self-education

Given that the number of factors that may impact individuals' sense of well-being is almost limitless, it is impossible for a body cognizant social worker to stay abreast of all research relevant to its maintenance. Nevertheless, it is important that workers remain aware of the *kinds* of factors that impact health and, thus, access literature from a wide range of disciplines and practice areas. Reading undertaken by a body cognizant worker would reach beyond subjects traditionally of interest to social work, that is, social psychology, family dynamics, adolescent health and so on, to environmental health, pharmacology and neuroscience, for example. Given the importance of social communication to individuals' well-being, workers may also want to read sociological literature on this area.

Above all, the body cognizant social worker must be a creative thinker and reader, retaining a lateral view of all areas of research that may be relevant to practice.

Part 2 Implications for Practice

Introduction to Part 2

In the first part of this book we discussed biological and sociological theories on the body relevant to general social work practice. In this second part, we expand on some of these theories and introduce others that have particular relevance for specific practice areas. We do not aim to provide an exhaustive discussion of ideas with applicability to our selected fields; the number of theories on the body with some potential significance for each practice area is seemingly endless. Instead, we emphasize those theories we believe to be most important.

Our selection of fields in Part 2 was influenced by three main factors: first, the fact that mental health, child protection, ageing, health and the field of alcohol and other drugs are central social work practice domains. Second, that within these fields, insight and knowledge from contemporary neuroscientific research and social theories on the body are, at this stage, only minimally incorporated into theorizing and practice. Third, that regardless of the fields in which social workers are engaged, they are likely to encounter clients whose main struggles are associated with these primary domains and, as such, require some familiarity with concepts and findings relevant to them.

Mental health issues are of special significance across all practice fields. For this reason, the first chapter in this second part, which looks at mental health and focuses particularly on neuroscientific perspectives on mental illness, is longer than subsequent chapters. The mental health chapter is followed by two chapters with a life course focus, namely, child protection and ageing. While both these chapters refer to fields of social work practice, they also provide the reader with an account of expected changes and adaptations characterizing human development at both the opening and closing stages of life. It is at these stages that changes are perceived as being especially rapid and profound. The last two chapters deal with social work practice in health care, and the field of alcohol and other drugs.

Each of the chapters in Part 2 concludes with an example of a practice scenario characteristic of situations encountered in the relevant field and how the Expanded Environmental Instrument might be used to guide practitioners' thinking.

The book concludes with a brief chapter which draws together the main arguments we have made.

6 Social Work, the Body and Mental Health

The main roles of social work are to promote social justice and enhance the quality of life of individuals and communities. Quality of life is determined by a number of things including individuals' material circumstances, social relationships or sense of group belonging, and general health. Particularly important to quality of life is psychological health and, in particular, emotional well-being. Emotional well-being may be influenced by a range of broad environmental factors but is also a significant determinant of how one experiences or copes with circumstances throughout life. Given the great importance of emotional health to all individuals – social work clients, as well as social workers – we place particular emphasis on mental health and the body in this second part of the book.

Mental illness, as few as five decades ago, was a topic little discussed outside of psychiatric hospitals and private clinics. Certainly, the ordinary individual knew very little about which symptoms characterize specific disorders. Today, mental illnesses are the subject of large-scale information campaigns throughout Western societies. Corresponding with the increase in public awareness of mental illness have been increases in diagnoses of each of the major categories of mental illness: depression, anxiety and compulsive disorder. Today, mental illness is understood to affect a significant proportion of the world's population; estimates of the World Health Organisation (2004) are that 450 million people are suffering from at least one mental illness at any given time.

Although there are few preferable terms, 'mental illness' or 'disorder' are problematic categories. Use of the term reflects beliefs in normal behaviour, affect and cognition. Yet 'normal' behaviour and thought are very difficult to delineate. Buss (1966, in Pilgrim and Rogers 1999) refers to four perspectives from

113

which behaviours or cognitions can be considered abnormal, each of which relies upon, or incorporates, one of the following: social and behavioural statistics; notions related to ideal human behaviour; ideas relating to adaptive and maladaptive behaviour; and ideas about what constitutes both realistic and distorted cognitions.

Behaviour, thought and emotion are determined not only by individuals' inherent and (conscious and unconscious) personal needs but also by social pressures, or culture. Thus, what is thought normal or deviant will vary amongst cultures and can be considered, in this respect, arbitrary. It is on this basis that some individuals – amongst them, social workers – have argued the concept of 'mental illness' acts as a form of social control; a means by which the removal of 'deviates' from society for 'treatment' can be justified. Indeed, throughout the centuries, dissenters, revolutionaries and 'troublemakers' of many shades have been marginalized or disempowered through punitive mental health 'treatments' (see Solomon 2002, ch. 8).

In more recent times, however, there is evidence to suggest that most of those who have been diagnosed with a mental illness are not, in fact, willing dissenters. Rather, a majority are individuals who have little or no control over their behaviour or thought processes, and are distressed by their condition or admit to being in need of help.

Other objections to the concept of mental illness are based on a belief that mental anguish is, in most cases, a response to social struggle. Those who hold this view argue the term 'mental illness' individualizes or masks the true causes of mental disturbance. The problem with this argument, however, is that mental illness is neither the inevitable outcome of oppression nor is mental illness, in every case, triggered by individual experiences of inequality, or the accumulation thereof.

There is a final objection to 'mental illness' that will be mentioned here. In some contexts, mental illness is seen as a temporary condition and psychiatric disability as more or less permanent (see McKenzie 1994). In other contexts, 'mental illness' and 'psychiatric disability' are used interchangeably. Some mental health service users reject the term 'psychiatric disability' with its implication that, at least for some individuals, recovery from mental illness is not possible. Others, influenced by the social model of disability prefer the term 'psychiatric disability'. This second group argues that, where 'mental illness' locates blame for an individual's suffering solely in the individual, the term 'disability' recognizes the role of the environment in its creation. Disability, according to Oliver (1990), can be defined as the disadvantage or restriction of activity by a social organization that takes little account of people with impairments (in Mulvany 2000: 584).

In Australia, psychiatric disability services have differed from traditional mental health services in the sense that they have placed less emphasis upon diagnosis and 'treatment', and greater emphasis upon support and recovery. The concept of recovery as developed by mental health consumers is highly complex; it differs considerably from the idea of being 'cured'. It can apply to those 'for whom the outcome of their disorder is uncertain' (Davidson, O'Connell, Tondora, Staehli and Evans 2004: 13) and can mean 'living well in the absence or presence of mental illness'(Mental Health Commission in Briscoe, Orwin, Ashton and Burditt 2004). Many argue that recovery from a psychiatric condition involves attainment of self-determination and a positive sense of self-worth, as well as social acceptance and equality of rights (see e.g. Patricia Deegan's work).

In recent times, some mainstream mental health services have focused more on concepts of recovery and otherwise adopted a more empowering approach to working with service users. Accordingly, the term 'mental illness' has become more acceptable to many.

Social work has a long involvement in service provision to the mentally ill. The first psychiatric social worker is considered to have been Mary Brooks Meyer who began her observations of psychiatric patients in 1904. Traditionally, social workers found employment in social work departments of large psychiatric hospitals. Since this time, however, and largely due to deinstitution-alization initiatives which began in many countries the during 1970s, the range of roles that social workers perform has expanded enormously.

The services that social workers currently provide in the area of mental health are a combination of those peculiar to their profession and those also provided by other mental health professionals, such as community or clinical psychologists or psychiatrists, occupational therapists, or psychiatric nurses. As discussed by Bentley (2002), services provided by social workers in the mental health arena include therapy, mediation, education, skills training, case management, and consumer and family consultation. Additionally, workers are required to participate in interagency and interdisciplinary collaboration, perform advocacy and community work, and undertake program evaluation and research and policy analysis. Ziguras and colleagues (1999) refer to arrangement of leisure activities and accommodation for those with a mental illness as other tasks regularly performed by mental health social workers.

Social workers in all fields, from aged care to housing, will encounter individuals under great stress, and thus at risk of mental illness, who have not had contact with health or other allied health professionals. For this reason, social workers also play an important role in preventing mental illness.

Regardless of the tasks undertaken, social workers in mental health bring a unique orientation to their work. Bland and Renouf claim that the breadth of social work's purpose, and, thus, the eclectic training they receive, has led social workers to look beyond illness and treatments to issues of individual and family welfare, and 'such concerns as identity and relationships, housing, work, and income security' (2001: 238). Documents such as the 'Mental Health Competencies', developed by the Australian Association of Social Workers (1999), state that workers in the field should have knowledge of 'social and political processes that shape the social environment', including social class and social control; and theories of social justice, including 'how disadvantage and social injustice works and its remedies'. No comparable stipulations are made within Codes and Ethics and similar for Australian psychologists or psychiatrists (see The Australian Psychological Society 1996; The RANZCP 1998).

Social workers' perspectives on mental illness have been informed by theories from a number of disciplines, some of which pertain to the *nature* of mental illness, and others of which refer to etiology or treatment. Use of theories is anything but uniform across the profession. Social workers based in mainstream public hospitals will, generally speaking, be especially influenced by concepts and findings from psychology and psychiatry. In particular, such workers are likely to view mental illness in 'medicalized' terms; that is, as a condition or group of conditions requiring treatment to be administered by appropriately trained professionals, and often medical professionals.

Perspectives on mental illness held by those working in community mental health services are just as likely to be informed by one or more social and sociological theories on mental disorder. Sociological theories vary in terms of the ontological status that they accord mental illness. Social causation theories, for example, accept some mental illnesses as legitimate, delineable conditions. As is evident by the name, these theories hold that many illnesses are caused by socio-environmental factors. The main occupation of 'social causationists' is identifying *which* social factors are responsible. Most social causationists believe that poverty and various kinds of disadvantage, based on sex or class, for example, are responsible.

Other social theories that have been persuasive in social work include social or critical realism. Social realism or critical realism, advocated by those such as Greenwood (1994) and Bhaskar (1978, 1989, as referred to in Pilgrim and Rogers 1999: 21), is a moderated form of social constructivism insofar as its proponents accept that a reality exists outside of discourse. Social realists are able to maintain simultaneous beliefs in material causation of a psychological condition and a critical stance in relation to how mental health problems come to be defined by a society. Whilst critical realists may accept that despondency or hopelessness can be 'biologically triggered', they are also likely to raise questions about how, and through what means, those feelings may be interpreted as signs of depression.

Theories that may be described as social work theories – that is, those that are most commonly taught in social work courses and drawn upon in a wide range of professional literature – deal surprisingly little with mental illness. This includes theories that focus specifically on interventions or practice approaches, through to those that provide comprehensive explanations of human nature. Exceptions here include psychodynamic theory, which provides detailed accounts of particular conditions. Depression is identified in earliest psychodynamic theories as the turning in of loss-associated anger towards the ego or internalized loved object. Depressed persons are believed to internalize loved objects either when those objects (individuals) no longer exist or where they do not want to actually hurt the love objects lest they become even more inaccessible (Gilbert 1992: 274).

Various radical theories and practice theories such as crisis intervention and task-centred theories provide scant discussion of mental illness. Particular radical theories sidestep the discussion of mental illness altogether where others conceptualize it almost exclusively in terms of how those enduring it experience or negotiate their social environments. Mental illness is characterized in most task-centred and crisis-intervention theories as a potential outcome of crisis, or failure to implement successful coping strategies but is, nevertheless, a marginal issue in the literature (e.g. Kanel 2003; Doel and Marsh 1992). Discussion of mental illness in central ecological texts is also relatively superficial. In general, ecological theory explains mental illness as the result of deficits either in individuals or their environments, believing that they can be minimized through effecting change in either the individual or the environment (see Germain and Gitterman 1996).

Overall, mental illness in social work theories is under-theorized. Notably absent in social work theories on mental illness are references to the body despite that, as discussed further below, most recent findings of importance on mental disorders have emerged from biology and, in particular, neuroscience.

Some individual social work theorists have attempted discussion of the relevance of bodies to the profession's work, either across fields of practice or specifically with the mentally ill, with mixed results. An article by Johnson and colleagues (1990) highlights the kinds of difficulties social workers' encounter in trying to discuss mind–body relationships. Johnson and colleagues, in an article calling for greater emphasis on the biological in the 'biopsychosocial' paradigm, demonstrate an appreciation for emotion and cognition as physiological processes but at different points distinguish between physical and mental events. At one stage, the authors claim that there are many instances where practitioners have failed to recognize 'biological causes for overt apparently psychological ones' (1990: 112) despite that psychological factors can themselves be conceived of in physical terms. At another point, Johnson et al. refer to physical factors *causing* psychiatric illnesses. At yet another point, the authors refer to the possibility that alcohol creates rage 'biochemically' (1990: 114) as though there were kinds of rage that were not biochemical in nature.

Johnson, in a later book chapter, tackles the topic of neuroscience and, at the time of writing, is amongst the few social workers to discuss its relevance for social work. In her chapter on emerging knowledge for social work, she states neuroscience has 'revolutionized our understanding of human behaviour in the social environment, mental health and mental illness' (2002: 362). Whilst recognizing there are still many gaps in neuroscientific knowledge, like Johnson, we argue neuroscience understands much that is of use to social work regarding the nature, etiology and treatment of mental illnesses. Below, we discuss some of the most important findings.

In 2003, when genetic scientists working on the Human Genome Project were near to identifying the full complement of genes in human DNA, there was great discussion about whether, in the future, particular illnesses could be eradicated through the elimination or manipulation of certain genes. There was much evidence from adoption and family studies that heredity played a significant role in a majority of mental illnesses. Before and since that time theories about which genes may be responsible for one or another mental illness have abounded. For example, two major studies in late 1980s found that a gene on chromosome 5 was possibly involved in schizophrenia (Cooper 2001: 94). Findings from these studies, however, were unable to be replicated. Findings regarding the role of other genes in schizophrenia, and genes in other conditions, have also generally been difficult to replicate. Most recent research, however, indicates that few, if any, mental illnesses are associated with just one or a handful of genes (Cooper 2001). Rather, it seems that what particular genetic profiles bestow is vulnerability to particular illnesses but also that pre-, peri- or post natal social or psychological triggers are, in most, if not all, cases, necessary to their onset. In several years' time it is possible that more will be known about which genes are central to different illnesses. In the meantime, gaps in knowledge about heredity have not stalled other important discoveries about the biology of mental disorders.

Neuroimaging has assisted identification of pathophysiological mechanisms underlying a number of mental illnesses. Significant discoveries have been made in relation to brain regions and pathways central to obsessive compulsive disorder, schizophrenia, anxiety and depression (see Andreasen 2001). Establishing which neural circuits and hormones are involved in given illnesses helps neuroscientists determine things such as other 'medical' problems with which the conditions may be associated and means by which such conditions might be remedied. A focused examination of findings on depression helps clarify the depth and breadth of neuroscientific knowledge on mental illness and its utility for social work.

Affecting as it does millions of people at any given time, depression is a leading cause of disability throughout the world (World Health Organisation 2004: 15). Over the years, the term 'melancholia' and subsequently, 'depression' have referred to many things from a curse, to a blessing, to a medically treatable condition. Currently, how it is defined is largely dependent upon the purposes for which it is being described. Of interest here is 'clinical depression', or depression as described in the Diagnostic and Statistical Manual of Mental Illness (Fourth edition, 1994). A broad clinical definition of depression includes anhedonia, or inability to experience joy, and low energy. Frequently co-occurring with low affect are problems relating to sleeping, eating, physical movement and/or cognition.

Although depression is a problem defined by persistent sadness it does not bear a simple relationship to a 'sadness' circuit. Whilst the broader symptoms of depression share similarities, the mechanisms underlying depression in different people seem to vary. Davidson points out that some groups of depression sufferers have as their main symptom an incapacity for joy, whilst others have high degrees of anxiety and negative affect as core symptoms (2002: 547).

There are particular areas of the brain that seem consistently to be affected by depression. Mayberg (2003) identifies these as the frontal lobes, in particular, the dorsolateral and orbitofrontal corticies. The dorsolateral and orbitofrontal areas both play a role in inhibition and control of behaviour; the dorsolateral areas are involved when a decision to be made is attentional in nature and the orbitofrontal regions become involved when the decision is based on affective information (Davidson 2002; Mayberg 2003). Changes in the cingulate and, in particular, the anterior cingulate are also common. The anterior cingulate cortex is a point of integration for visceral, attentional and affective information (Thayer and Lane 2000: 211). Other main areas of the brain frequently affected by depression are the amygdala which, amongst other things, is responsible for directing attention to emotionally salient stimuli and indicating, to higher parts of the brain, that further processing of stimuli is necessary. The hippocampus, also central to depression, is involved in the creation of conscious memories and performs a range of regulatory functions (Davidson 2002). Whilst these areas appear to be important to all types of depression, in some cases they are over-active and in others, under-active. Davidson has proposed that there may be an anterior cingulate-based depression – characterized by a lack of will to change – and a prefrontal cortex (PFC)-based subtype. Those with a PFC-based depression might be aware of, and thus more anxious about, their inability to improve their condition (2002: 555).

Shenal, Harrison and Demaree (2003) have developed a model for subtyping depression based on dysfunctions in different areas of the prefrontal cortex. They suggest that dysfunctions or under-activation in the left anterior area of PFC, for example – which is more active when individuals experience positive emotion and is associated with approach or proactive behaviours – might produce, amongst other things, limited positive affect (including deficits in processing and executing positive behaviours), sparsity of speech, behavioural slowing and restricted social approach behaviours. The neuropathological mechanisms causing dysfunctions in these different areas may differ from individual to individual. That is, whereas left anterior dysfunction might always produce the same symptoms, how dysfunction comes to occur in that area might vary. For some individuals, a hormonal problem could lead to dysfunction. In other individuals, a neurotransmitter dysfunction could be responsible.

An area of uncertainty for neuroscientists is whether depression, or depression types, in children have similar neural underpinnings to those experienced by adults. Research into childhood depression is lacking. A great deal is known about the manner in which adverse circumstances impact the immature brain (discussed further in Chapter 7). However, neuroscientists are uncertain as to whether circuits underlying emotion in the young are the same as those in adults. In the case of the elderly, depression has been associated with reduced orbitofrontal volume and increased lesion density in the orbitofrontal region, which is potentially related to apoptosis, or natural cell death (see Ballmaier et al. 2004). A number of studies have found that there is a direct relationship between depression and decline in cognitive performance in the elderly (Elderkin-Thompson et al. 2003).

Depression has often been referred to as a stress-related disorder. There are significant gaps in the various neuroscientific theories about the mechanisms through which various stressors enact their effects. And, as should be clear from what has been stated already about different physiological abnormalities giving rise to comparable symptoms, how a given stressor is able to produce a depressive response will differ according to the individual affected. However, some important discoveries about the routes different stressors use have been made.

Psychological stressors encompass those social in nature, such as extended periods of isolation or frequent contact with hostile individuals, and other more general stressors – for example, losing a favoured item – to which most individuals are vulnerable. They also include things to which only some individuals – on the basis of their prior experiences or concepts about world and self – will find stressful. All stressors impact stress systems in the same way: when an individual enters a situation, information regarding her external environment is processed by her sensory systems before being fed by her temporal lobe to the amygdala, that part of the brain, mentioned elsewhere, involved in emotional appraisal. The temporal lobe simultaneously projects to the hippocampus, that region devoted to, amongst other things, memory tasks; the hippocampus will help match information about the individual's current situation with images she has formed in the past about comparable circumstances, rapidly and mostly unconsciously. When an individual is stressed, the hippocampus then signals hypothalamic-pituitary-adrenal, (HPA) axis, described presently, and two different neurotransmitter systems (Seeman 2001).

The HPA axis, along with the sympathetic nervous system (SNS), is involved in the fight or flight response. As mentioned in Chapter 2, constant stress over an extended period of time can lead to an over-abundance of cortisol circulating in the system, a condition called hypercortisolemia. This condition can lead to damage to the hippocampus. Aside from inducing poor affect, a damaged hippocampus is thought to lead to cognitive and memory impairments, other problems associated with depression (Meyer, Chrousos and Gold 2001). Such a process is thought to underlie depression in at least 50 per cent of cases (Nestler, Barrot, DiLeone, Eisch, Gold and Monteggia 2002).

Countless studies have documented that a disproportionate number of individuals of lower socio-economic status suffer from depression (*Muntaner, Eaton, Meich and O'Campo 2004*). Many explanations have been offered for this, including that those poorer have less access to health care and nutritional food (Siefert, Heflin, Corcoran and Williams 2004). Other studies have found that living in noisy, polluted and/or crowded environments creates psychological vulnerability whilst others have found that unemployment, or a lack of engaging or 'meaningful employ-ment' can predispose individuals to illness (Link, Lennon and Dohrenwend 1993; Weich and Lewis 1998). The fragmentation in families or social isolation that often occurs as a result of inse-cure housing arrangements have also been offered as the link between depression and poverty. A recent analysis of longitudinal data pertaining to over 100,000 psychiatric patients admitted to a hospital in Massachusetts supports that financial stress, inde-pendent of any other factor, creates risk of one of several mental illnesses, including depression (Hudson 2005). What is certain is that those from poorer backgrounds are more likely to experience multiple concurrent stressors (see Baum, Garafalo and Yali 1999) and, as such, are more vulnerable to depression. Research utiliz-ing both self-report and biological measures have supported that those of low socioeconomic status experience more stress (see McEwen and Seeman 1999; Meyer, Chrousos and Gold 2001).

Regardless of the position from which one commences, decline in socio-economic status is also likely to occur once individuals have experienced mental illness. Re-employment or retention is often difficult after a period of illness due to the stigma attached to the illness, a loss of confidence on the part of the sufferer, or cognitive and memory impairments incurred during the illness (see e.g. Lerner et al. 2004).

Exposure to high levels of cortisol in early life is considered to be particularly detrimental for an individual's emotional develop-ment. There is some evidence to suggest that exposure to a high level of glucocorticoids pre-natally, as a result of maternal stress, can lead to hippocampal damage and the attendant problems of vulnerability to depression, and cognitive and memory impair-ment mentioned above. (See Field et al. 2004.) Findings from developmental psychology that parental indifference, inconsistency, neglectfulness or abusiveness greatly increase the chance of a child later developing emotional or cognitive problems are well supported by neuroscientific evidence. Children who have been subject to abuse have been found to have elevated round-the-clock levels of cortisol (Meyer, Chrousos and Gold 2001). This may reflect permanent damage to the endocrine system, a sign of a child being at significant risk of developing depression. (Emotional disorders in children are discussed further in Chapter 7.)

It is not the case that all individuals suffering from depression exhibit high levels of cortisol or a dysregulated HPA axis, however. Heim and colleagues found a group of patients whose stress functioning was normal (Heim, Newport, Wagner, Wilcox, Miller and Nemeroff 2002), and Gold and Chrousos (2002) found a group whose stress response was under- or hypo-responsive. Those with symptoms corresponding to the 'atypical depression' subtype are most likely to have a stress system that is hypo-responsive.

Both hypo-and hyper-responsive stress systems are correlated with various illnesses and conditions. An under-production of the hormone cortisol (caused by the hypo-responsive state), for example, can lead to inflammatory diseases, such as arthritis. An over-supply of this hormone, resulting from an over-active stress system, can cause the immune system to be suppressed (Robles, Glaser and Kiecolt-Glaser 2005). Emotion and illness are mutually impacting. Various infectious, autoimmune and neurodegenerative diseases are thought to contribute to the development of depression. Cytokines are small protein molecules that are the main messengers of the immune system. Cytokines stimulate the hypothalamus to produce corticotropin-releasing hormone (CRH), a chemical messenger released by the hypothalamus during the stress response. CRH activates the HPA axis and triggers the production of cortisol and so forth, leading to the same negative consequences mentioned above (McEwen 1999).

Dietary factors can be responsible for inducing depression in particular individuals. Trytophan is an amino acid essential to the production of serotonin, one of the most important mood-impacting neurotransmitters in the body. Trytophan is found in various foods (with turkey and bananas having particularly high concentrations). Dietary-induced trytophan depletion can lead particular depression-prone individuals to relapse (Booij et al. 2002). Low levels of folate, a nutrient found in high quantities in spinach, chickpeas and lentils are also strongly correlated with depression (Paul, McDonnell and Kelly 2004).

Caffeine can be particularly problematic. Aside from inducing anxiety in a large proportion of the population, exacerbating psychotic symptoms in some patients with schizophrenia and causing insomnia in a wide range of individuals, caffeine can disturb treatment of depression through such means as increasing lithium clearance. It may also cause problems relating to information processing and motor coordination in those whose anti-depressant medications rely on the same isoenzymes as caffeine for metabolism (Paton and Beer 2001). The dangers of caffeine are particularly alarming in light of the fact that waiting rooms of community mental health agencies in many parts of the world are stacked with free tea and coffee for the consumption of clients.

Smoking is another problem. Some data shows that serotonin formation and secretion in patients with mental illness are influenced by chronic smoking. Smoking inhibits the activity of monoamine oxidase B, which is responsible for breaking down several neurotransmitters (Haustein, Haffner and Woodcock 2002).

Work by Chesler (1974) and Busfield (1996) remind us that statistics pertaining to women and mental illness should be interpreted cautiously; madness and deviance has, throughout the centuries, often been linked with female behaviour and preferences. Nevertheless, it appears that females are somewhat more vulnerable to depression than males. Findings are that women are up to twice as likely, after the onset of puberty, to experience a depressive episode than males (Kornstein 2001: 11). Women are also more inclined to experience a greater range of symptoms than male sufferers. A number of social theories have been offered for this, including that women have less economic, social and political power than men, and are thus exposed to more stress, or that women are more reactive to stress (Macijewski, Prigerson and Mazure 2001). Other theories focused on hormones have been offered.

In general, depression in some women may be related to a preexisting vulnerability to depression – as bestowed, for example, genetically or through early childhood experiences – in combination with the natural hormonal turbulence that characterizes such events as the onset of puberty and the pre-menstrual phase. At puberty, young women experience an increase in estrogen and the beginning of a cyclic and diurnal variation in its production. These changes increase the sensitivity of neurotransmitters – which may also, at this time, be impacted significantly by psychosocial and other stressors – and thus susceptibility to emotional disorder (Steiner, Dunn and Born 2003: 71). Pre-menstrual Dysphoric Disorder (PDD) may be related to increased levels of androgen, a hormone that has been linked to sex drive and aggression; an imbalance between progesterone and its metabolite, allopregnanalone, or alterations in the sensitivity of a type of serotonin receptor (Steiner, Dunn and Born 2003: 75). A recent study has found that women who suffer from PDD have abnormal norepinephrine function (Blum et al. 2004). Post-partum disorder (PPD) is suspected to be associated, in some cases, with HPA functioning and cortisol production and, in others, with thyroid dysfunction (Wisner and Stowe 2004). Changes in receptors for serotonin function have also been found in some women with PPD (Newport et al. 2004).

Chances are that, in the not-too-distant future, evidence for gender-specific triggers for depression in men will also in be discovered.

It is not necessarily the case that identifying the trigger for a depressive episode will assist in figuring out the best treatment. That is to say, it will not always follow that because an individual's most recent depressive episode was caused, for example, by loneliness, that an increase in his social activity will bring about remission. Whether an increase in social support will work is dependent on the particular pathological mechanism responsible for his depression. Different dysfunctional mechanisms are responsive to different types of treatment. Put another way, types of treatment impact the brain differentially, although there is some overlap in the brain regions treatments affect.

It is likely that, in the future, neuroscientists will be able to determine, through establishing which kinds of abnormalities have given rise to an individual's suffering, which treatments will best work for a sufferer. Work to this end is already taking place. Mayberg and her colleagues are endeavouring to find particular biomarkers, or biological abnormalities, that will predict what kinds of treatment different individuals will respond to (see Mayberg 2003). Genetic scientists have also come that much closer to identifying which classes of anti-depressant medications are suitable for different groups of people. Scientists have had the ability since 2003 to conduct a particular kind of test called the Drug Reaction Test that has recently been made available to the public in the United States (for a fee). The test determines, amongst other things, the functionality of certain enzymes. A large number of individuals are thought to have genetic variations that affect one or more of the eight to ten enzymes in the liver involved in the metabolism of most drugs (see Kaplan 2005).

Just as the distinction between physical and psychological illnesses is false, so too is the distinction between physical and psychological therapies. Psychotherapy, or counseling, can be considered a physical therapy, inasmuch as, it has a direct impact upon the brain. A number of researchers have used neuroimaging to work out how individuals' brains change in response to psychotherapy. One study by Goldapple and colleagues found that CBT responders showed increases in the hippocampus and dorsal cingulate region, and decreases in dorsal, ventral and medial regions of the frontal cortex. By contrast, those subjects who were treated with paroxetine showed increases in both prefrontal areas and the hippocampus. These findings are interesting in light of the known role of the hippocampus in emotional monitoring and memory, and the respective roles of the dorsal, ventral and medial regions in working memory, self-referential processing, and cognitive ruminations (Goldapple et al. 2004: 37). Another study found that responders of interpersonal therapy (IPT) versus paroxetine, IPT responders, like the CBT responders, showed decreases in the right PFC. As mentioned, the right PFC is associated with negative emotion. Responders also showed changes in the left anterior cingulate gyrus – that area of the brain that undertakes conflict monitoring (Brody et al. 2001). Whilst neuroscientific findings indicate psychotherapy works, more research pertaining to how it works is needed; there is a measure of inconsistency in findings across studies.

As discussed in Chapter 2, negative affect is related to a greater amount of activity in the right PFC, and positive affect with more activity in the left. Thus, there is reason to believe that engaging in tasks such as abstract reasoning or meditation that stimulate the left PFC do not so much 'distract' us from our negative thoughts, as help diminish them.

Frequent positive social contact is thought to not only prevent depression – attentive affectionate care is essential to children's development of healthy emotional regulation – but also alleviate it. Countless studies have found, in fact, that recovery time from depressive episodes and quality of life amongst depressed individuals correlate with self-reported levels of social support (see e.g. Nasser and Overholser 2005; Kuehner and Buerger 2005). Given the strong association between our relationships with others and how we see ourselves and the world, positive social support is most likely to work through means similar to psychotherapy. Given that both human touch, and the hormone oxytocin – a hormone that facilitates bonding and affection – have been found to have mood-enhancing effects, there are also questions about their relevance to the ameliorating effects of social contact upon depression.

Whereas psychotherapy is considered to work through 'top-down' mechanisms meaning that those parts of the brain concerned with conscious thought are being trained to gain control over the so-called limbic brain areas – those areas from which emotions originate and over which individuals, most of the time, have very little control – anti-depressants medication, on the other hand, can be described as having a bottom-up effect. This means that the major sites of action for most anti-depressants is the nuclei in the brainstem, the lowest part of the brain and that which is most strongly identified with autonomic processes. Effects eventually filter up into the higher parts of the brain (Goldapple et al. 2004). But there is some common ground in terms of the brain regions that the different therapies affect.

Although different classes of anti-depressants have different modes of action, most work by making the hormones serotonin and norepinephrine more available to the body. Monoamine oxidase inhibitors (MAOIs) inhibit the enzyme monoamine oxidase which helps break down serotonin and norepinephrine; tricyclics inhibit the nerve cell's ability to re-uptake serotonin and norepinephrine, whilst selective serotonin re-uptake inhibitors (SSRIs) block the presynaptic serotonin transporter receptor (and has an indirect effect on norepinephrine). There are other anti-depressant medications that do not fit into these classes such as buproprion and nefazodone, the mechanism of which is slightly different (Andreasen 2001, ch. 9). There is increasing controversy about the use of anti-depressant medication given that other interventions, such as exercise, have been shown to be, in some cases, as effective at alleviating depression whilst not giving rise to the same kinds of side effects (see below). The side effects of medications can be severe. MAOIs, for example, whilst producing a positive response in many, impairs the body's ability to break down tyramine, a substance found in many foods including aged cheese, wines, and most nuts. Consumption of food containing tyramine whilst taking MAOIs can cause dangerously high blood pressure. Other medications cause weight gain, agitation, poor concentration and other adverse cognitive effects in many (Stein and Strickland 1998). It is expected that future neuroscientific research will lead to the development of medications that have more precise mechanisms of actions and a reduced capacity to disrupt a range of bodily systems.

As mentioned above dietary deficiencies are frequent triggers for depressive episodes. Whereas those depression sufferers with sufficient levels of folic acid and trytophan will not benefit from increasing their intake of these elements (see e.g. Bell, Hood and Nutt 2005) there are many individuals whose depression will be seriously impacted by dietary changes.

Physical exercise is also understood to decrease the effects of depression. A handful of recent studies have, in fact, found that exercise can be as successful at treating mild to moderate depression as pharmacological treatments, particularly in older people but also in others (Blumenthal, Babyak, Moore and Craighead 1999; Craft and Landers 1998: 353). Explanations for its efficacy include that it provides participants with a greater sense of self-efficacy or social interaction (Bodin and Martinsen 2004). Other theories include that exercise disrupts HPA functioning (O'Neal, Dunn and Martinsen 2000: 123) or stimulates the release of b-endorphin, which is an endogenous opioid (a kind of natural painkiller) (Brosse, Sheet, Lett and Blumenthal 2002: 753).

Experimentation with sleep manipulation also holds promise as a treatment for depression. An important recent finding is that one night's total sleep deprivation leads to a complete remission of symptoms for between 40 per cent and 60 per cent of depression sufferers for between one and several days. Other depression sufferers have achieved success with partial sleep deprivation (Giedke and Schwarzler 2002). There are a number of theories about why sleep deprivation works, but most understand it to be related to changes in dopaminergic and/or serotonergic function (Wu, Buchsbaum and Bunney 2001).

Whilst neuroscientific theories have, as their focus, a relatively stable and ultimately knowable internal body, external or 'public' bodies are open to endless reinterpretation and manipulation.

Humans do not have access to one another's thoughts. In trying to establish something about strangers and, in particular, the threats they pose to us, we watch one another. We are constantly observing one another's bodies and are having our bodies observed; how we hold ourselves, the gestures we use, the activities we engage in, indicate to others our understanding of (or, at least, interest in) social codes.

Labelling theory, as proposed by Howard Becker and developed further by those such as Scheff, looks at the appraisals we make of others that are relevant to mental illness. Mentioned above is that how individuals' behaviour is judged – whether as normal/sane or abnormal/insane – will depend largely upon the norms of cultures to which persons, judging have been exposed. Labelling theorists argue, further, that judgements made of individuals will differ according to the social roles they inhabit (Scheff 1974: 449). Where, for example, a poorly paid cleaner might not be expected to be exuberant, subdued behaviour in a wealthy and successful actor, or even an expectant parent, might be taken by many as a sign of depression. The roles that individuals occupy can change over time meaning that particular of their behaviours that in some contexts seem normal will, in other contexts, be considered deviant. Labelling theorists argue that behaviours are more likely to be judged as deviant when exhibited by those who have already been diagnosed with a 'mental illness' (Pilgrim and Rogers 1999: 22).

Our bodies are not only the object of judgement but also the means by which we are controlled. In eighteenth century Europe, mental illness came to be seen as a threat to the social order. This change in status coincided with the increased 'medicalization' of mental illness. In Foucault's view, doctors formed a kind of shock troop that helped to isolate the ill in 'treatment centres' and administer a range of brutal treatments. Treatments provided by Pinel, a doctor whose influence was significant throughout Europe at this time, included forcing the mentally ill into freezing showers and straitjackets (Foucault 1989, ch. 9). Particular social theories help highlight that whilst giving one's body to the care of science may lead to the end of mental anguish, it may also lead to harm. In this light, the idea of self-care and providing those who are ill with the means to administer it becomes particularly important.

Whereas, in some instances, control of behaviour is effected by external sources, those experiencing mental illness can be encouraged to suppress their own behaviour, to either positive or negative effect. Foucault (1977) argues that all treatment of 'deviants', including the mentally ill – from the most punitive through to the more benign measures of contemporary social institutions – can cause the relevant individuals to judge and censor those aspects of their behaviour, however harmless, that they have come to see as abnormal. Recent work by those such as Parr provide support for this thesis. Parr, who spoke to a number of individuals who were diagnosed mentally ill, found that his interviewees sought out 'insane spaces', places – such as bedrooms, parks and cafes – where they could be 'themselves'. Parr's data suggests that his respondents' identities were influenced by their 'interpretation of their mental attributes' (Mulvany 2000: 592) and the 'common sociocultural codings and understandings about how the self should be in every day life' (Parr 1997 in Mulvany 2000). They were aware of the meanings others attributed to their behaviours and sought to avoid the rejection associated with being identified as 'different'. Fear of rejection has led other individuals who have received a diagnosis to limit opportunities for being observed and judged altogether by removing themselves from social life. This self-imposed isolation, however, leaves them vulnerable to relapse (Link, Cullen, Struening and Shrout 1989).

There is an interesting question about the extent to which the regulation of behaviour is able to regulate thoughts – in particular, unwanted thoughts – and emotion. Ekman (1993: 388) has found that arrangement of facial muscles into particular expressions can, in very little time, stimulate neural and endocrine activity associated with the emotion it suggests. Similarly, Kataria (1999) has found that making facial expressions and sounds associated with laughter can eventually induce a spontaneous version of the same. Much research has found that spontaneous (non-malicious) laughter has a range of health benefits. (See e.g. Bennett, Zeller, Rosenberg and McCann 2003.)

Stoppard is interested in how 'embodied' experiences – the living of life through a body – contributes to the incidence of mental illness and, in particular, depression, amongst women. Taking a material-discursive position, which conceptualizes the body as 'simultaneously a physical and symbolic artifact' (Lock in Stoppard 2001: 92), Stoppard argues depression can result from a woman's efforts to 'meet socially constructed standards defining the good woman' (108). Much is expected of the 'good woman' that can 'exhaust a woman's body, while undermining her morale and sense of well-being' (92). She is required, for example, to take on the majority of caring work in families and housework, often in addition to paid work. Further, acceptance amongst peers can rely on a woman's ability to maintain a pleasing appearance and/or be sexually attractive to men.

Certainly, women's bodies are more vulnerable to domestic violence, the incidence of which is strongly correlated with mental illness and, in particular, depression (Roberts, Williams, Lawrence and Raphael 1998). As well as living in constant fearful anticipation of the next attack, women subjected to domestic violence may experience themselves as physically devalued and vulnerable, which is in itself extremely stressful.

Widespread sexual objectification of women within mass media has also been detrimental for the mental health of many women, to which high rates of eating disorders, body dysmorphic disorder and general appearance-related anxieties stand in testament (see Bordo 2004). Individuals – both male and female – with any of a range of 'physical' disabilities or permanent injuries are especially vulnerable to negative self-appraisal, and negative appraisal and treatment by others, based on their appearance or inability to achieve 'physical perfection' (see Stone 1994 and Taleporas and McCabe 2001).

Bordieu (1984) argues that the way in which individuals conceptualize and use their bodies – in social communication and work, and otherwise – is also determined by (whilst also determining) social class. Charlesworth (2000) and Wainwright and Turner (2003) argue that working class men are more inclined than others to objectify their bodies, to view their bodies as instruments for hire and, consequently, experience a sense of alienation or distance from their bodies. The frames of reference that individuals use to think about their bodies can lead to greater or lesser sympathetic treatment of self and better or worse mental health.

Sociology reminds us that the visible or social body together with the experienced body is as important for our understanding of mental illness as the biological body.

Corporeal capacity

As stated in the first part of this book, corporeal capacity refers to an individual's psychological and 'medical' health, and his skills and self-perception together with his sense of hopefulness or optimism. It is a term that simultaneously acknowledges the client as a biological and social being. It also reflects appreciation of the significance of a client's past experiences and environments to his development of capacity and the importance of his current and immediate environments to its expression. It is social workers' role to help clients develop corporeal capacity and establish or find environments in which capacity may best be exercised.

Social workers have a particular responsibility to care for the psychological and, in particular, emotional health, of their clients. As stated throughout this text, emotions are central to human life; they are the means through which the impact of our environments are sensed and their existence the reason why our relationships with others are meaningful. Thinking in terms of clients' corporeal capacity and applying knowledge of the body – or 'body cognizance' – is essential to selecting and implementing interventions relevant to emotional health.

Body cognizant social worker

The body cognizant social worker will be aware of the relevance of individuals' perceptions and use of their bodies – for work, and as instruments of communication and signification – (as well as how their bodies are perceived by others) to the maintenance of mental health. She will also be aware of the relevance of findings from biology to understanding, preventing and treating mental illness.

Findings by neuroscientists on mental illness and by social theorists on mental illness and the body suggest some new roles for social workers and provide support for forms of intervention already in use.

Frequently, clients feel guilty about experiencing mental illness, believing it to be caused by a weak will or another personal deficit that they feel they should be able to control. A task of social work and other mental health professionals, consequently, has been to help clients understand the significant challenge that recovery from psychiatric conditions can present. Some uncertainty exists as to whether particular kinds of brain lesions or physiological abnormalities correlated with different disorders occur prior or subsequent to initial episodes of illness. Nevertheless, making clients aware of brain abnormalities commonly associated with their disorders can help workers convey to clients the 'realness' of their conditions.

Neuroscientific findings, as discussed, support findings from epidemiological studies and social research that individuals of lower socio-economic status are more prone to stress and mental illnesses such as depression and anxiety. The body cognizant social worker can use this knowledge to further 'normalize' clients' illnesses and discourage self-blaming by clients who have experienced or are currently experiencing illness. It may also be used to encourage clients into forms of social action that may benefit both themselves and others vulnerable to mental illness.

A familiarity with findings from neuroscience that any of a range of pathophysiological mechanisms may underlie a given mental illness will also ensure that the body cognizant worker avoids treating individuals' experiences of mental illness in a standardized manner; that she does not, in other words, make immediate assumptions about which particular treatments will be most appropriate for a client and so forth, based on the perception or knowledge of the client as depressed, for example.

The body cognizant worker would also convey hypotheses regarding the (physiological) relationship between stress and mental illness as a way of encouraging both clients with and without a history of mental illness to develop strategies for dealing with and avoiding stressful events. Amongst tactics for avoiding stress, the worker may introduce to clients meditation and other forms of relaxation, and cognitive behavioural and other strategies aimed at helping clients to develop a sense of independence, positive self-image and belief in their potential for change. Given findings on the ability of abstract mental tasks to inhibit right-sided prefrontal (brain) activity, or diminish negative affect, the body cognizant worker could also encourage clients to undertake mental tasks – such as word puzzles, mathematical games or solving of practical problems – during the experience of a slightly to moderately poor mood.

The worker would inform clients about how – from a physiological perspective – relaxation and problem-solving techniques are thought to impact affect and either prevent, or assist recovery from, mental illness. Having such knowledge not only provides clients a greater sense of confidence in the activities – with optimism itself having positive benefits for mental health – but also provides clients with a greater sense of control over their body states (or moods).

The body cognizant social worker would be aware that some individuals, either due to cognitive effects with which their illnesses are associated, or use of illegal or legal drugs they are taking to treat it, will have trouble learning new kinds of behaviours or patterns of thinking. This would remind the worker to attempt to establish a client's cognitive abilities before persevering with more cognitively sophisticated forms of intervention.

The body cognizant worker would also provide intensive education around such things as diet, exercise and how these factors impact mental illness. Depending on work context, workers might also assist clients who are currently suffering or have recently recovered from mental illness, with such things as meal planning. Particular impetus is provided for helping clients who suffer from anxiety or depression to access aerobic activity.

Given that affective disorders frequently co-occur with a repressed immune system, a body cognizant social worker would inform those suffering from such conditions about their greater vulnerability to a range of illnesses and how immune functioning and emotion are related.

The body cognizant worker would discuss with clients the relevance, for recovery or maintenance of good mental health, of how individuals conceptualize and use their bodies in every day life. The worker would assist clients with negative views of their bodies to change their perceptions of their bodies. As a means to facilitating their better social integration, the worker might help clients to become aware of how they communicate with others physically. She might also help clients to understand how various postures and facial expressions can either facilitate relaxation or exacerbate psychological distress.

Currently, mental health funding is focused on primary care. There is much debate over the desirability of the increased role of primary practitioners in treating those who are mentally ill. General practitioners do not have the time or, in most cases, the expertise to undertake anything other than infrequent, superficial counseling of patients. Doctors are also likely to prescribe medication over any other forms of treatment. Recent findings of the efficacy of alternate forms of treatment – from increased social activity through to exercise – for treating particular mental health conditions should be used to support funding applications for community mental health programs, support groups and other kinds of socially based intervention programs.

The body cognizant social worker working in policy might want to draw attention to neuroscientific findings suggesting the viability and, in some cases, (given the frequent side effects of medication), of non-pharmacological forms of treatment for a range of mental illnesses. He would also stress the importance of making provisions for those experiencing mental illness to receive *long-term* counseling and support, and greater opportunity to partake in activities that will increase their sense of self-belief and optimism.

Below we refer to the manner in which the Body Cognizant Assessment Guide (BCAG), as discussed in Part 1 of this book, may be used to assist work undertaken by the body cognizant worker.

Client profile: The client is a 19-year-old woman who suffers from dysthymia. She has experienced one lengthy episode of major depression – which began shortly after her father died – from which, with the help of antidepressant medication, she has only recently recovered. The client, who was living with her father just prior to his death, is currently living in temporary accommodation with friends. She has one older brother whose whereabouts are unknown, and has recently made contact again with her mother with whom she shares an ambivalent relationship. As she is unemployed but unwilling to receive unemployment benefits, the client has approached the community health agency seeking financial advice. Her other main concern is increasing feelings of anxiety and fear of slumping back into depression. The client has been attempting to reduce her feelings of anxiety through regularly drinking alcohol. This, at times, exacerbates her low mood but, she is unwilling to use medication again.

	Potential sources of client vulnerabilities/strengths		Targets for amelioration/enhancement	
	Adversive	Protective	Adversive	Protective
Macrosocial factors	**What:** e.g. Lack of employment opportunities available for those with little previous working experience. **How (impact):** e.g. Means client has lack of money which makes meeting basic needs independently difficult. Inability to secure work affects her self-esteem.	**What:** e.g. Existence of community mental health services; one of which is close to her current accommodation. **How (impact):** e.g. Provides the client with a sense of having somewhere to go if she is feeling emotionally vulnerable.	**(Address) What:** e.g. Reluctance of businesses to take on employees with no working history. **(Address) How:** e.g. Suggest the local newspaper run positive articles on businesses who have taken on staff with no work experience in their particular industries.	**(Address) What:** e.g. The existence of training schemes available through government-run services for the unemployed. **(Address) How:** e.g. Encourage the government to provide free short-term training for those who are looking for work but do not necessarily want to receive benefits.
Community scale biological/chemical or physical factors	**What:** e.g. Prevalence in client's age group of young people drinking alcohol. **How (impact):** e.g. Increases likelihood of the client continuing	**What:** e.g. The wide availability of anti-depressant treatment. **How (impact):** e.g. The client has had recent success with a prescribed SSRI, i.e.	**What:** e.g. Common abuse of alcohol by young people. **How:** e.g. Encourage client to discuss with friends some of the risks associated with	**What:** e.g. The recent discovery of dietary conditions that can exacerbate poor mood, and inclusion of label warnings on, and healthy 'additives' (such

Continued

Continued

	Potential sources of client vulnerabilities/strengths		Targets for amelioration/enhancement	
	Adversive	**Protective**	**Adversive**	**Protective**
	to be a part of a subculture based around frequent and excessive drinking. Problematic given the effect of alcohol upon her.	having experienced alleviation of symptoms, and few side effects.	drinking to excess, ways to reduce drinking, and activities available in the local area that may help them get out of the habit of frequent drinking.	as Omega 3) in, commercial food. **How:** e.g. Increase the chance of the client receiving required nutrients.
Small scale biological/chemical or physical factors (as afflicting person or home environment)	**What:** e.g. The client regularly drinks excessively. **How (impact):** e.g. Regular use of alcohol exacerbates her low mood where sudden discontinuation increases her anxiety.	**What:** e.g. The client has temporary accommodation at a friend's house. **How (impact):** e.g. Having proper accommodation for the last few months has allowed the client to have proper rest at night, thus lowering her risk of illness and serious relapse into depression.	**What:** e.g. The client's use of alcohol as an anxiolytic. **How:** e.g. As the client has a fear of 'anxiety medication' due to friends' experiences, inform client of 'alternative' other forms treatments, such as St John's Wort (which has also been successful for treating mild to moderate depression).	**What:** e.g. The client's development of good sleeping and other lifestyle habits, including regular walks to the park. **How:** e.g. Encourage the client to increase either her physical activity or interest in the outdoors.

Intersubjective/ interpersonal factors	**What:** e.g. Client is emotionally distant from her mother. **How (impact):** e.g Client's relationship with her mother consumes a considerable amount of her energy, making her feel, at times, angry and, at other times, guilty. Client believes her feelings towards her mother 'hold her back' in various areas of her life.	**What:** e.g. The client is relatively popular and has good memories of her relationship with her father. Whilst she has not seen her brother for months, she has always got along fairly well with him. **How (impact):** e.g. The client has derived either explicit support from her friends during her most difficult emotional times, and at least some sense of comfort from 'just being around them' at other times of feeling low.	**What:** e.g. The client's relationship with her mother. **How:** e.g. Assist the client to think through the various reasons for her feelings towards her mother and of potential ways these feelings might be resolved, e.g. through writing a letter to her mother to tell her how she feels, or by accepting that non-contact with her mother is, at this stage in her life, preferable.	**What:** e.g. The client's relationship with her brother. **How:** e.g. Given that the client has previously been close to her brother and is missing the one other family member she has been close to – her father – terribly, she might be encouraged to make contact with her brother.
Intrapersonal/ intrapsychic factors	**What:** e.g. The client is prone to depression and, more recently, anxiety.	**What:** e.g. The client feels a sense of duty towards her father to make the best out of her life.	**What:** e.g. The client's experience of depression and anxiety.	**What:** e.g. The client's ability to find the strength to keep living, even when at her lowest point.

Continued

Continued

Potential sources of client vulnerabilities/ strengths		Targets for amelioration/ enhancement	
Adversive	Protective	Adversive	Protective
How (impact): e.g. The client often feels hopeless and, lately, as if something terrible will happen to her. She often feels indifferent as to whether she lives or dies.	**How (impact):** e.g. This has prevented the client, to this point, from attempting suicide and encouraged her to talk to someone when feeling down even when she hasn't felt like it.	**How:** e.g. Assist the client to recognize destructive cycles of thought and social attitudes that exacerbate her feelings of hopelessness and anxiety. Assist the client to identify a range of positive 'physical' activities that she can build into her daily routine.	**How:** e.g. Assist client to think of other more positive reasons – (or reasons beyond a perceived debt to her father) – to keep living and trying to improve her life. Help her to record these reasons in a way that will be capable of 'reaching' her when she is feeling at her lowest.

7 Social Work, the Body and Child Protection

Within social work practice, the body of the child is most visible when it bears the evidence of abuse, in the form of physical injuries or through body language exhibited by the child. Conceptualizing individuals as embodied beings, we argue throughout this book, assists our understanding of human need and attempts to limit suffering. Considering children, also, in terms of their corporeality allows us to better grasp their immediate and future needs and the range of factors that influence their development.

The protection of children the world over is as much a challenge as ever. Reports of emotional, physical and sexual abuse and neglect of children in most Western societies remains high and, in some countries, continue to rise (Creighton 2004). A number of protective concerns are particular to contemporary times. Advances in medical technology means that children who might not, had they been born in earlier decades, survived for more than a few days are living well into middle childhood and beyond. Children with complex or multiple care needs are at particular risk of harm or rejection given the difficulties and expense associated with providing their provision of proper care. Whilst reports of abuse have risen, the means to preventing or ending abuse – including provision of financial, emotional, social and educational support for parents with low income, few social contacts, ill health, disabilities or a substance dependency – have become harder to secure. Nevertheless, there is much evidence that child protection measures throughout the Western world have already prevented or limited suffering for thousands of children. Given a range of improvements – such as better distributed funding and a better educated workforce – there is reason to believe such services can become more effective still.

It is only relatively recently that the protection of children has been of sufficient social concern to attract intervention by government and non-government services. The first child protection services were established in the United States and England in the 1880s. The earliest child protection agencies were legally authorized to remove abused children from the care of their parents and place them, permanently, with approved families or in orphanages (Scott and Swain 2002: 4). Whilst these early protective efforts likely resulted in some positive or even preferable outcomes for children, many actions taken by agencies were questionable or – from a contemporary standpoint – deplorable. Many of the new homes children were placed in were no better, and often worse, than the homes they had been removed from. Moreover, many protective agencies participated in an insidious form of cultural engineering. In Australia, many indigenous children who were at no risk of harm from their parents were removed from their homes and, ostensibly for their own 'moral protection', placed in orphanages or dormitories or with white families (National Inquiry into the Separation of Aboriginal and Torres Strait Islander Children from their Families 1997).

Since the 1960s, protective services throughout the world have reflected more complex understandings of abuse and, generally, become more sensitive to the needs of both children and parents. There is considerable diversity amongst contemporary protective systems which, nevertheless, fall into three broad categories as defined by their practice orientation. As identified by Gilbert (1997) services have either a child protection orientation, which emphasizes legalistic interventions; family services orientation where reporting of abuse is mandatory; or a family service approach where reporting is not mandatory. Systems or services with the second or third approach are based on the understanding that abuse may be prevented where all family members are helped to meet particular needs. The first model clearly identifies the child as its client and has often led to punitive or alienating treatment of parents. However, those systems that have traditionally had an exclusive 'child orientation' – as in England, Australia, the United States and Canada – are slowly broadening their focus. Tomison states that, in Australia at least, child protection no longer 'drives the system but merely becomes one important facet in an overall welfare assessment of the family' (2001: 53).

Across practice models, protective workers – a significant proportion of which are social workers – perform a handful of common tasks. These include, correctly determining if a child is subject to maltreatment, and the severity of any abuse that has occurred; establishing the risk of the child being mistreated in the future; and developing means to assist the child (Tomison 2001: 50). Necessarily then, workers must also possess knowledge about such things as child development and child needs.

Social workers – as reflected by the professional literature (See e.g., Harms 2005) – continue to draw much of their knowledge on child development from a handful of common theories, namely, attachment theory as developed by Bowlby and Ainsworth, and the theories of Piaget and Erikson. Following discussion of these theories we present biological perspectives on child and adolescent development and issues pertinent to child and adolescent well being and, thus, also protection.

Attachment theory, as initially developed by Bowlby, posits that infants identify their primary caregivers from a very early age and, understanding their reliance upon them, use all and any means to keep them within close proximity. In most instances, Bowlby claims, infants will become anxious upon separation from their caregivers – as demonstrated through behaviours ranging from visual searching to vocal signalling – which continue until mother and caregiver are reunited. Where an infant is not reunited with her caregiver for some time she will eventually become quiet and still through exhaustion (Bowlby 1977). On the basis of infant observation undertaken by Mary Ainsworth, it was established that infants, in fact, have a range of attachment behaviours or attachment 'styles'. Which attachment style an infant develops will depend upon temperamental characteristics she has inherited together with kinds of interaction that occur between herself and her caregiver. Attachment relationships can be more or less healthy or adaptive. Contemporary attachment theory identifies four attachment styles – secure, insecure-avoidant, insecure-ambivalent and insecure-disorganized – and emphasizes the importance of infants' attachments to individuals besides mothers, such as siblings (Lopez 1995). Bowlby and Ainsworth, as well as contemporary attachment theorists, argue that the relationship an individual forms with his primary caregiver and other close individuals will have significant bearing on all relationships subsequently formed, as well as general mental health (see Mikulincer, Shaver and Pereg 2003).

Erikson's theories, which deal largely with identity and social role formation, are regularly criticized for their cultural specificity and resistance to empirical scrutiny. Nevertheless, as constructs, they have aided thinking about kinds of internal conflict that have confronted humans since the inception of industrial society. Erikson (1968) argues that individuals pass through different stages at specific ages that manifest, or are experienced, as conflicts or 'crises'. Any crises that go unresolved create the possibility of great emotional anguish, social ill-adjustment and, potentially, mental illness. Between infancy and adolescence individuals confront the following conflicts: trust versus mistrust, during which an infant determines the extent to which individuals and her environment can be relied upon; autonomy versus doubt, during which a child struggles to perform a number of crucial tasks independently; initiative versus guilt, when a child learns to balance desire for greater self-determination with childish impulses; industry versus inferiority, which relates to the struggle of children in middle childhood to achieve social success and competencies equal to their peers; and identity versus role diffusion. This last conflict occurs in adolescence and requires reflection upon all previous lessons learnt about life and self (Erikson 1968: 96).

Whereas attachment theory focuses largely on children's emotional and social development, Piaget's theories are concerned with cognitive development. Piaget posited that, as a result of interaction with their environments, children will move through four main stages (or three, with the middle two being considered sub-divisions of one stage). These include a sensorimotor stage (between the ages of 0 and 2) during which the main tasks are development of motor skills and goal directed behaviour; a pre-operational stage (between the ages of 2 and 7), which is characterized by egocentrism and intuitive, as opposed to logical, thinking, but also by a development in representational abilities; a concrete operations stage (between the ages of 7 and 11), during which children are able to reason about concrete objects or tangible information; and a formal operations stage (between the ages of 11 and 15). During this final stage individuals can apply abstract and hypothetical reasoning (Goswami 2001: 258).

These theories and related others have been enormously useful in assisting social workers, psychologists and others to understand children's needs. Nevertheless knowledge of these theories, we argue, needs to be supplemented by knowledge of recent neuroscientific findings or, preferably, re-examined in terms of their compatibility with such. Neuroscience provides an insight into mind-brain processes that cannot be gained through means such as behavioural observation, ethological study and interviews that were available to Piaget, Erikson and other social theorists and psychologists.

There are a number of gaps in neuroscientists' knowledge about which brain regions and mechanisms are associated with particular tasks and implicated in given disorders. With respect to some functions, less is known about children's brains than those of adults. For a variety of reasons, research on emotion in children has proven especially difficult. One challenge has been that kinds of brain activity involved in the detection and production of emotion are more similar in young children than in adults. This has made drawing conclusions about such things as children's emotional reactions to facial expressions particularly trying. And still to be determined is the level of stability in children's emotions over time and, thus, how easily, if at all, emotional *states* and emotional *traits* can be distinguished in children as they can be in adults (Davidson and Slatger 2000). Nevertheless, in recent times, much has been learnt about the manner in which the brain develops from conception through to adulthood, as well as kinds of stimuli that may positively or adversely affect a child's health.

Many things may influence proper development of a foetus, including an individual's genetic makeup, viral infections, accidents endured by the mother and maternal metabolic disorders. For some time, it has been known that particular of a mother's behaviours during pregnancy, including her consumption habits, can also affect her foetus. There is some evidence, for example, that maternal smoking causes, amongst other problems, hyperactivity, aggressiveness, tendency to seek conflicts, anxiety and depression. One means through which nicotine may cause such effects is by altering the function of acetylcholine – a key neurotransmitter throughout the brain, (through changes in the expression of particular receptors in the brainstem and cerebellum)

(Falk, Nordberg, Seiger, Kjaeldgaard and Hellstrom-Lindahl 2005).

Regular consumption of large amounts of alcohol by pregnant women causes at least some manifestations of foetal alcohol syndrome (FAS) in 30–40 per cent of children (Ornoy 2002: 122). FAS is associated with a particular pattern of facial features as well as pre- and postnatal growth deficiency and cognitive and behavioural problems linked to central nervous system dysfunction. Episodes of binge drinking (considered to be five or more standard drinks) during pregnancy can also result in offspring experiencing delays in development of language and numerical skills (Ornoy 2002). Illicit substances such as cocaine and heroin also impact the foetus, although findings pertaining to the duration of effects postnatally are inconsistent. (See Chiriboga 2003.)

Children of women who were malnourished during pregnancy are at risk of a variety of problems, from cardio-vascular through to endocrinological and metabolic problems that can persist into later life. Such problems may occur, Godfrey proposes, because changes in the in-utero environment spark changes in 'expression of the foetal genome' and developmental adaptations that confer an initial 'advantage to the foetus, but ... predispose to degenerative disease in post-reproductive life' (2002: 22).

More recently, a mother's emotional state during her pregnancy has been discovered to be a significant determinant of a child's well being. Several recent studies have found that maternal anxiety during pregnancy can cause, in addition to pre-term delivery and low birth weight, a number of behavioural problems in offspring (Van den Berg, Mulder Mennes and Glover, 2005). Children of a range of ages who were born to mothers who experienced either intense or prolonged periods of stress during pregnancy have been found to have, variously, poor concentration, poor impulse control and emotional difficulties. Available evidence suggests that these effects are related to dysfunctions in the developing child's hypothalamic-pituitary-adrenal (HPA) axis, 'limbic system' – those parts of the brain considered crucial for emotion and attention – and the prefrontal cortex (PFC). There is uncertainty about the mechanisms through which maternal anxiety impacts the developing child, but one theory is that the foetal environment is changed by alterations in maternal levels of cortisol (Van den Berg, Mulder, Mennes and Glover 2005).

Depressed mothers are also more likely to give birth prematurely and have babies of low birth-weight. Newborns of mothers with depressive symptoms have been found, by Field and colleagues, to have higher levels of cortisol and lower levels of dopamine and serotonin as compared to other children. This is similar to the physiological profile of mothers themselves during the prenatal stage (Field, et al. 2004). Physiological abnormalities are reflected in such things as poor habituation, motor skills, and depressed behaviours.

Neuroscientific findings have supported a number of traditional child development theories developed by psychologists and social scientists. Amongst the most significant theories for which neuroscience has provided support are those concerning the importance of an infant's interactions with her primary caregiver for healthy cognitive, social and emotional development.

The first two years of a child's life are the most significant time of brain growth. Because 'the infant brain is designed to be moulded by the environment it encounters' (Schore 2001a: 12), what happens to an infant during this period, and the range of stimuli to which an infant is exposed, is of particular importance. All brains begin with an excess of connections between regions which require 'pruning back'. Which connections are retained depends, to some degree, upon which are most useful for the earliest environments in which infants find themselves (Johnson 2001). Environments that provide infants with appropriate levels of intellectual and sensory challenge, and in which they can derive strong emotional support, will assist their achievement of healthy neural development.

One of the most important mediators of good mental health in infants is a secure attachment relationship. Such an attachment allows an infant to develop the physiological capacity to cope with stressors and, in particular, social stressors (Schore 2001a). Playful interaction between a mother and infant usually begins within the first months of an infant's life, at a time when an infant's brain is sufficiently mature to allow for communication. During 'play', which is based around the exchange of visual and auditory stimuli, a mother will reflect her child's movements and facial expressions; at times consciously and, at other times, unconsciously. As, at this stage in an infant's life, the mother is the most 'potent stimulus in the infant's social environment'

(Schore 2001a: 18) this synchronization is enormously pleasurable for the infant. A mother providing good care for her infant will recognize and reflect her infant's positive emotional states and attempt to amplify them. Where, on the other hand, she has inadvertently caused stress by causing 'misattunement', she will match the infant's emotions before leading herself and infant to a more positive state. During play, mother and infant alternate between attentive engagement and periods of inattention (See Hsu and Fogel 2003 for full discussion on mother-infant interaction). 'The more a mother tunes her activity level to the infant during periods of social engagement, the more she allows him to recover quietly in periods of disengagement' (Schore 2001a: 18) or, in other words, develop the skills to regulate his own emotions. Whilst a mother can choose to convey one or another emotion states to her infant, she may also transmit fleeting emotions of which she is unaware which will be, all the same, registered by and impact – for good or bad – the infant's emotional state.

Emotions reflect particular physiological states. As maturation of a number of brain sites are experience-dependent, some affective states enhance, whilst others provide a toxic environment for, brain growth (Cirulli, Berry and Alleva 2003). Where a mother facilitates many moments of joyful exchanges between herself and infant and the infant's swift recovery from distress, she assists the infant to develop the neural capacity for normal emotional regulation. Schore suggests attachment is, by and large, mediated by the right PFC, the development of which is, in turn, enhanced by secure attachment relationships (Schore 2001a, Schore 2001b). There is some evidence that the HPA and the sympathetic adrenomedullary system – the main mediators of coping strategies – are both largely under the control of the right brain (Wittling 1997).

Where a caregiver is either frequently abusive or neglectful, including emotionally neglectful, thus often leaving her child in 'an intensely disruptive psychobiological state' (Schore 2001b: 210), the infant is denied kinds of socio-emotional learning opportunities crucial to healthy development. Due to dysregulation of vital brain functions, children who experience trauma in early life are at great risk of developing a range of problems that will persist through time (a number of which can also be caused by other kinds of neurological insults). Aside from emotional difficulties, they are likely to develop poor social and cognitive skills and, in extreme cases, severe psychopathologies (Galderisi and Mucci 2000: 44). Eighty per cent of infants who have experienced trauma have a Type D, or disorganized/insecure, attachment style (Carlson 1989 in Schore 2001b: 214). Infants with such an attachment style – which indicates the existence of some cognitive dysfunction – are highly ambivalent towards their caregivers and respond badly to challenge.

Schore argues that when infants experience prolonged episodes of distress or attachment disruptions they will move from a hyperaroused state, which is mediated by the sympathetic nervous system – reflected at a behavioural level as crying and screaming – to a passive or dissociated state. This latter state is controlled by the parasympathetic system. Extreme and rapid alterations between these two states create 'chaotic biochemical alterations' (Schore 2001b: 212) as the infant is exposed to toxic levels of neurotransmitters. The accumulation of negative experiences can result in permanent changes to the function of a range of neurotransmitter systems that underlie emotional and other functions, through damage to particular brain regions. Dysfunction has been found in dopamine, norepinephrine, serotonin, opiate and corticotropin releasing hormone systems in children who have experienced trauma (De Bellis 2001). Structural changes have been found in the PFC, the hippocampus, the amygdala and corpus callosum, (which connects the left and right hemispheres) (Diseth 2005).

Particularly influential, Schore suggests, would be dysfunction in the orbitofrontal regions of the brain. A loss of connections between one part of this region and other brain areas is thought to lead to anhedonia, where a loss of connections between the medial part of this region and segmental forebrain-midbrain circuit can lead to an inability to suppress 'hyperarousal' states such as terror and rage (Schore 2001: 226). The orbitofrontal region in the healthy brain is also able to exert a level of influence over the amygdala, but damage, including trauma-related damage, to these connections would lead to an over-active amygdala, thus, excessive emotional reactivity. As the orbitofrontal region is a kind of 'executive control' for the right side of the brain, damage to this area can compromise a variety of right-brain functions from processing of visual and vocal interpersonal stimuli, formation of social relationships to experience and regulation of affect (Bechara, Damasio and Damasio 2000). Evidence from a range of studies suggest neglected and abused infants have dysfunctional right-sided activity (Schore 2001b: 237).

Levels of dysfunction are also thought to underlie 'insecure organized' and 'insecure avoidant' attachment styles. Infants with either of these attachments styles, however, demonstrate retention of particular coping strategies: the former, a passive coping style of autoregulation, and the latter, an 'active' coping style. Infants with a disorganized insecure style can implement neither coping strategy and, thus, generally experience more distress (Schore 2001b: 244).

De Bellis (2000: 557) suggests that abuse of a child by a parent is often a sign that the parent herself suffers from an abuse-related emotional disorder. A range of stimuli may precipitate emotional states in a parent with such a disorder that undermine her capacity to care for her child. A child's cries, for example, may give rise, in a mother (or father), to a strong emotional memory that causes her to dissociate – a reaction that, in many cases, will ultimately bring about a dissociative response in her child. Where an emotional memory is unaccompanied by a conscious memory, the mother may be unable to identify the trigger for her emotional response and thus be unsure of how to prevent such reactions in the future. (Emotional memory versus conscious memory is discussed in greater detail in Chapter 2.) This indicates the need for mothers who struggle to provide proper care for their infants to receive intensive emotional support and counselling and, in some cases, pharmacological treatment, in addition to any 'parenting training'.

Individuals' capacity to be affected by adverse social environments and relationships continues throughout life and is particularly significant until the end of late adolescence or early adulthood. Between infancy and late adolescence, the brain continues to undergo periods of rapid growth, substantial synaptic pruning and myelination (the process by which nerves gain protective sheaths that allow them to communicate with one another) that may be affected by a range of environmental factors. How stressors impact in later years, however, will depend not only upon kinds of socially sculpted brain changes that have occurred but also moment-to-moment events such as how individuals interpret a given stressor.

To what extent children who have been neglected or abused are able to recover normal brain functioning in later years is dependent upon a range of factors including kinds and severity of damage sustained and quality of care received later in life. Some children are able to recover from severe abuse or emotional deprivation, whilst others – regardless of the level of emotional, social and cognitive support provided – will retain serious deficits throughout life. McLean's review of the research literature (2003) concerning children who spent their first several months in orphanages (and thus, typically, without a consistent carer) found that such children are more inclined to have personal, social, gross motor, fine motor-adaptive and language difficulties later in life than others, but that being an orphan does not guarantee that a child will suffer psychopathology or developmental arrest. Research with non-human primates suggests that the timing of abuse, or age at which abuse or neglect is experienced, is a significant determinant of an individual's ability to recover (see Nelson, Bloom, Cameron, Amaral, Dahl and Pine 2002). It is likely that human babies have periods in which they are more or less vulnerable to separation.

To emphasize the importance of relationships between caregivers and, in particular, mothers and their infants, is not to deny the influence that others may have upon a child's cognitive and behavioural development. Particular of an infant or child's relatives or associates may offer comfort where a parent cannot or, alternately, cause considerable stress for which protection from a caregiver cannot entirely compensate. As a child gains independence her opportunities to forge significant relationships outside of the home increase. Harris argues that the relationships children develop with non-family members are at least as significant for children's development as their familial relationships. She refers to studies that found the 'operative environmental influences' for alcoholism and criminal behaviour are 'in the neighborhood, not in the home' (Harris 2000: 714). Further, Harris suggests that many behaviours and roles children learn through interaction with their parents are context specific, meaning that, for example, a child who appears withdrawn with family members may be outgoing in the school yard or at friends' houses. The nature of relationships with peers are thought to determine behaviour in these other contexts.

Lupien, King, Meaney and McEwen (2001) have also found evidence that peers significantly influence the well-being of children and, in particular, older children. In one study Lupien and colleagues found that young children from lower socio-economic backgrounds have higher morning salivary cortisol levels (or more cortisol in their saliva) – a sign of an over-active HPA system – than their peers. This was interpreted as an effect of an emotionally challenging home environment, or one characterized by familial and economic instability. One explanation the researchers offer for the 'equalization' of cortisol expression amongst children at secondary school level is that peer relationships amongst children of this age are more important than relationships with parents. Where a child is accepted by, or happy amongst, his peers, peer identification may offer protective effects.

Peer groups, through provision of emotional support and/or a sense of identity, can have *direct* positive impact or, conversely – through such means as exploitation or periodic rejection – negative impact upon the health of a child. Peer groups may also affect an individual's health *indirectly* through their encouragement of particular behaviours.

Particular biological factors predispose adolescents towards 'risk-seeking behaviour'; this term referring, here, to behaviour with the potential to be injurious to health or another aspect of self. Evidence suggests that at the beginning of adolescence, individuals experience a change in 'reward sensitivity' meaning that they require higher levels of stimulation to achieve the same subjective feelings of pleasure as previously experienced. This, Steinberg (2004) offers, is due to alterations in the limbic system associated with the neuroendocrinological changes that occur in puberty. On the other hand, the capacities to regulate emotion and behaviour and weigh consequences are not fully developed; regulatory capacities involve the PFC – and, in particular, the dorsolateral PFC (Giedd 2004) – which does not reach maturity until early adulthood. Being in the company of valued friends creates a high level of emotional arousal for adolescents and frequently, as a consequence, a desire to try new things (Steinberg 2004: 55). Some adolescents, however, will be more inclined to take risks than others. Amongst things determining this will be genetic factors, value systems, social milieu and opportunity.

Many risks that adolescents take are beneficial to their psychobiological (or emotional and social) development, where others are particularly harmful. Amongst the most dangerous behaviours commonly adopted by adolescents is the regular or excessive consumption of alcohol. High levels of alcohol consumption are thought to have a number of effects upon the adolescent brain. Adolescent individuals who drink heavily show reduced hippocampal volumes, irregularities in the white matter of the brain and a number of abnormalities in brain response, while performing challenging cognitive tasks. This is reflected, at the cognitive level, in poor attentional skills, and poor performance on tests assessing verbal and non-verbal skills. It is not clear at this stage how long-term abstinence affects recovery of such abilities (Brown and Tapert 2004).

It is during adolescence that a number of mental illnesses emerge, many of which are thought to occur as a result of interaction amongst individual genetic factors, social experiences and biological changes that occur during normal adolescent development. Puberty stimulates change in a range of neuroendocrine axes, including reproductive and adrenal axes. Such changes can modulate stress systems in the brain, where the stress systems can impact reproductive and adrenal systems (Cameron 2004). Adolescence offers much opportunity for extreme stress: increases in social and intellectual challenges and expectations are usually accompanied by greater levels of self-consciousness or self-awareness, and scrutiny by others. As such, many adolescents are at risk of stress-related or affective disorders.

Those social workers working within protective services are increasingly exposed to neuroscientific theory concerning child development, whether through agency-related training, personal reading or attendance at multi-disciplinary conferences. We argue, however, that all social workers need some knowledge of neuroscientific theory and, thus, that all undergraduate courses should include units providing systematic discussion of such. Understanding how particular activities or environments impact behaviour, cognition and emotion, helps workers prioritize areas for interventions, make sense of certain of their clients' thinking patterns and behaviours, and begin to draw inferences regarding the suitability of given interventions.

Whether an individual sees his or her own body primarily as a vehicle for experience, an instrument of competence, a means to communication or an aesthetic object, has significant implications for well-being. Attitudes towards these aspects of self begin to form during childhood, through interaction with peers and caregivers. Thus, such things as perceptions of relevance to a child's body that are consciously or unconsciously expressed by others; restrictions or expectations placed on a child's body; and the manner in which others communicate with a child physically, will be important for the child's sense of safety and self, as well as health.

Children or children's bodies have not always been viewed, unambiguously, as objects worthy of protection. Rather, documents pertaining to early protective efforts reveal that, in mid-nineteenth century, children in many Western societies were viewed simultaneously as vulnerable (to corruptive influences) and – through their susceptibility to corruption and, especially in the case of the poor, vast neediness – threatening (Scott and Swain 2002: 10). Resultantly, a range of restrictive measures – designed to both protect impoverished children from vice and society from them – were imposed upon them by agencies charged with providing their care.

By the start of the twentieth century, children were more likely to be viewed as innocent than dangerous, and in need of protection and guidance from adults. With their better development in mind, during the 1900's children's bodies were made subject to a new range of disciplinary practices. Advances in psychological and paediatric sciences gave rise to a range of milestones and standards children were expected to achieve and methods for achieving them (Howson 2004: 143). Meanwhile, school and home became 'crucial sites for observation and monitoring of children to ensure they met the markers for normality established ...' (Donzelot 1979 in Howson 2004: 143). Whilst advances in knowledge about child health and development and educational methods have led to many benefits for children in general, they have also encouraged, in many parents, a perfectionistic attitude towards childrearing. Armed with 'knowledge' about what their children should be capable of given the 'right' circumstances, many parents have pushed their children, through deprivation or other forms of punishment, to obtain certain physical (or intellectual) standards or feats.

More recently, an escalation in concern about children's safety has led to new impositions upon children's freedom, in the form of restrictions upon with whom and where children play. Giddens (1992) argues that contemporary society is characterized by preoccupation with risk. Those such as Brownlie (2001) argue it is with risk to children that society is particularly concerned. A spreading panic about the harm that may befall children – fuelled, amongst other things, by frequent media reports of child molestation and abduction – has led to attempts to keep children 'indoors', and the development of 'children only spaces' (see Scott, Jackson and Backett-Milburn 1998). Whilst the physical containment of children may temporarily keep them from harm from strangers or other environmental hazards, preventing their exploration of the broader world can deprive them of crucial opportunities to develop confidence and independence.

Where children are largely kept indoors, they are often denied the chance to take physical exercise or engage in physical play. Sports and various types of physical exercise, as discussed in Chapter 6, are believed to stimulate neurotransmitter activity capable of undermining negative emotion. In addition, (where children do not have 'winning' as a preoccupation), physical activity can be a means via which children develop a sense of competence and, through the social interaction and sense of identity it can provide, healthy self-esteem (Richman and Schaeffer 2000; Pederson and Seidman 2004; Eppright, Sanfacon, Beck and Bradley 1997). It is not only over-protective parents that prevent children from undertaking physical activity, but also a lack of 'play' spaces. Young children who live in high density accommodation, for example, find it particularly difficult to play physical games; in some cases, because there are no large outdoor areas located nearby and, in other cases, because outdoor spaces have been 'colonized' by adults. (See Romero 2005 for discussion of barriers for children from low-income families to outdoor play.)

Adults impact children's well-being not only through kinds of expectations and restrictions they place on children's activities, but also by influencing children's experience of, or relationship to, their bodies. Connell (2000: 92) has argued that what individuals notice about their bodies is, to a large extent, socially mediated. This is to say that kinds of feelings and body parts that individuals notice, and the ways in which they interpret or view them, depend upon such things as self-perception, the development of which is partly contingent upon social experience. One subject in Connell's research recalled being overcome with shame when, running down a beach as a child he noticed his untoned flesh 'wobble'; a sign to him of his lack of athleticism. Connell argues that the special value given to athleticism in males in Western societies encourages such self-consciousness in male children.

Many messages children receive from society through social practices, transmission of values and ideals, or from individuals children come in contact with, influence the kinds of experiences – both negative and positive – children have of their bodies. Mentioned elsewhere in the text is that children with low self-esteem can interpret sudden unpleasant emotion associated with certain kinds of spontaneous physiological activity as caused by their own wrongdoing. In other words, they interpret feelings of anxiety or similar as a form of punishment, regardless of how difficult they find identifying behaviour for which it might have been administered. Making negative inferences and judgements about proprioceptive or other such experiences can cause neutral sensations to feel unpleasant or exacerbate negative feelings or conditions.

Children who have suffered serious abuse can, as a particular manifestation of dissociation, become desensitized to pain and discomfort (Scaer 2000). Others, particularly those who have been sexually abused, may dis-identify with their bodies and/or come to see them as objects of disdain. Milligan and Andrews (2005) interviewed women who had been sexually abused as children about their self-harming practices. The most frequent reason cited by their subjects for their self-abuse was 'bodily disgust'.

Children's relationships to their bodies may also be affected through observing the attitude adults hold in relation to their bodies. A number of studies have found that the priority girls place upon their appearance is as much affected by their mothers' attitudes towards personal physical appearance as anything that may be communicated to them directly (Shuster, Blackmore and Fox 2004; Woodside et al. 2002). Dissatisfaction or preoccupation with such things as physical appearance can be extremely harmful, as evidenced by high rates of eating disorders amongst young girls and reports of low self-esteem based on appearance. Thus, adults in a position to influence children have a responsibility to examine and modify their own body-based attitudes and behaviours. This is especially so given the powerful messages children, and particularly girls, receive through the media about the unacceptability of imperfect looking (or performing) bodies (see Bordo 2004).

There are a number of means through which children establish and reaffirm social relationships and a sense of identity through use of bodily communication. Warin (2000) and Neppl and Murray (1997) discuss how children shore up a sense of identity through rehearsal of activities and personal or interactive behaviours associated with their gender. Children also have a tendency to mimic other children as a way of demonstrating their affiliation with them. At times, children mimic each other unconsciously, an exchange that has been found to strengthen social bonds. (See Chartrand and Bargh 1999b for a discussion of the social effects of 'mirroring'.) Also well accepted is that children who are most popular are often physically confident, either as a result of or as demonstrated through, sporting ability or their use of their bodies in social communication. The quality of social relationships children acquire at school can have a significant effect upon their self-esteem and, consequently, a variety of future outcomes. For this reason, and those others discussed above, attitudes children hold in relation to their bodies matter.

Corporeal capacity

Throughout this book we argue that individuals' interaction with their social and broader environments impacts, from moment to moment, their cognitive capacity or, in other words, their emotional and general well-being together with their general abilities. It is during childhood that neural activity responds most dramatically to positive experiences and environments, and, likewise, insult. When experienced during childhood, circumstances such as material deprivation, can have long-lasting effects. Financial stress, for example, can lead parents to neglect one or several of a child's needs or frequently express frustrations towards the child. It may also dictate that a family lives in a neighbourhood unlikely to provide the child with positive play experiences or – due to a high crime rate, pollution or high levels of ambient noise – that causes the child fear or significant discomfort. As discussed in detail above, neglect and stress can impact a child's emotional regulation capacities and cognitive development and, resultantly, overall health. The lack of opportunities a child has for creative play and socialization are also likely to be detrimental to a child's self-esteem and emotional well-being and, potentially, long-term emotional regulation. Emotional disposition and the skills an individual acquires throughout life, in part, determines the quality of an individual's future experiences: the kinds of company and opportunities she will seek, where she chooses to live and so on.

Body cognizant social worker

Many findings within neuroscience and sociology pertaining to the body provide clearer rationale for current social work interventions, whilst others suggest new foci for practice. Below we provide a handful of implications of findings on the body for social work with children and parents.

Findings regarding the importance of maternal well-being to the development of the foetus suggests expectant parents and women who desire to become pregnant require education on the potential effects of emotional state upon the developing child and, thus, techniques for controlling stress. It also suggests that emotionally vulnerable expectant mothers require intensive support in the form of regular counselling sessions, relaxation classes or groupwork.

Research undertaken by Schore and others regarding the long-term consequences of neglect or abuse for children's neural development, and the particular level of plasticity of the brain during infancy, justifies the current emphasis of many protective systems upon early intervention. Findings concerning the importance, for children's emotional development, of 'attunement', or regular interaction, with emotionally 'stable' others, suggests a focus that a social worker may give to parenting training. It also suggests the need for social workers to organize, for children who do not have a dependable or regular caregiver, regular appointments with a counsellor who may act as a kind of 'emotional regulator'. The tasks of such a professional would be to attend to, and validate, a child's emotions states, and through both compassionate response and provision of age appropriate cognitive and behavioural strategies, enable the client to recover from negative emotion. Many questions remain as to the efficacy of play therapy – a style of intervention that recruits kinds of symbolism and creativity associated with normal play – for treating psychological and emotional problems in children. Nevertheless, given that play therapy techniques do not require abstract reasoning or highly developed verbal skills, they may assist young children to think about and regulate their emotions. Certainly, as Hall and Kaduson (2002) discuss, stress reduction and relaxation techniques can be presented to children in a playful and non-threatening manner. The particular utility of play therapy for children is an area ripe for research by multi-disciplinary teams comprising those with social psychological training and those whose training is in the biological sciences.

Knowledge concerning the ease with which infants can trigger negative emotional states in mothers and that mothers can unknowingly communicate negative emotional states to their infants (thereby, in turn, causing the infant distress) supports the argument for compassionate treatment of abusing parents and, thus, current trends in the focus of child protection systems. (See above.) Parents not only require information about better parenting practices and support to change practices potentially of harm to their children. They also need ongoing counselling (as provided by the social worker or another) to assist them to address their own emotional challenges, and assistance with any significant problems – material or otherwise – that may exacerbate these problems.

Due to kinds of neural activity stimulated by particular emotional states, cognitive – and, in particular, attentional – difficulties often arise in conjunction with emotional dysregulation. Having an awareness of such can alert social workers to the possibility that a child who appears distractible or is slow to grasp concepts appropriate to her age is also at risk of, or is currently suffering, an emotional disorder.

The evidence that stress hormones normalize when children reach secondary school suggests that experiences with peer groups can compensate for a stressful home environment. For this reason, workers should be aware that assisting an older child to remain at school or find a regular set of friends may be almost as important if not as important as assisting them to secure accommodation with a caring family.

The physiological evidence of the influence peers have upon adolescents' well-being and impetus to act supports the argument made by those such as Ronson (2004) for the use of groupwork with adolescents. Social workers should seek to involve adolescents at risk of emotional or psychological disorder through neglect or abuse, in educational, 'therapeutic' or purposive groups attended by others of their own age.

Social research together with neuroscientific research indicates that children's self-esteem impacts how they experience their bodies which, in turn, affects their physiological activity and overall health. Social workers should discuss with children who suffer from considerable anxiety such issues as how they think about their bodies and how they interpret uncomfortable physiological sensations. Particularly important is helping children who either dissociate in stressful situations or self-harm to understand their right to bodily integrity, and to both value their bodies and attend to their bodies' needs.

Particular social research indicates that children's development of self-esteem is aided by an experience of their bodies/themselves as physically capable. Neuroscientific research supports that physical exercise can lead to the amelioration of stress and anxiety. These findings together suggest workers should ensure that young clients are provided with the opportunity to partake in regular physical activity. Children with any of a range of physical disabilities should also be provided opportunities to test and enjoy the capabilities of their bodies, whether through individual or group activities.

An aspect of self from which one derives self-esteem and a sense of identity is physical appearance. Appearance becomes particularly important where an individual lacks stable affiliations or a sense of place that might otherwise provide him with a sense of identity. Social workers should ensure that children are encouraged to consider their 'public' or 'visible' bodies as instruments of communication, or means to *actively* creating relationships and opportunities, as opposed to objects to be judged and upon which fate merely acts. A worker should recognize the particular importance of assisting children with minor through to significant disabilities to develop a positive sense of body. Children with significant disabilities are likely to benefit from socializing and participating in activities with children facing challenges comparable to their own.

A body cognizant worker at the community level may attempt to arrange activities that allow children who have little opportunity for physical skill development and outdoor play, to participate in both. He may also choose to organize local presentations for parents and expectant parents that discuss, in simple terms, current neuroscientific findings relevant to both child development and emotional processing. In addition, he may arrange relaxation and stress management classes for parents.

Amongst other things upon which a body cognizant worker at the policy level may want to focus are ways in which more funding can be provided for long-term counselling for parents as well as children. Her awareness that parts of the brain involved in decision-making and the assessment of risk do not mature until early adulthood, and can be significantly compromised by long term neglect or other forms of abuse, may be used in arguments for extending kinds of support available to adolescents who are exiting state care.

Given that most social workers will at some stage encounter children in need, we argue that neuroscientific theories and theories on the body relevant to children should be included in all social work courses. Such theories sit comfortably alongside of particular theories – such as Bowlby's – relating to child development that have traditionally been taught in social work courses, whilst providing useful challenges to the claims, or at least the lack of specificity, of others. Experiential learning activities supportive of a focus, in education, on the body, include infant observation.

Infant observation involves observing an infant in her own home environment, typically for an hour every week, for a given period of time. This activity allows the worker to gain an understanding of infants' needs: their emotional, their social and cognitive development, and their methods of communication, whilst 'not burdened by the direct responsibility for managing' a case (Briggs 1992: 49). The worker is more than a passive observer; by looking at or interacting with the infant she impacts the infant's behaviour. The response she elicits from an infant in turn affects her behaviourally and emotionally. Thus, an observer may also learn from her observations something about herself and what she brings to her assessments (and also how to tolerate emotionally uncomfortable situations) (Briggs 1992: 49). The observer, through watching how infant and carers interact with, and affect, one another, also gains an understanding of what it is that infants need from carers. It is harder to think of an activity more focused on watching and interpreting the movements of one's own and others' bodies and bodily sensations as structured infant observation.

The Body Cognizant Assessment Guide (BCAG) is as useful for interventions with children as it is for work with parents or adult clients. The following is an example of how the Instrument might be used by a child protection worker.

Client profile: Luke is an intelligent but anxious boy of nearly four years of age who has recently come, through a neighbour's complaint, to the attention of Protective Services. Luke's mother is 22 years old and was, herself, a client of Protective Services. Luke's mother provides inconsistent care, at times lavishing her son with affection and, at other times, yelling and occasionally hitting Luke. In an attempt to live what she calls a 'normal young person's life', Luke's mother virtually ignores Luke for days whilst she entertains friends at her house.

	Potential sources of client vulnerabilities/ strengths		Targets for amelioration/ enhancement	
	Adversive	Protective	Adversive	Protective
Macrosocial factors	What: e.g. Inadequate funding in public health system to ensure the client's mother can receive sufficient on-going counselling for emotional and social difficulties. How (impact): e.g. Increases chance of client being removed from mother's protection.	What: e.g. Ability of the court system to place children in temporary stable care. How (impact): e.g. The power of the courts to remove the client may provide extra incentive for mother to improve care for her child. Court's powers increase client's chance of experiencing – whether at home or a placement – attentive, supportive and consistent care.	(Address) What: e.g. Raise awareness of abusing parents' need for intensive supportive counselling. (Address) How: e.g. Undertaking / encouraging and publicizing relevant research.	(Address) What: e.g. Widespread view of children as vulnerable and in need of protection. (Address) How: e.g. Initiate a 'primary prevention' campaign promoting understand-ing of children's neural plasticity.
Community scale biological/ chemical or physical factors	What: e.g. Client has no safe spaces to play in with other children.	What: e.g. Client's neighbour often takes client to Before School Breakfast programme organized for commis-sion housing residents.	What: e.g. Lack of children's safe play spaces.	What: e.g. Breakfast programme.

Continued

Continued

	Potential sources of client vulnerabilities/ strengths		Targets for amelioration/ enhancement	
	Adversive	Protective	Adversive	Protective
	How (impact): e.g. Client missing opportunities to develop relationships with peers as well as physical abilities/sense of self as physically capable.	**How (impact):** e.g. Client has chance for brief interactions with other children and to receive nutrition.	**How:** e.g. Petition council to address this.	**How:** e.g. See if client's mother wishes to become involved in running of the program as a way of increasing her social circle and participating in community life.
Small scale biological/ chemical or physical factors (as afflicting person or home environment)	**What:** e.g. Client lives in a house (a) that is full of cats that is often dirty and (b) in which loud music in often played late at night. **How (impact):** e.g. (a) Potential vulnerability to disease (b) potential negative impact on client's hearing and sleeping and, thus, learning.	**What:** e.g. Enough room in current residence for client to escape to when he is scared or uncomfortable. Contains telephone. **How (impact):** e.g. Opportunity to escape sense of danger minimizes negative feelings/arousal.	**What:** e.g. Loud music in the home. **How:** e.g. Try to educate mother about hazards. Purchase headphones for the mother and/or encourage mother to choose particular times of the day or week to listen to music.	**What:** e.g. Client has separate room in which he feels safe when his mother is angry. **How:** e.g. Encourage client's mother to decorate this room and to provide the client with comforting objects and intellectually stimulating toys (some of which client and mother can maybe make together).

Intersubjective/ interpersonal factors	**What:** e.g. Client appears to feel both protective towards his mother as well as frightened of her. **How (impact):** e.g. Potential to cause significant emotional dysregulation.	**What:** e.g. Client has occasional contact with paternal grandmother in whose company he appears relaxed. **How (impact):** e.g. Client has some opportunity for calm, peaceful time and to develop an understanding of being cared for and, thus, improved self-esteem.	**What:** e.g. Client's experience of inconsistent care. **How:** e.g. Work intensely with client's mother around both parenting issues and the mother's own personal issues.	**What:** e.g. Client's relationship with his grandmother. **How:** e.g. See if the relationship between client's mother and grandmother can be supported allowing client more opportunity to see his grandmother.
Intrapersonal/ intrapsychic factors	**What:** e.g. Client often appears withdrawn. **How (impact):** e.g. Client's tendency to withdraw when stressed suggests vulnerability for significant depression.	**What:** e.g. Client appears to have attentional and language skills slightly advanced for his age. **How (impact):** e.g. Acquisition of age-expected learning abilities suggests robustness of particular neural pathways and bodes well, at this stage, for his future ability to apply good analyses of interpersonal and other situations.	**What:** e.g. Client's tendency to socially withdraw and become emotionally inexpressive. **How:** e.g. Provide client with the opportunity to experience and express anxiety/unpleasant emotion and, subsequently, age appropriate support and training in stress reduction.	**What:** e.g. Client's intelligence. **How:** e.g. Encourage client's intellectual curiosity and mother's (or grandmother's) provision of not only emotional support but also intellectually stimulating play.

8 Social Work, the Body and Aged Care

Age as a chronological marker is of central importance in our society. The question 'how old are you?' is a primary reference point for thinking about ourselves and others. We assume that the answer will enable us to identify, categorize and classify someone in terms of their likely physical health, the nature of their experiences, their eligibility for services, the extent to which their behaviour and social capacities are 'normal' and so on. Age then, matters because it carries the assumption that ageing follows a typical and predictable course and a course to which labels such as 'child', 'adolescent', 'old person' can be applied. Around these categories, our beliefs and social practices are constructed and organized (Witkin 2000). Age, as Kunkel (2003: 131) points out, serves often as a proxy for a stage or transition in the life course, in particular, however, as a proxy for identifying increased risk of health problems.

While age is most frequently understood as chronological decline, Witkin (2000: 22) invites us to think differently: 'rather than express our age in calendar years, we could use cellular age, subjective experience (such as how old we feel), physiological age (such as health and fitness level), spiritual age, contextual age (how old we feel in a particular situation), or all of these together'. Nevertheless, biological ageing is a 'brute fact': 'ultimately our bodies are not endlessly renewable' (Turner 1995: 249).

In late life, perhaps more than at any other time in the life course, the body becomes of central importance (Heikkinen 2003), very much 'making its presence felt' in the everyday lives of older men and women. For many of us physical ailments, decline in the capacity to undertake mundane tasks, pain and disablement reduce our ability to participate in social and collective life in the same way as in earlier years. Even more so, those who

167

experience the three major neurogenetic diseases associated with late life – Alzhiemer's disease, Parkinson's disease and cardio-vascular disease – endure considerable suffering and increased need for care from family and community. Curiously, however, while human bodies in contemporary society are of central concern (Turner 1995: 257), (witness for instance post modern celebrations of the possibilities of endless life (Wahidin and Powell 2003)), there has been a reluctance (at least in sociology and cultural theory) to think about bodily decline and death (Featherstone and Wernicke 1995: 2). Rather, the focus has been placed on isolating old age from the rest of the life course (Hareven 1995: 119), with interest directed towards the effects of the aging process on the body and the symptoms of bodily decline in later life (Featherstone and Wernicke 1995:1). A consequence of this has been the dominance of biomedical perspectives in aging research (Wahidin and Powell 2003) which serve to highlight mind-body separations, working to reinforce the stigma and fear of an ageing and declining body as 'other', and ageing itself as a social problem to be solved (Kunkel 2003: 130).

Aged care is a key and increasingly important site of social work practice. The latter half of the twentieth century witnessed a demographic revolution, at least in Western liberal democracies, what Hokenstad (2000: 26) calls an 'age quake'. For the first time, people are living longer and populations are growing older. The implications of an ageing population are cutting across generations as families of several generations share caring responsibilities. As Sharlach, Damron-Rodriguez, Robinson and Feldman (2000: 523) point out, demographic changes and increased longevity have meant that families may now contain four or five generations, fewer members and an increase in the number of dependent persons at both ends of the age spectrum.

The International Year of Older Persons in 1998 spurred social work academics and practitioners in the ageing field to recognize the significant role social work could increasingly develop – within hospitals, in the design and evaluation of health care services for older people, in providing support, information and respite to carers (especially where carers themselves are elderly), and in advocating for the protection of older people from abuse and neglect (Keigher, Fortune and Witkin 2000).

The five core principles of the International Year of Older Persons – independence, participation, care, self-fulfilment and dignity – resonate well with social work's values, beliefs and practices. They provide helpful guidelines for the major focus characterizing social work practice in the aged care field, namely, the social situation of older people within political and economic structures, and the social components of health and well-being impacting in late life. Social work practice in aged care is focused towards providing a 'holistic culturally competent model of health and long term care services ... (recognizing) the important interaction of health, mental health and social and cultural factors' (Galambos and Rosen 2000: 17). Sharlach, Damron-Rodriguez and Witkin (2000: 253) concur, arguing that social work goals in working with older people should include preserving their independence, optimal functioning, dignity and quality of life through developing and maintaining empowering practice approaches and services.

The tasks social workers undertake in the aged care field require, in the first place, an understanding of how advanced age affects the client's experience (Sharlach, Damron-Rodriguez and Witkin 2000: 526). This means that it is very important for social workers to apply a 'biopsychosocial approach to understanding (the) physical and mental health' of older people (Gardner and Zodikoff 2003: 383). Thus making assessments will include paying attention to integrating biotechnical and scientific advances in gerontology whilst maintaining a sensitivity to the interactions of health and age, race, ethnicity, gender, socio-economic status and cultural background on the well-being of the client (Gardner and Zodikoff 2003: 384; Geron and Little 2003).

Because social workers frequently work in multi-disciplinary settings such as aged care assessment teams, hospitals and community health services, they become players in what Neysmith (1999: 2) refers to as the 'contested terrain' of defining old people's needs and determining how they are to be met. Given social work's prevailing concerns with the impact of structural features in affecting life chances, social work practice in aged care can bring these insights to bear in recognizing the political and economic forces which operate to marginalize, exclude and oppress. In particular, social workers need to understand that the experience of ageing is gendered. More women than men live to late life and the stigmatized and oppressive images of the aged female body stand in contrast to the socio-cultural value placed on bodies which are young, male, able-bodied and heterosexual. As Neysmith (1999: 8) points out, 'so-called frailty does not occur in a degendered, universal body. The body being scrutinized *is* old, but frequently it belongs to other devalued social categories ... it is often female, poor, or visibly ethno-racial'.

Scharlach, Damron-Rodriguez, Robinson and Feldman (2000: 536) provide a useful summary of the knowledge and skills social workers in the aged care field require: 'Gerontological social work, by virtue of its holistic person-in-environment perspective, its distinctive attention to psychological and social functioning, its integrative focus, and its commitment to meeting the needs of underserved and disadvantaged groups, is especially well suited to help meet the challenge faced by our ageing society'.

In previous chapters, we have offered critique of social work's person-in-environment and life course perspective and argued for the inclusion of both biological and sociological theories regarding the body. We now turn to explore these issues in greater detail in relation to social work in the aged care field.

As we have noted, social work relies solidly on its conceptualization of person-in-environment and the life course, with emphasis on the individual's capacities to adapt to life transitions and stages in development. The provision and availability of adequate resources nurture an individual's resilience and coping ability. In late life, recognition is given to the influence of accumulated risks and deficits which may play an important role in affecting the quality and quantity of an individual's life (Germain and Gitterman 1996; Harms 2004).

Criticisms of life course approaches refer to tendencies towards reductionism, individualizing, and simplification (Hagenstad and Dannefer 2001) with lack of recognition of the fact that social processes are constantly impacting on human ageing, that ageing is in fact a life long process (Bury and Wadsworth 2003: 109). Nevertheless, while life course approaches acknowledge the interaction of micro and macro perspectives, how this interaction actually occurs remains largely unexplained (Kunkel 2003: 129).

Within gerontology there has been considerable theoretical development in recent years, drawing upon work in sociology, critical theory and cultural studies. Kunkel (2003: 130–132) usefully refers to these as occurring within three generations.

The first generation of the 1970s conceptualized ageing as inevitably negative, associated with physical decline and social loss. Powell and Biggs (2003) note that the biomedical study of ageing has dominated the development of gerontology, an outcome of which is to see medical science as offering the only solution to the 'problem' of ageing. The social problems of ageing were seen as being due to the incapacities of older people, evident in behavioural problems and their failure to adapt to the environment. Old age was understood in this generation as primarily a biological phenomenon (Kontos 1999) with the mind and body conceptualized as separate and decontextualized.

Concomitantly within sociology, functionalist theorizing (derived from Parsons) emphasized the importance of the social system of a harmoniously balanced social world, in which older people were to be encouraged to progressively disengage from earlier social roles without disturbing the system's equilibrium (Cummings and Henry 1961 in Aldwin and Gilmer 2004). Critiques of functionalism and its reflection in Disengagement Theory refer to the inability of such theorizing to deal with the conflict, inequality and social contradictions inherent in society (Dannefer 2003), and in fact serve to discourage systematic examination of social diversity and inequality.

The second generation – 1980s and 1990s – saw the emergence of critical gerontology where attention was focused on understanding the structural features which influenced individuals' life trajectories. Research using cohort studies moved thinking away from individual perspectives towards emphasis on the processes of ageing and how these influenced and differentiated the experience of ageing, lending recognition to the heterogeneity and diversity of late life created by social and economic location.

Critical gerontology has a particular resonance for social work with its identification of the significance of structural factors in affecting late life trajectories, especially with regard to marginalized and oppressed groups (Neysmith 1999, Gardner and Zodikoff 2000). However, it has also been subject to critique for its perpetuation of mind-body dualisms characterizing biomedical perspectives (Kontos 1999) and continuing adoption of universal notions of the body. Nevertheless, critical gerontology has contributed significantly to our understanding of the social problems attending late life – poverty, isolation, the gendered differences in experiences. It invites consideration of the connection between the denigration of late life and the loss of social and work roles. For example, in societies which place a premium on production, those outside the work force become the object of social and cultural marginalization.

The third generation of the 1990s took up recognition of diversity in the ageing experience with efforts to synthesize both micro and macro perspectives and the role of human agency in determining the differential experience of ageing. Post-modern perspectives emerged alongside these, as sociology and cultural theory became increasingly interested in the body and its centrality to human experience and self-identity (Turner 1995). As Turner (1995: 258) remarks, the experience of the ageing of the body in late life creates a tension between our sense of our own inner self and awareness of the outer 'biological degeneration' of the body. The meaning of the body is socially constructed and culturally mediated (Nettleton and Watson 1998, Hareven 1995, Powell 2003), allowing quite different significance to be placed on it in different cultures and at different historical periods. In Western liberal democracies in the contemporary period, old bodies are frequently denigrated, which we see reflected especially in language (Witkin 2000) – 'doddering', 'senile' – while youth is celebrated (Hareven 1995). Featherstone and Hepworth (1991) refer to this biofeedback-like process as the 'mask of aging'. They contend that older people make sense of the biological reality of their aging bodies as if bodies are a mask concealing the real subjective self underneath. From this perspective, age can be viewed as a fluid rather than fixed process, and interest is placed on the meaning of the experience of late life (Williams 1995).

The emergence of discourses around 'successful ageing' coincide with biomedical advances and opportunities to reconstruct the ageing body. Opportunities for older people to attend to diet, health and exercise promote individuals' capacities to enhance and extend late life, learning how to manage one's own ageing body to achieve a 'successful' or 'good' old age. Critiques of these perspectives point to the pressures placed on old people to 'make an effort' in order to retain their place in mainstream society, prompting Tulle-Winton (1999: 283) to ask whether successful ageing is, in effect, 'a technique of regulation which serves to deny old people the legitimate right to bodily disfunction and even perhaps cultural disengagement?' Such perspectives also tend to homogenize and reduce old people to their chronological age, ignoring the diversity of health, social and economic location which has been demonstrated to be highly significant in empirical studies of cumulative advantage/disadvantage (Dannefer 2003).

Each of these perspectives – biomedical, critical and post-modern – contribute valuable insights into ageing. Social work theory and practice in aged care has maintained its person-in-environment and life course perspectives and, to an extent, has drawn upon understandings generated within each of these three. Our interest in this book is to place the body in the centre of our thinking and to draw from this implications for social work practice. We have already offered critique of aspects of person-in-environment formulations and life course perspectives through the conceptual frame of corporeal capacity. In the next section, we want to draw all of the foregoing together by arguing for an approach which draws together both sociological and biological understandings for social work theory and practice in the field of ageing.

We begin with an account of the biological changes that occur in late adulthood and interweave these with understandings from sociology and cultural theory which recognize the physiological realities of the ageing body while retaining emphasis on the meaning and experience of ageing, acknowledging the importance of individual agency within a social and material context.

Featherstone and Wernicke (1995: 1) highlight that 'ageing is about the body, yet in the study of ageing, we often lose sight of the lived body'. Nevertheless, as Mrak, Griffin and Graham (1997) point out, it is difficult to provide a 'non controversial, non trivial' definition of ageing, anatomical, cognitive and functional changes are part of the ageing process. Why these changes occur has been a question tackled by evolutionary biologists (Kaye 2002; Martin 2002), offering perspectives of considerable credibility. These refer to the fact that contemporary humans live far longer than our earliest ancestors because of economic, health and public health developments in recent times. Thus, the human brain comprises the genetic adaptations to life achieved more than seven thousand generations previously, a brain which was 'not specifically adapted for extended longevity' (Kaye 2002). It is likely that 'we age because of a variety of gene actions that escape the force of natural selection' (Martin 2002).

Viewing ageing through the framework of corporeal capacity acknowledges the parallel actions of genes and environment over the lifespan. The dynamism and plasticity of genes supports the notion that the lifespan is modifiable rather than a fixed dimension of human existence, and as Martin (2002) comments, 'the good news is that life span parameters are plastic'.

In contrast to approaches which single out late life as a separate phase in the life course, biological research points to the variability and difference in the ways in which individuals age (Kraemer, Bherer, Colcombe, Dong, and Greenough 2004). For different people, in different locations and at different times, the process of ageing differs. For some, physiological changes associated with ageing occur rapidly; for others, more slowly. Three physiological levels combine to account for the ageing process (Lamberts 2003; Aldwin and Gilmer 2004: 43–53). These are genetic elements, molecular/cellular elements, and systems level factors. The rate at which the human organism ages is affected by the complex inter- actions and transactions of all three – genetic, cellular and systems level factors. The physiological system, however, has some degree of plasticity and flexibility which means that interventions – social as well as biological and biotechnological – can result in positive as well as negative outcomes, accelerating or slowing the ageing process.

As genetic factors account for less than half of the variance in late life illness and mortality, it would appear that environmental and psychosocial factors play a major role, not just in the speed with which the body ages, but the nature and character of the ageing process (Longo and Finch 2002; Lamberts 2003; Aldwin and Gilmer 2004: 62–64). For example, research has found that the ageing process may be slowed by exercise, meditation, moderate alcohol intake, social support and stable personal rela- tionships, as well as a 'calm disposition' (Aldwin and Gilmer 2004: 62). By way of contrast, older people are more vulnerable to physical stressors because their physiological capacity to regulate homeostasis declines. This may account for their increased sus- ceptibility to chronic illness. Other research, in contrast, has found that a person's earlier experience of surviving and 'going on' despite the stresses of life, assists them in becoming more rather than less resilient (Aldwin and Gilmer 2004: 63).

The body has sophisticated regulatory systems organized through the sense organs, nervous system (brain and spinal cord), endocrine and immune systems. These regulatory systems communicate with and coordinate the internal organs which are responsible for digestion, and the circulation and processing of nutrients and fluids (Aldwin and Gilmer 2004: 119–207).

The endocrine system experiences a decline in circulating hormone concentrations and a decrease in the activity of growth hormones. At menopause, the drop in circulating estrogen levels is associated with vasomotor reactions, sleep disturbance, changes in skin and body composition. For males, testosterone levels decline after the age of 40 and, while it is unclear whether a reduction in sexual activity, muscle mass and strength are causally related to this, lower testosterone is associated with decrease in performance on tests of cognitive functioning and the increased likelihood of depressed mood (Lamberts 2003).

The production of cortisol impacts memory and cognition with higher cortisol levels being associated with memory decline, especially for women. Growth hormone levels are also associated with the speed of information processing, higher levels being associated with less cognitive decline (Lamberts 2003).

As people age, the levels of growth hormone declines, leading to decreased muscle and bone mass and strength. This clearly has implications for people's functional abilities and consequently, may impair their quality of life (Lamberts 2003). As Isaacowitz and Smith (2002) report, everyday functioning is linked with satisfaction in old age, especially for women. We know that more than half of the adult population suffer from osteoporosis and osteoarthritis which bring with them pain and disablement due to decline and failure in the musculo-skeletal system. In order to prevent or delay the onset of these conditions, attention needs to be placed on ensuring that the skeleton, muscle and skin receive adequate calcium and other minerals. These are essential for metabolism, nerve transmission and movement.

The ageing of the healthy brain (see Mrak, Griffin and Graham 1997; Kaye 2002; Rosenberg 2002) undergoes a number of predictable changes, beginning in young adulthood. Brain volume decreases with more white than grey matter apparent, indicative of cell death especially in the hippocampus and frontal lobes. There is a loss of myelin which acts as a protective cover to nerve cells, a loss of synapses and dendritic arbor, as well as an accumulation of neurofibullary tangles and myloid deposits in the brain and blood vessels. These changes are implicated in decreasing capacity for cognition and memory.

As these changes occur to all human brains over time, while there may be variability of the age at which problems emerge, it is more a question of time, when rather than whether an individual will 'neurologically succumb' (Kaye 2002).

On a more optimistic note however, although the brain is a postmitatic organ, meaning the neurons cannot be added but will decrease in number as we age, it also has significant plasticity until age 90 (Mrak, Griffin and Graham 1997). In a recent review of the literature on cognitive and brain ageing, Kraemer, Bherer, Colcombe, Dong and Greenough (2004) found evidence across a number of studies that allow us to be 'cautiously optimistic ... with regard to the modifiability of age-related changes in cognition and underlying brain function. Factors such as lifestyle, education, occupation, expertise, and fitness have been found to influence the trajectory of cognition from young to old adulthood' (2004: 949).

Two types of cognitive processes occur in humans. The first, crystallized, refers to knowledge-based abilities, such as verbal knowledge and comprehension. These are maintained or improve with age. The second, process-based cognitive functions such as reasoning, the speed of information processing and those abilities not dependent on experience decline with age.

The variability of aging decline and the heterogeneity characterizing people in late adulthood may be accounted for in relation to environmental and socio-economic factors (Lamberts 2003). For example, both longitudinal and cross-sectional studies demonstrate that education has a key role to play in maintaining cognitive and memory functioning. Indeed, lower levels of education are the strongest predictor of cognitive decline in measures of verbal and non-verbal memory, conceptualization and non-verbal activities. Autopsy studies support this. In the brain the field of neurons in language-associated regions is increased with education but, as Kraemer, Bherer, Colcombe, Dong and Greenough

(2003: 943) point out, 'whether brain complexity gives rise to educational attainment or vice versa cannot be determined'.

Studies of the influence of environmental factors also demonstrate that an engaged lifestyle which is rich in stimulation can delay cognitive decline. Particular regimens of fitness and exercise training have also demonstrated positive affects on cognitive functioning, particularly when they included strength and flexibility activities engaged in for more than 30 minutes. In these studies, cardio-vascular fitness and brain health were marked by reduced decline in grey and white matter in the frontal, prefrontal and temporal regions of the brain.

While Kraemer, Bherer, Colcombe, Dong and Greenough (2004) in reviewing the available research in this area, caution that more research is needed to increase our understanding of the 'nature and limits of cognitive plasticity across the adult life span' (2004: 950), nevertheless such findings challenge contemporary thinking about the inevitability and immutability of decline in late life.

Maintaining the healthy functioning of key regulatory systems in order to prevent disease and delay disease onset is vital to the rate and character of the ageing process. Behaviour which ensures good nutrition, exercise and the avoidance of damaging behaviours such as smoking, over-eating, and living in toxic environments (e.g. with very loud music or ultraviolet light) can enhance the quality and quantity of life.

While it is well recognized that the interface between physical and emotional well-being is complex, research findings are contradictory with respect to whether or not emotional stability, emotion regulation and optimism may be protective in late life (Aldwin and Gilmer 2004: 253). Interestingly, Isaacowitz and Smith (2003) report findings from their research into affect in late life that personality is more important than social relationships in predicting subjective well-being in the oldest old – those aged 85 plus. People with high extroversion scores reported positive affect while those with high neuroticism scores predicted negative affect. However, the effects of stress have been noted at genetic, cellular and systems levels. For example, stress may upset homeostasis leading to damage at the cellular and genetic levels.

It is possible that the experience of chronic stress during life may have a role to play in the development of chronic illness in later life (Aldwin and Gilmer 2004: 281). There is however, considerable variation in the effects of stress on the body, perhaps referring to individuals' particular styles of coping with problems. Indeed the role of social support in dealing with stress has been well-documented. Those with strong social support have both greater longevity and better health (Isaacowitz and Smith 2003; Aldwin and Gilmer 2004: 294). Although the physiological mechanisms whereby social support is related to physical health are not well understood, they possibly include an ability to adapt to stress, the availability of help and resources, as well as skilful coping capacities. Very importantly however, Aldwin and Gilmer (2004: 296) point out that psychosocial factors only weakly predict the development of disease, with genetic make-up, health behaviour habits and exposure to environmental toxins playing a more significant role. Nevertheless, should an individual be afflicted by disease, their personality and disposition and the availability of social supports may play a role either in their recovery or their decline.

The most common diseases of late life – Alzheimer's, Parkinson's and cardio-vascular diseases – are related to both genetic and environmental effects, and none of them are to be regarded as the inevitable consequences of aging (Mrak, Griffin and Graham 1997). Rather, the aging brain accumulates many of the pathologies expected (and described above), but these are not uniformly associated with neurological impairment (Kaye 2002). Indeed it has been found that, while low levels of education are associated with a greater risk of Alzheimer's disease, high levels of education can delay cognitive decline 'even in the face of increasing cerebral atrophy' (Kraemer, Bherer, Colcombe, Dong and Greenough 2004: 944). The gradual changes in cognitive ability which accompany healthy brain aging may represent one disease process or one elemental pathological event (Rosenberg 2002), so that, for example, a mild cognitive impairment may be 'just that', or it could be a precursor to Alzheimer's Disease. Thus, those factors such as diet, exercise, stimulating intellectual activity, ongoing learning, social support, and a healthy environment which have been found to be protective of brain functioning in late life assume considerable importance in measures to either prevent and/or delay the onset of difficulties. While limited to studies of primates, fascinating discoveries have already been made which demonstrate that when these animals are placed in enriched and stimulating environments, some neurogenesis was evident in the hippocampus as well as improvements in performing tasks of spatial learning and memory were observed (Kraemer, Bherer, Colcombe, Dong and Greenough 2004: 945). The potential these discoveries hold for the aging human brain are exciting.

Corporeal capacity

Ageing occurs 'not only in the body, but in time, in place, in history, and in the context of lived experience' (Kontos 1999: 687). Or, in our terms, the life-long process of ageing can be thought of as elaborating corporeal capacity. By late life one's corporeal capacity will, through the many events and environments in which it was sustained, be changed, altered, enhanced or assaulted. Late life may herald the extinction of corporeal capacity, but until that happens, the human body remains in active engagement with life processes.

These processes, as we have noted, simultaneously comprise and influence the environment both internal and external to the body. While the body is a biological organism and system, it cannot be reduced to that alone. The intentions, beliefs, meanings and assumptions which people hold concerning their bodies, derived from culture and society and located within history and time, also shape the body and shape the experience and the manifestation in the body of the ageing process. In this sense then, we can talk about the plasticity of the body. As Bury and Wadsworth (2003: 111) argue, while society shapes ageing at the individual level (for example, discourses around 'successful ageing') changes in the health and ageing profile of populations (e.g. increased longevity), also shape and change society and the culture of society. Human agency, (e.g. the decisions to choose particular health behaviours) and the interactions between social knowledge and social practices (e.g. the application of effective biological knowledge through public health measures) mitigate and/or increase the potential risks to health and well-being across the life course. As a person ages, the advantages and disadvantages found in both the internal and external environment and the behavioural responses to them (on individual and collective levels) can accumulate and increase the potential for disease and/or strengthen resilience and survivorship as the person ages towards late life (Dannefor 2003).

Despite the plasticity of the body, it is also the case that, as Bury and Wadsworth note (2003: 116; see also Aldwin and Gilmer 2004: 296), many health problems are also strongly associated with biological age. Linked to this are the developments in pharmacology and biotechnology which mean that many people live longer with disabilities and chronic illnesses, including of course, those whose impairments occurred at birth or during earlier years (Putnam 2002).

The work of epidemiologists including Kuh and Ben-Shlomo (1997) and Kuh and Hardy (2002) advance a life course approach grounded in empirical research which places particular emphasis on analysing a wide range of biological and social experiences in childhood and adolescence which combine to influence adult disease risk. Kuh and Ben-Schlomo's (1997: 7) concept of chains of risk includes both those chains which can be advantageous and disadvantageous in influencing the risk of adult disease occurrence. They argue that health damaging exposures and/or enhancing opportunities are socially patterned by the social stratifications of socio-economic status, race and gender, and opportunities for education, occupation and relationship formations. By way of contrast to person-in-environment and life course perspectives drawn on in social work, this epidemiological approach to the life course is not directed towards studying health and health problems at each life stage but rather how risks to later health might originate in early life and accumulate across the entire life course (Kuh and Hardy 2002: 13).

This perspective also receives support within the current social gerontology literature where the theorizing of age and cumulative advantage/disadvantage has taken a cohort-based rather than individual-based approach (Dannefer 2003), demonstrating that, as a cohort ages, increasing health and economic inequality and variability occurs. The effect of structural factors in the distribution of opportunities and resources accounts for this variability, indicating not just the significance of structural forces but also the difficulty of treating an ageing cohort as homogeneous.

Body cognizant social worker

Social workers should be encouraged by findings such as those of Grenier and Gorey (2000) which demonstrate the effectiveness of gerontological social work services in being 'practically helpful' (2000: 230) to the majority of service users in their meta-analysis of 89 published studies. However, what we have conceptualized as body cognizant social work practice might suggest that attention to some of the following might significantly increase the benefits of social work interventions.

Social work practice in aged care which places the body at the centre of theory and practice would draw on some of the developments in the understanding of the physiology of the body, theoretical contributions from critical and social gerontology, sociology of the body, and cultural theory as we have sketched them here from within a corporeal capacity framework. This would allow for a richer and more complex practice base. Thus, the overarching goal for social workers in this field might be both a preventative one in which effort is made to increase the years of healthy life we can all enjoy with the full range of our functional and mental capacities until the last stage of life (Lamberts 2003), as well as practise interventions informed by biological and sociological understanding which maximize the potential for older people experiencing impairments and disabilities to enjoy as satisfying a quality of life as is possible. Knowing the major factors which control rates of brain health span mean that we can appreciate the time period when the brain is optimally functional and concentrate our efforts at that point (Kaye 2002).

Such a project might begin by reconsidering prevailing life course perspectives and recognizing an ongoing life-long rather than age and stage approach to human development, thereby avoiding a tendency to isolate ageing as a stage rather than as integral to the life course. The perspective advanced in this chapter has emphasized the centrality of the body at the interface of social, historical and cultural processes which influence the nature and character of the ageing body and the experience of embodiment. The body is marked in real and corporeal ways through the operations of social, political and economic structures of gender, race and class. The plasticity of the body provides both evidence of its physiological make-up as well as its location within social and cultural processes. This plasticity even in late life reinforces the appropriateness of social workers' role in intervening to provide the opportunities to enhance health and well-being of older people and to reduce the allostatic load, or accumulating impact of wear and tear, (see Chapter 2) on the body's systems.

Body cognizant social workers then need to be informed about the kinds of behaviours and practices which may slow the ageing process, or perhaps more importantly, prevent decline once disease has occurred. On a practical level, this might mean that social workers ensure older people eat nutritious food, take moderate exercise, meditate and so on. Efforts to break down the potentially isolating conditions for older people, particularly those whose mobility is compromised, or who have limited or reducing social networks, may become a priority. Research has reinforced what social workers have often believed to be of considerable importance in late life, namely, the provision of social support and the building of social networks which buffer the effects of stress and build resilience.

Post-modern theorists have brought to our attention the considerable importance of exploring meaning in lived experience for those who have lived for many years. This accumulated experience is a rich storehouse to draw upon in interpersonal and community interventions. The relationship between constructing a sense of one's identity which can change over time brings with it recognition that what it means to be an aged person with an ageing body is open to many different interpretations and not fixed within biomedical discourses of decline and degeneration. Rather, contemporary discourses such as those surrounding notions of positive ageing may be of value in liberating individuals to see themselves differently, as persons with agency and the capacity to choose different (health promoting) lifestyles. Concomitantly, their right to a self-identity as frail and disabled must also be accommodated.

A body cognizant approach might mean that the assessments which social workers make in regard to users of aged care services could include 'attention to the links between thoughts, emotions, and physical health, exercise and nutrition, and skills or attitudes developed to maintain emotional and physical wellbeing' (Tangenburg 2002). They might also pay attention to environmental factors such as the person's living conditions and financial security.

Taking corporeal capacity as a framework for practice in aged care may also mean that social workers retain their critical perspective in relation to analysing social policies and practices which may serve to manage, regulate and monitor older people's lives – and bodies. Dominant constructions of older people as non-productive, dependent and helpless when reflected in social policies and practices serve to further marginalize older people (Tulle-Winton 1999). In addition, a body cognizant social worker may retain awareness of issues to do with their presentation of self, the likelihood that there will be a significant gap in age from the client and that the presentation of their more youthful and possibly more socially valued body could raise difficult emotions for the client. For themselves too, recognition of the (often unconscious) prejudices that may arise when confronted with older bodies may require admission and consideration to avoid unintended and unhelpful communication.

Social workers have always valued self-determination and empowering practices, and in working within aged care, this must remain a priority. While the positive ageing discourse is premised on notions of individual agency and choice, there are older people for whom this is of little relevance, perhaps because of their social and economic status, or perhaps because of their physical frailty. Models of social disability, especially their strong emphasis on disability rights, may offer parallel and relevant perspectives for social workers in aged care to draw upon (Putnam 2003).

In line with this more critical perspective, body cognizant social workers in aged care may also usefully increase their knowledge and practice base by learning more about the patterning of health risks across the life course and the cumulative influences of advantages and disadvantages. This may lead social workers to ask questions about how human actions reproduce social forms, for example, how class-based inequalities are reproduced, exploring the relationship between individual-life trajectories and the social forces – intergenerational, interactional, ideological – that shape them and that are evidenced in the body (Dannefer 2003). As Williams, Birke and Bendelow (2003: 8) comment, '(The) relations between the biological and the social are lived, experienced and expressed in and through our embodied being-in-the-world, with all the contingency and uncertainty this entails, from birth to death'.

The contributions of biological and sociological research on ageing reviewed in this chapter can be brought together in applying the Body Cognizant Assessment Guide (BCAG) to this hypothetical example.

Client profile: The client is a 79-year-old woman who has been widowed for many years. She lives in her own home which is somewhat dilapidated, has a large rather wild garden and is poorly heated with many potential hazards such as loose rugs and a bathroom and toilet some distance from her bedroom. She receives a part pension and superannuation payments. Her children are supportive, but all work full-time although some live quite close to their mother. They are able to shop and prepare meals for her. Recently, she had a knee replacement operation and since then has been depressed at times and has lost confidence. She is becoming increasingly frail and immobile. Her house is on a busy road, and the footpath is in poor condition. She does not drive. Her daughter contacted the social worker at the local council, concerned at her mother's increasing depression and isolation.

185

	Potential sources of client vulnerabilities/ strengths		Targets for amelioration/ enhancement	
	Adversive	Protective	Adversive	Protective
Macrosocial factors	**What:** Stigmatizing and homogenizing of aged as burden and non-productive. Social value placed on images of youthfulness **How (impact):** Lowered self-esteem, depressed mood, sense of rejection and uselessness; anxious that she will be forced to move into residential care and out of mainstream life	**What:** Policy focus on 'ageing in place'. Availability of range of services **How (impact):** Knowledge that services exist to enable her to remain in own home reduce anxiety and depression	**(Address) What:** Stigma and social rejection of aged **(Address) How:** Advocate continued resourcing of 'aging in place' policy; action to pressure media for alternative and positive representations of aged people	**(Address) What:** Ageing on policy agenda **(Address) How:** Utilise services; document how they ameliorate individual situations; identify and record service gaps
Community scale biological/ chemical or physical factors	**What:** Busy road, poor footpath, lack of adjacent parking	**What:** Physiotherapy program for elderly offered by local community health service; GP makes home visits	**What:** Address parking, busy road, poor footpath	**What:** Physiotherapy programme, GP home visits, supportive family

Continued

Continued

	Potential sources of client vulnerabilities/strengths		Targets for amelioration/enhancement	
	Adversive	Protective	Adversive	Protective
	How (impact): Anxious about leaving house; unable to cross road; fearful of fall on footpath; difficult for visitors to park and/or take her out in car	**How (impact):** Program available to increase mobility and build confidence; regular health checks from GP; build strength and reduce anxiety, lift mood	**How:** Consult planning and engineering sections of local government for improvements, consideration of pedestrian crossing nearby client's home, argue for priority parking space designated near her home	**How:** Support re regular monitoring of her health, opportunities to build muscle mass and mobility will increase confidence; reduce anxiety about having to leave home, elevate mood. Chance to socialize with others at physiotherapy may reduce isolation and increase mental well-being
Small scale biological/chemical or physical factors (as afflicting person or home environment)	**What:** Old house, difficult to heat; some hazardous furnishings **How (impact):** Possibility of illness; likelihood of fall. Client often stays in bed for warmth; is anxious and	**What:** Supportive family assisting with shopping and meal preparation; family not pressuring mother to leave home **How (impact):** Client less isolated on	**What:** Old, cold house with some hazardous furnishings **How:** Work with client and family to identify hazards; consult with OT, housing advice from RAIA on	**What:** Issues causing stress and lowered mood being addressed **How:** Client being put in contact with helpful services, thus feeling less isolated, more confident with consequent

	stressed about falling – therefore takes little exercise which further increases immobility, muscle decline and depressed mood	weekends; eating nutritious food; client keen to reassure family that she is OK at home	possibility of renovations and adjustments to improve safety and comfort	elevation of mood; becoming motivated to undertake physiotherapy
Intersubjective/ interpersonal factors	**What:** Most contemporaries either dead or similarly immobile **How (impact):** Feelings of isolation, loneliness, being a burden; client withdraws more, immobility increases through lack of exercise; some cognitive slowing and memory impairment. Client 'picks up' her children's anxieties re her ability to manage and this creates additional worries for her	**What:** Good family support from children **How (impact):** Frequent visits and outings when possible reduces loneliness	**What:** Feelings of sadness and loss of confidence; anxiety re possibility of having to leave her home **How:** e.g. Encourage outings to group activities, e.g. physiotherapy. Encourage her to use phone more to call friends	**What:** Good relationships with children and friends **How:** e.g. Reflect on this and what she has contributed to others and can go on contributing, even in new group situations

Continued

Continued

	Potential sources of client vulnerabilities/ strengths		Targets for amelioration/ enhancement	
	Adversive	**Protective**	**Adversive**	**Protective**
Intrapersonal/ intrapsychic factors	**What:** Loss of confidence since knee replacement **How (impact):** Feels depressed, withdraws which leads to further physical decline and immobility	**What:** Client has survived many losses in her long life **How (impact):** Ability to remember good and bad times, and to have constructive outlook on limits and capacities of self and others. Her longevity indicates biological advantage which can be a strength to augment	**What:** Anxiety re managing; depression **How:** e.g. Provide opportunities to reflect on her strengths and life experiences. Perhaps encourage joining journal club or narrative therapy (life history) project	**What:** Client's intelligence and cognitive capacity **How:** e.g. Build on this strength and encourage client that these capacities are valued and will continue to be enhanced the more she engages with others, takes on new experiences, attends to physical fitness

9 Social Work, the Body and Health Care

From the earliest days of the profession, social work has evidenced recognition of the impact of poor economic and social conditions in the generation of health problems, disease and illness (Schlesinger 1985, Finger and Abramson 2002). It was through recognition of the central role that poverty and material conditions play in affecting (if not determining) the life chances and opportunities of people that social work's predominant concern with the person in their psychosocial situation had its genesis.

Social workers have been working in hospitals and health care settings in Australia since the 1930s (Browne 2005: 109) and were a presence even earlier in other countries. Their ongoing association with health delivery services has changed and evolved over the years. However, there is a detectable difference in emphasis over this time from a concern with the impact of social conditions on health and well-being, to a concern with the impact of accidents, illness and disease on those afflicted and their families. This is a shift away from a structural focus towards a concern with how people function and manage their lives when confronted with ill health. In the contemporary era, there is also an emergent focus on the meaning and significance for individuals of these stressors and, in the light of this, emphasis on identifying and working to develop and strengthen individual and family resilience and coping capacities.

We might think of these changing emphases as indicative of paradigmatic shifts away from more critical perspectives towards more social constructionist positions. Such shifts are also reflected in – and no doubt influenced by – the changing nature of the contexts in which health social workers work.

In this chapter, our concern is with the health care field rather than specific sites of social work health service delivery such as paediatrics or oncology units. Our purpose is to discuss some of the factors which influence practice in this field such as debates that the discourses of biology and sociology are competing rather than mutually informing, and the impact on thinking and practice of perspectives which distance, if not oppose, biological and sociological perspectives.

All health settings – hospitals, primary care centres, community health services – are primarily medical settings in which the medical and nursing professions dominate. The so-called medical model is generally seen as underpinning their philosophy and practice. This model has been noted to comprise the following key features (Mishler and Amara Singham 1981):

1. Disease is understood as a deviation from normal biological functioning.
2. Specific diseases are caused by specific micro-organisms: this is the doctrine of specific disease aetiology.
3. Universally, disease impacts on humans in the same way, regardless of culture, time and place.
4. Medicine is considered to be scientifically neutral.

Criticisms of this model relate to an apparent absence of recognition of contextual factors, limited consideration being given to the different ways in which people might experience disease, as well as concerns about the extent to which the causative logic of the model fits with other perspectives on health, specifically those with a disability focus.

Among practitioners in contemporary health care practice however, the terms of reference for this debate are more likely to be conceptualized in relation to a perceived opposition between social/psychological training and training in the biological sciences rather than the medical model per se. Nevertheless, the role of social work in health settings has been, by and large, to complement the work of doctors and to offer patients and families services targeting aspects of their social functioning. Schlesinger (1985: 79) argues that, for social workers, 'Health involves not the absence of disease but the capacity to cope in physical and psychological terms, and is related to the quality of social relationships and the ability to carry out a variety of activities consonant with age, interests and physical and mental capacities'.

The dominance of the so-called medical model has made it the target of, at times, unwarranted attack, accusing it of failing to address the social context of human lives and of perpetuating reductionist mind–body dualism (see Crossley 1995). In reply, those working within the medical model counter that it provides a more contextualized perspective taking into account social, spiritual and environmental factors, evident, for example, in the clinical practice of doctors, than is recognized. Its success is apparent in highly significant achievements in terms of treatments and cures, and at least in the West, the reality of declining mortality rates and improving quality and extension of life (see Weissman 1996; Sampson 1996). Indeed, social workers working in hospitals do recognize the acknowledgement that nursing and medical professionals currently accord to the influence of psychological and social factors impacting on patients' health (personal communication, Jane Miller).

For social workers, it is the biopsychosocial model which is seen as underpinning practice. This model is drawn from systems theory, proposing that all three elements – biological, psychological and social – are interconnected and interdependent. Within this model, in addition to biological disease factors, the psychological and subjective experience of illness and the implications of social and material conditions in regard to health can be accommodated simultaneously. However, the dominance of social constructionist perspectives in social work has tended to filter out the 'bio' elements, leaving social workers more firmly committed to a psychosocial understanding – and leading to growing concern from some contemporary writers in the social work health care field about the absence of the 'bio' and the necessity to reclaim it: 'In social work the bio in the biopsychosocial model has been largely ignored. We call ourselves "social" workers but in the future we will have to be *"biopsychosocial workers"*' (Pecukonis, Cornelius and Parish 2003: 10. See also Volland, Berkman, Phillips and Stein 2003). It may also be that the different sociological and biological perspectives somewhat forced together in the biopsychosocial model have created what Crossley (1995) terms a 'jumbo model'. He considers biological and sociological discourses to operate from different perspectives, each of which has different 'vices and virtues'. What is needed, from his point of view, 'is a genuinely "dialogical" perspective which admits of the value of different perspectives and refuses to prejudge which, or which combination, will be of most relevance in any given instance' (1995: 248).

Research and practice in the health field is dramatically changing as we enter the twenty-first century with the development of new technologies, understandings and innovations which have accompanied the human genome project, the bio-technology revolution, globalization, increasing interest in holistic health and natural healing, media expansion and Western cultural 'colonizing' of greater parts of the world. Turner (1995: 257) comments that contemporary society has placed the body as a project of 'ultimate concern' as evidenced by a prevailing focus on organ transplants, gender plasticity, sexuality, gay and feminist politics, AIDS and HIV, the technological possibilities of the body, and the production of new bodies.

In addition, the demographic shifts resulting in larger numbers of people living longer has meant an increase in the numbers of people living with chronic illness and disabilities. These very rapid developments – particularly in the West – have also sensitized us to the prevailing conditions of inequalities in health, and questions about who experiences poor health, and how we can explain health inequalities.

In the contemporary world, health care systems continue to undergo radical change, driven by a number of factors. These include demographic (ageing of the population), economic (fiscal) and technological (e.g. genetic and pharmacological) changes and developments. Medical sociologists and other social theorists (e.g. Giddens 1991) argue that there is a new paradigm of health apparent in the twenty-first century – a 'regime of total health' (Nettleton and Gustafsson 2002) in which ordinary people are encouraged (perhaps even required) to monitor and maintain their own health. Fewer people receive care within institutions, placing greater responsibility on communities and families to care for themselves. The close to universal (in the West) access to the internet means that health information (and sometimes online health services) is widely available. Medical professionals are under scrutiny from the wider public for the first time, as lay people are encouraged to seek out information and become critical health consumers. Technological developments, for example, new vaccines and interventions, increase the range of choices available for patients to make in regard to their health care. Where previously debates about the merits and risks of various treatments may have been confined to the medical establishment, today they are vigorously debated in the media and in cyberspace. Greater awareness of choices around health treatments and of the risks involved in them, devolves greater responsibility to social workers in particular.

Social workers have always been located at the boundary between patients and the health care system, advocating for and assisting patients in accessing health services. Today, however, there is need for them to have a far greater understanding of the increasing complexity of treatments in order to ensure that they are fully cognizant of the risks and able to interpret these in relation to their knowledge of the vulnerabilities and material conditions of patients' lives. The same holds true of course, with regard to social workers and their work with service users in all settings, for whom such health-related information can be vital. Health, as Browne points out (2005: 107), is 'the business of all social workers.'

In addition, the organizational arrangements in contemporary health care systems mean that social workers are often working alone and autonomously within teams comprised of other health professionals. Separated organizationally, and often geographically, from professional colleagues places social workers in situations of needing to be both well informed of the nature of medical interventions and able to interpret the implications of these for their patients (see Volland, Berkman, Phillips and Stein 2003). This requires a strong knowledge base and clarity about social work's particular contribution to debates about patient care, perhaps made more difficult in contemporary times when the certainty that used to characterize medical and scientific knowledge seems no longer to prevail, for example, in relation to end-of-life issues (see Nettleton and Gustafsson 2002: 6 for a discussion).

Social constructionist approaches, as we have noted in Chapter 1, have been the bedrock of much social work theorizing. There we noted their limitations in relation to tendencies to absent corporeality and materiality of the body. In the area of health care, this undoubtedly poses considerable conceptual and practice difficulties, especially when combined with the 'etherealizing' of the 'bio' within the biopsychosocial model, espoused as central to social work practice in health care.

Awareness of this problematic has emerged in calls by some social workers in health to adopt more holistic or mind–body practices, for example, using meditation, biofeedback and guided imagery interventions with patients (see Finger and Arnold 2002; Henderson 2000; Cook, Becvar and Pontious 2000; DeCoster 2000) in recognition of growing evidence of the effects of bodily states, including emotion, on health.

While the proponents of holistic and mind–body approaches argue that these are challenges to the dualism and separation of mind and body thought to be exemplified by the medical model, such approaches themselves fall victim to the same charges. Williams (2003: 40) argues persuasively that these therapies retain the mind–body dualism, with primacy going to 'mind' as healing the body (see also Weissman 1996; Sampson 1996). Further, the causes of ill health are 'returned' to the individual with responsibility for personal change, possibly also entailing 'life style' change, and thereby deflecting attention away from structural and societal sources. Rather than holistic or mind–body therapies being viewed as 'liberatory', Williams suggests (2003: 40) that they reflect instead a 'drastic increase in the medicalization of life in late Western society'. Sampson (1996: 196) takes this argument further, proposing that the commodification of holistic health has as its object 'the appropriation of the political and social power now in the hands of physicians and scientists, and its attendant economic rewards'.

Our intention so far has been to sketch and critique the prevailing theoretical and practice models influencing social workers in health care settings, with emphasis on the importance of the contemporary health care context in creating the particular conditions and requirements of social work practitioners. We now want to revisit the concept of corporeal capacity and explore its particular relevance in relation to the health field.

Corporeal capacity

As we have previously noted, 'corporeal capacity', provides a framework for recognizing our location as environmentally embodied beings, adapting, changing and shaping ourselves and the material and social world as our lives unfold. A social worker working from a corporeal capacity framework will see the world through the three 'lenses' – widescreen, middle distance and close-up – we have described earlier, recognizing the interpenetration of those broad 'levels' of social and material reality which are simultaneously and continuously 'producing' the immediate situation which we are trying to understand and to work with.

An individual's corporeal capacity is determined by limitations of the species, and her particular inherited strengths and weakness in addition to kinds of environments – social, political and natural or chemical – that an individual has been exposed to. Corporeal capacity refers to an individual's developmental stage, psychological and 'medical' health, her skills, self-perception together with her sense of hopefulness/optimism. The opportunities an individual will have to express her capacity is determined by her immediate and current environment. 'Immediate environment' refers to the situation that an individual is in at any given moment. Her capacity to deal with a specific situation will be better or less well developed depending upon her prior experiences. An individual's current environment, on the other hand, refers to the people and chemical, biological and physical hazards with which she may come into contact on a day-to-day basis. Her ability to change her environment will depend upon the nature of the change desired, the level of resistance the relevant environmental factors offer and her own corporeal capacity.

As Williams, Birke and Bendelow (2003: 6) point out, health is a key site for exploring the impact and significance of the relationship between biology and society. It also requires careful analysis in order to avoid what Birke (2003: 48) refers to as 'the abyss of determinism' when we consider biology, and the 'abyss of relativism' when we consider sociology. Bringing understanding from these two fields together is complex and demanding – but central to any effort to 'bring back' the body to social work in health.

In a concept sharing similarities with corporeal capacity with a specific health focus, epidemiologists Kuh and Ben-Shlomo (1997) and Kuh and Hardy (2002) propose the 'life course approach' as a conceptual framework which synthesizes biological programming and social models. 'Biological programming' can be understood, here, as referring to both an individual's specific genetic heritage as well as those features common to all humans.

'Life course epidemiology is the study of the contribution of biological and social factors acting independently, interactively, and cumulatively during gestation, childhood, adolescence and adult life on health outcomes in later life. The purpose is to identify long-term risk and protective processes that explain variation in individual disease risk and changing patterns of disease over time and across populations' (Kuh and Hardy 2002: 14).

Kuh and Hardy's work is centrally concerned with how risks to health in adulthood may originate in early life and accumulate across the entire life course. Although methodological issues challenge longitudinal research designs, there is mounting research evidence to support their life course perspective. Several concepts derived from this approach are particularly useful: the notion of chains of risk and chains of protective factors (Kuh and Ben-Schlomo 1997: 7) in which certain experiences in early life, such as low birth weight, may in turn lead to a change in risk of adult disease. For example, a child who is smaller than others is at greater risk of coronary heart disease and, added to this, may have lowered self-esteem which triggers behaviour which may damage health such as excessive alcohol use. The social patterning implicit in an individual's response to life opportunities refers to the availability of resources and opportunities which are constrained by social factors such as gender or race. These factors change over time and differ in different societies.

Attempts to understand why health inequalities prevail have led to many studies analysing the relationship between social class and health. These include epidemiological studies as well as longitudinal studies of age cohorts. Such studies do demonstrate that poverty and social exclusion are correlated with poorer health. However, questions remain as to why this is so, how social characteristics are perceived by individuals, processed into biological signals which then convert them into disease. Blaxter (2003: 74) refers to this, quoting Tarlov (1996) as the 'sociobiological translation'.

Blaxter's explanation draws on the concept of 'health capital'. This metaphor interprets health in similar terms to wealth – both can accumulate or decline, can be lost or augmented over the life course in ways which can be measured but not always predicted.

The foundations for 'health accumulation' are laid down in utero and then elaborated at birth, during infancy and childhood. Such factors as maternal health, education, family life and occupation provide opportunities and challenges to the accumulation of health capital for adult and later life. A person's behaviours can deplete the stocks of health capital, for example, through poor diet, smoking and so on, but eventually such stocks will run out as the individual ages and dies (see also Williams, Birke and Bendelow 2003: 5).

Health capital is also affected by historical and often class-related events such as epidemics, depressions, war and conflict. Thus the context of an individual's life is related both to historical factors and the age and class cohort of which they are a part.

The notion of health capital is useful in bringing together in interaction, biological and social factors. Elements which affect the body's defences – such as the stresses associated with social locations of oppression, of lack of control, low income, prejudice, stigma and conflict – as well as exposure to infections and other hazards can be brought together in ways which recognize their complexity.

As Blaxter (2003: 81, 82) summarizes, the health capital metaphor has strong explanatory power regarding health inequalities which accepts both the constructed nature of social facts and physical biological facts. It takes us back too, to the discussion in Chapter 2 of the concept of allostatic load, coined by McEwan (1998) and elaborated by McEwan and Lesley (2004).

Allostatic load refers to the accumulation of stress over the life course which causes wear and tear on the body's systems. The stress reaction is generated by the body's attempt to adapt to feelings and experiences of insecurity, problematic social interactions, sense of lack of control over such things as one's job, poor diet, lack of adequate sleep, little exercise, few opportunities for holidays and relaxation. The impact of exposure to stress for sustained periods results in damage to the mechanisms through which insulin controls glucose levels in the blood as well as having the potential to disrupt aspects of immune system functioning. The outcome of this is to increase the individual's propensity to become vulnerable to illness and disease.

Elstad (1998: 60; see also Lillquist and Abramson 2002) pointed out that psychosocial stress, for example, sustained exposure to abuse, may, through its impact on the immune system, either directly affect disease development or, more indirectly, motivate the stressed person to engage in health-damaging behaviours such as smoking and problematic alcohol use. Williams (2003: 50–58) takes Elstad's findings further, demonstrating that socio-economic power and status differentials result in different emotional modes of being. For example, occupying a powerless social status increases the likelihood that a person will experience unpleasant emotional modes of being, where emotions such as anxiety, fear, anger and resentment will emerge.

Further, occupying a minority or stigmatized status, for example, belonging to a minority racial group or living with psychiatric disability, might bring with it not only material deprivations with their own health consequences (poor housing, poor nutrition, poor education) but also target such people as the objects of discrimination and victimization which increase the burden of unpleasant emotional states, isolation and lowered self-esteem.

It comes as no surprise then, that those with low incomes, poor levels of education and little control over their lives demonstrate higher levels of disease vulnerability, evident, for example. in cardiovascular disease, certain kinds of cancer, arthritis and so on. In fact, McEwan and Lesley (2004) argue that allostatic load (which can be measured in relation to quantities of adrenaline and noradrenaline in urine as well as measures of body function such as abdominal fat deposits) can serve as a predictor for disease onset.

Body cognizant social worker

We have earlier argued that a social worker who is body cognizant will practise in a way that indicates that the social worker is aware of (a) environment, and human behaviour, affect, information processing and learning, from a 'biological' perspective, or relevant findings on these from biology and (b) meanings ascribed by the worker, client and wider society to bodies, and the significance of this for client well-being, as well as ways in which the body is used by any of these parties in communication.

In the health care field, the significant developments in neuroscience and epidemiological research which we have noted above point to the importance of social workers 'taking on board' this information as they work with clients in the health care field.

Placing emotion at the interface of body and society enables us to think differently about the credibility and effectiveness of social work interventions in health. Already there is a growing body of research, coming principally from outside social work in the fields of psychology, medical sociology, neuroscience and psychoneuro-immunology which examines the relationship between psychosocial interventions and health maintenance. Of especial importance is the research undertaken in cancer, heart disease and mental health.

While research findings concerning the relationship between psychosocial support and increased cancer survival have yielded mixed results (Lachman 2000; Andersen 2002), psychotherapy has been found to be highly effective in improving quality of life. In other areas, for example, heart disease (Ornish 1990) and diabetes (Viner, Christie, Taylor and Hey 2003; Kennardy, Mensch, Bowen, Green and Walton 2002) group intervention and support led to improvements in physiological functioning.

Andersen (2002) has developed the 'biobehavioral model of the psychological (stress and quality of life), behavioral (compliance and health behaviors), and biological pathways from cancer stressors to disease course' (2002: 591). On the basis of a review of outcome studies measuring quality and quantity of life following interventions to ameliorate stress, she concluded that '(p)sychological interventions may moderate the effect of adverse psychologic, behavioral, or biologic responses, on disease outcome' (2002: 591).

Salovey, Rothman, Detweiler and Steward (2000) review research on the impact of positive emotional states and health behaviour patterns in relation to cardio-vascular and immune responses. Positive emotional states can facilitate healthy behavioural practices by providing the resilience that people may need to confront the possibility that they might have serious health problems, for example, engaging a person's willingness to undergo screening tests. While optimism may offer people the opportunity to consider and plan for future outcomes and in so doing motivate helpful health behaviours, humour has been identified as both a protective factor in building resilience (Curtis and Cicchetti 2003) as well as helping people cope with life stressors.

Social support is related to lower mortality, lower prevalence and incidence of coronary heart disease, and faster recovery from heart disease and heart surgery. Positive social relationships do promote health and well-being, and the availability of social support may insulate people from experiencing increased degrees of stress. Thus, feelings of security coming from social support may play a significant role in increasing an individual's resilience to physical illness (Curtis and Cicchetti 2003). The cascade-like effect of a positive mood may become a critical component in encouraging further social support to be offered.

Recent research into the placebo effect has demonstrated that the expectation, the hope of finding relief or cure is registered in the brain, altering brain pathways. Interestingly, different pathways to those altered by mood-altering medication, for example, for depression, are implicated. Such research reinforces our everyday understanding of the significance of offering and generating hope in those who are challenged by the vicissitudes of life, that building on the resources of patients who are depressed or have low morale actually makes a tangible and measurable difference to both the quantity and quality of life (see also Salovey, Rothman, Detweiler and Steward 2000). Thus, when psychotherapeutic interventions are offered as well as pharmacological treatments, maximum advantage might be gained in attaining and maintaining a positive emotional state.

As DeCoster (2000: 8) points out, it is social workers amongst all health service providers who most often assume most of the responsibility for dealing with the emotions of patients and families. Being ill or injured, or even attending a routine health check, can be highly emotionally charged events.

The nature, source and intensity of emotions are, as we know, the very 'stuff' of the therapeutic and helping relationship which is (usually) the principal medium through which social workers engage with their clients. More than this though, as we noted earlier, emotions demonstrate the connection between bodies and the social context, and indeed are the means through which we enter into and construct social relationships and signify their meanings. Emotions comprise physiological elements, bodily feelings and cognitive processes and, as such, interpenetrate the material and psychosocial dimensions of everyday life.

So, given the foregoing discussion, what can these findings tell us about the place of social work interventions in health care?

There has been a recent upsurge of interest amongst social workers in the study of emotion (Lillquist and Abramson 2002; Finger and Arnold 2002; DeCoster 2000) with recognition of its importance in social work in health care. DeCoster (2000: 10), for example, noting the absence of a conceptual model of emotion in social work, developed her own. This she located firmly within the social constructionist paradigm, identifying emotion as a socially learned response, reinforced in interactions, with interdependency amongst its four elements – situational cues, physiological cues, expressive gestures and demystifying labels (e.g. anger, fear). DeCoster's interest was in the cognitive and behavioural strategies that social workers used in what she termed 'emotional treatment ... (to) therapeutically modify the actual emotion experienced by the client' (2000: 11).

Lillquist and Abramson (2002) reviewed research findings pertaining to psychosocial interventions and cancer survival, noting social work's long-standing and primary role in providing emotional support and in coordinating community support networks for patients. The importance of social workers informing themselves of research work in this field is emphasized, the authors noting that 'the consideration of both the individual and his or her environment inherent in a social work approach has the potential to both broaden and strengthen interventions and survival' (2002: 77).

The experience of illness or disease and perhaps the treatment the patient receives may be highly stressful for different people. A person's reaction to illness might depend on the nature of the condition, the circumstances in which it occurred, the developmental stage which the person has reached, the duration of the injury or disability, whether, for example, it will resolve over time, or become a chronic ailment or whether it will cause further deterioration and death. For example, a 20-year-old man who receives severe spinal cord injuries in a car accident resulting in permanent disability and quadriplegia may be highly traumatized both by the event and by contemplation of the future. Similarly a 75-year-old woman who fractures her hip may be traumatized by the possibility of moving into residential care. Again, a young woman with a diagnosis of breast cancer requiring mastectomy and chemotherapy may be severely traumatized by the loss of a highly valorised part of her anatomy as well as the implications for childbearing which chemotherapy might imply. Receiving a cancer diagnosis for most people is also a severely stressful event.

In all these situations, social workers would be advantaged by understanding the nature of stress reactions and the possibility such reactions might overwhelm the client, exacerbating and perhaps further complicating their health situation. What seems to be emerging from recent research is the recognition that different people show varying levels of resilience in the face of adverse events (Curtis and Cicchetti 2003). As Curtis and Cicchetti (2003: 779) point out, the individual's pathway to psychopathology or resilience will be influenced by a complex mixture of 'the individual's level of biological and psychological organization, current experience, the social context, timing of the adverse event(s) and experiences, and the developmental history of the individual'. Elsewhere we have discussed the plasticity of the human brain and its ability to change and recover from the damaging effects of stress. Whether those who are classified as resilient have an increased capacity or plasticity above the normal levels which assists recovery, or whether the person's brain has greater than normal resistance to the impact of adversity may be unclear (Curtis and Cicchetti 2003: 982). However, plasticity remains characteristic of the brain throughout the lifespan. This provides a strong argument for the incorporation of social interventions such as counselling and psychotherapy in conjunction with pharmacotherapy to ameliorate or at least prevent damage to the brain. These interventions, working together with the brain's inherent self-righting tendencies, may increase the likelihood that maladaptive processes which can lead to abnormal perturbations in the brain, manifested in behaviour such as depression and anxiety, can be circumvented, allowing the brain to stabilize and prevent the occurrence of enduring psychopathologies.

Reviewing social work practice in health care from a corporeal capacity and body cognizant point of view offers a framework which makes sense of what social workers already do, and do well, for example, offer support, engage clients in relationships, maintain hope and work to build clients' optimism and resilience in the face of difficulties. The body cognizant social worker might place greater emphasis on the importance of patients attending to issues of adequate sleep, a nutritious diet and regular exercise. In counselling or casework situations, the body cognizant social worker will recognize the impact of the body's responses to ill health, when the work of the body's immune system is fighting the disease by creating it's own chemical reactions, which in turn may affect the patient's energy levels, leaving them feeling sleepy and lethargic. Recognizing the impact of this on what can be achieved in the counselling relationship might guide the mode and timing of one-to-one meetings.

The important finding regarding the role of a sense of lack of control over events might play in increasing levels of stress may suggest that social workers consider using empowering and patient-directed interventions, for example, working closely with consumer representatives, employing more group-based interventions, involving patients where possible in decision-making processes. In these ways, the social worker might conceptualize their practice as being primarily focused on reducing the patient's allostatic load, that is, offering a range of interventions – counselling, group work, family work, information and guidance on diet, exercise and relaxation – which have as their overall purpose the reduction of influence of those negative or noxious environmental factors which play a determining role in health outcomes.

Body cognizant social workers' actions to influence health policy might be those which take account of the long-term consequences of social inequality on health, issues of access to education, child care, safe working environments, both in relation to physical surroundings and staff relationships. It clearly has implications for community-focused interventions and strategies which target capacity building, social cohesion and attention to the built environment, as well as the planning and design of communities. This new knowledge about the causal factors implicated in poor health should also be one of the considerations that social workers include in their work as advocates addressing those social and material conditions arising from injustice and inequality in social relationships. (See Browne 2005: 118, for further discussion.)

While social workers already do many of these things, the body cognizant social worker may do them for different reasons, namely, because they hold a different understanding of the impact of what they do on the material bodies of clients. Being able to see these as 'real' or 'actual' interventions with 'real' or 'actual' implications for changing clients' bodies and lives, suggests that social workers should be aware and knowledgeable about the actions they take and their bodily consequences. This means not only keeping up to date with research findings, but thinking strategically about how, with whom and where to target interventions so that they can be of maximum benefit. Salovey, Rothman, Detweiler and Steward (2000: 117) while arguing from the point of view of psychology, reinforce the exciting potential of a 'body centred' health care for social work practitioners: 'in the (21st) century, the biopsychosocial mechanisms accounting for these remarkable correlations (the effects of emotions on physiological function and health) will likely be untangled, and these scientific breakthroughs could then serve to expand the basis for relevant clinical practice'.

Social workers in health care settings are often members of health teams, although less frequently are they in positions of power within these teams. Given the point we have made earlier about the stressful nature of work environments where one has little control over what happens, it may be very important for social workers to pay attention to their own allostatic lead. Working within authoritarian hierarchies or non-democratic organizations (often experienced in hospitals and in teams where power is located in other dominant players) may have 'fundamental influence on the content of social relations and social interactions, hence health' (Williams 2003: 57). This suggests that social workers might need to ensure that they receive adequate support and acknowledgement for their work and are given appropriate and recognized opportunities to assert their own needs for autonomy where this is relevant.

In detailing these kinds of interventions which flow from a body cognizant perspective, it also becomes clear that how social workers and other health professionals work with patients are mutually beneficial. A body cognizant approach does, as we have discussed, recognize that social work interventions (providing practical assistance, support, counselling) are more properly understood as corporeal or body-targeted interventions. Treating the emotional reactions of patients is equally 'interventive' as is surgery or pharmacotherapy. Acknowledging that social work practices hold the same significance and importance for patients' health as do other biological interventions can, perhaps, goes some way towards dissolving social workers often experienced sense of occupying a subordinate role in the health care team.

It is also relevant to urge that social work might give careful consideration to a return to the profession's first preoccupations with the relationship between health and the environment that characterized the earliest days of the profession. Contemporary epidemiological and other research which we have described in this chapter are forcefully demonstrating the crucial nature of environmental impact on health and its differential effects in relation to the stress-inducing character of social structures and social stratification such that poverty, low levels of education, social isolation, abuse and neglect dramatically influence the quality and quantity of human health and life. This is where social work in health care began, and perhaps, it is where the body cognizant health care social worker should re-focus.

We conclude this chapter with a case example, demonstrating by using the Body Cognizant Assessment Guide (BCAG), how the ideas of corporeal capacity and body cognizant practice might be adopted by social workers in the health care field.

Client profile: The patient is a 51-year-old single woman recently diagnosed with primary breast cancer. There is no family history of this disease, and the client was diagnosed following routine breast screening. She has been treated with lumpectomy and a course of radiotherapy. She is referred to the hospital oncology social worker because of her emotional distress at diagnosis and difficulty with transport to radiotherapy appointments. The client is a secondary school teacher at a large outer suburban high school teaching year 9 and 10 boys (aged 15 and 16). She lives alone in a semi-rural area. Her mother suffers from dementia and is in a nursing home. She has a brother whom she is close to, as well as good friendships amongst colleagues at school.

	Potential sources of client vulnerabilities/strengths		Targets for amelioration/enhancement	
	Adversive	Protective	Adversive	Protective
Macrosocial factors	What: Stressful work – 'difficult' and challenging students. Often feels she is not in control in classroom; classroom and recreation areas overcrowded and chaotic at times How (impact): Relationship between stress and lowered immunity may be significant in her response to treatment	What: Screening programmes for breast cancer How (impact): Client has received early diagnosis and no disease progression so far	(Address) What: Stressful workplace (Address) How: Involvement of union and OH & S re more empowering work practices; attention to adequate, safe facilities	(Address) What: Strong union presence and involvement in education sector (Address) How: Encourage patient to talk with union and OH & S representatives – or instigate this with patient's permission
Community scale biological/ chemical or physical factors	What: Overcrowded recreation areas at school How (impact): Stressful for teacher in charge, feeling hyper-alert and constantly 'on guard' to avert problems	What: Short journey to work; regular holidays How (impact): Able to drive short distance on quiet roads to work/home in peaceful state of mind; able to plan for and take regular 'time out' for relaxation	What: Overcrowded recreation area, stressful and chaotic How: Encourage discussion at school to consider alternative arrangements	What: Availability of information and resources re breast cancer both through community groups and on-line How: Enable client to gather all relevant information so she is able to

				ask questions of medical staff, is aware of range of treatments and services
Small scale biological/ chemical or physical factors (as afflicting person or home environment)	**What:** Lack of public transport; relative geographic isolation of residence **How (impact):** Difficulty getting to/from radiotherapy treatments; infrequent social contacts when at home	**What:** Pleasant semi-rural environment; non-polluted air; low noise levels **How (impact):** Minimal stress in environment; opportunities for relaxation, enjoyment of physical beauty of surroundings	**What:** Relative geographic and social isolation **How:** Sometimes lonely, feeling vulnerable and 'cut off' from support services and social contact	**What:** Pleasant non-polluted home environment **How:** Encourage relaxing activities possible in this setting – meditation, painting, walking
Intersubjective/ interpersonal factors	**What:** Does not always feel in control of students **How (impact):** Raises anxiety and stress levels when they are unruly	**What:** Good relationships with colleagues **How (impact):** Feels supported and cared for by them. Time out for medical treatments accommodated without difficulty	**What:** Lack of social support outside work – all her friends are in paid workforce **How:** Connect her to sources of support, e.g. local government services, community health centre, groups for women with breast cancer	**What:** Good relationships with colleagues **How:** Reflect on her capacities for friendship and importance of extending networks beyond workplace

Continued

Continued

	Potential sources of client vulnerabilities/ strengths		Targets for amelioration/ enhancement	
	Adversive	**Protective**	**Adversive**	**Protective**
Intrapersonal/ intrapsychic factors	**What:** Feelings of being responsible for illness; uncertainty of illness outcome **How (impact):** Increased anxiety, lowered capacity to concentrate, irritability with students	**What:** Intelligence and competence in managing demanding job and independent life **How (impact):** Realises that she can regain emotional stability; confidence in seeking resources and assistance	**What:** Previous history of feeling emotionally overwhelmed when under stress **How:** Assist exploration of earlier events and identification of coping mechanisms she has and also needs to acquire	**What:** Capacities to form good supportive relationships with others; motivation to engage in protective health behaviours **How:** Identify these strengths and provide opportunities to enhance and extend them, e.g. on-going individual counselling and group work with others with breast cancer

10 Social Work, the Body and Alcohol and Other Drugs

In almost all fields of social work practice, issues concerning the abuse or problematic usage of Alcohol and Other Drugs (AOD) arise. Whilst social workers might work in specialist services or agencies specifically addressing the needs of people with problematic AOD use, in other settings such as health, mental health, prisons, child protection, family work, work with young people, aged care, the behavioural and practical difficulties that frequently arise in relation to the problematic use of AOD may require consideration as they impact on the service user and/or their family and social relationships. The frequency with which complications relating to the problematic use of AOD are encountered within social work agencies reflects the ubiquity of their influence in the wider community.

In Western liberal democracies such as Australia, AOD are part of the fabric of everyday life, used by the majority of adults and often seen as a prerequisite for the smooth social functioning of the community. However, when their usage becomes labelled as problematic, those whose behaviour is recognized as affected are variously considered to be lacking in moral fibre (unable to resist the lure of intoxication) or deviant (subversive or rejecting of society's guiding rules and principles) or ill (in the grip of a condition over which they have limited control). Significant stigma attaches to the label of 'addict' or 'alcoholic' and as a consequence their access to treatment received at services may be less than optimal.

However, it is true to say that all of us use AOD for more or less the same reasons: to lift our mood, to relax, to energize ourselves, to alter our mental state, to socialize more easily, to forget even briefly those issues or concerns which burden us. But we also know that it is the moderate or controlled use of AOD that achieves these outcomes and that excessive use can have deleterious and unwanted effects – depression, anxiety, engaging in risky behaviour and so on. Because such general knowledge about the effects of AOD is available in the community, those for whom it becomes problematic – whose lives seem out of control and whose behaviour poses dangers to themselves and others – prompt questions about why it is that some people are more susceptible to these effects, and why some continue to use AOD to excess even when the impact can be so devastating on themselves and those around them.

Social work has long been interested in the field of AOD, partly because of the impact of problematic usage across service sectors and within families and communities, and partly because of social workers continuing interest in working with those on society's margins, many of whom engage in problematic AOD usage. Interestingly, it appears that in this field more than others, social workers have been alert to incorporating developments in neuroscience as they pertain to the addictions (see e.g. Spence, DiNitto and Straussner 2001 editing writings from the Summit on Social Work and the Neurobiology of the Addictions held in 2000 in Texas, United States). The publication issuing from this Summit offers a different view from prevailing dualistic conceptions of person-in-environment such as van Wormer's (1995) who, while arguing for inclusion of biological dimensions in addictive behaviour, retains the separation of biological, psychological and social causative factors, being critical of what is termed the 'disease model' of addiction. The so-called disease model proposes that addiction is associated with biological abnormalities which can significantly alter brain function and physical health. However, van Wormer's view (1995: 323) that 'Alcoholism ... is a truly *biopsychosocial* phenomenon' does accord with the perspective offered here, although we shall utilize the concepts of 'corporeal capacity' and 'body cognizant social worker' rather than the ecological model as a framework for theory and practice in this field.

In beginning then, we shall outline the knowledge required by the body cognizant social worker in the field of AOD. This has two aspects:

1. understanding the impact on the brain of AOD and
2. understanding the impact on the brain of AOD at various points across the life span.

At the outset, it is important to distinguish between what is meant by addiction and what is meant by physical dependence. A person with a physical dependence on a drug will become physically ill when the drug is no longer taken, but this is not the same as being addicted. For example, some drugs can cause physical dependence but not addiction, and vice versa. When people have an addiction, say to alcohol, their physical dependence may be treated during the withdrawal process, but this will not affect their addiction, that is, the symptoms of withdrawal such as cravings will remain as will the potential for relapse.

Addiction, by contrast, refers to a loss of control over drug use, or the compulsive seeking and taking of a drug regardless of its consequences (Nestler 2002: 1076). Addiction is thus a chronic, relapsing and sometimes fatal disorder which is characterized by compulsive, often uncontrollable drug seeking. It is generally considered to be a brain disease (Spence, DiNitto and Straussner 2001: 1; Meijler, Matsushito, Wirshing and Janda 2004) with genetic risk factors accounting for perhaps 50 per cent of a person's vulnerability, although the precise genes involved have yet to be identified (Nestler 2002: 1076; Azmitia 2001: 58).

In thinking initially about what the brain is, we need to bear in mind that it is a closed biological system of living cells. It is thus a system which strives always to retain homeostasis and balance in order to function optimally. So, whenever one chemical system is activated, it immediately effects millions of other cells, and following this reaction, adjusts to accommodate any changes in activity (Azmitia 2001: 42–46). As Azmitia (2002: 46) points out, the more dramatic or pronounced the change occurring, the more dramatic the brain's response. These changes are subjectively experienced as moods or emotional states and, in the wake of a drug-caused reaction, such mood changes may last for weeks, months or even permanently. As we have noted elsewhere, the brain has plasticity and flexibility which makes it not only capable of responding to alterations in the external and internal environment – perhaps the very reward the person taking a particular drug seeks – but also exposure to the drug can lead to modifications in the brain's size, shape and function. The interconnections between neuronal systems are particularly vulnerable to the damaging effects of drugs, depending as we shall see later, on the stage of development of the brain itself.

So, what actually happens when a person takes alcohol or a psychoactive drug such as heroin, cocaine, marijuana, ecstasy?

All drugs work on the 'reward centre' in the brain which comprises a number of brain structures – the ventral striatum, mid brain, amygdale, prefrontal and other limbic cortical regions, as well as the hippocampus and hypothalamus (Nestler 2002: 1076). When a drug is taken it interacts through the neurotransmitters (chemicals released from nerve fibres which stimulate other nerves) creating a surge of dopamine which leads to intense feelings of reward and well-being. The brain's dopamine pathway reaches many parts of the brain – that concerned with emotion, pleasure, memory of emotional events and decision making capacity for emotional events (Erickson and Wilcox 2001: 11). At the same time, it raises the level of dopamine in the neurotransmitters.

This change to the chemical balance – homeostasis – in the brain may create long-term changes which can endure even after the person has stopped taking the drug. The first change to occur may be the development of tolerance to the drug, so that in the future, the brain will require more of the drug in order for the person to gain the same feelings of pleasure. This tolerance occurs because the large surges of dopamine released into the brain cause the brain to have fewer receptors for dopamine, desensitizing the brain to its own normal brain dopamine. The subjective experience of low dopamine may be feelings of low mood or depression with a lack of sensitivity to the everyday pleasures of life.

Overtime, with repeated exposure to the drug, long-lasting memories are created. Even after prolonged periods of withdrawal, stressful events can trigger an intense craving for the drug, laid down in the memory, which may precipitate relapse (Nestler 2002: 1076).

The range of events considered stressful, and the responses individuals make to them will, of course, vary greatly and bear a relationship to the individual's age, social circumstances and genetic make-up. The initial decision to take AOD as a means of dealing with or in reaction to challenging situations perhaps refers to their availability as much as to the rewards which are registered in the brain, prompting a repeat of the behaviour. For example, where a child is exposed to the chaos, anxiety and insecurity of family life dominated by the drug-seeking behaviours of addicted parents, it may be understandable that they too may seek similar soothing and comfort from drugs and alcohol, perhaps sharing the genetic propensity for addiction to occur from their parents. Crucial to the body cognizant social worker's understanding of the effect of AOD on the brain is recognition of the different stages of brain development over the course of an individual's life. (For an expanded discussion, see Azmitia 2001.)

We have earlier (in Chapter 7) noted the importance of critical periods in the developmental trajectory, those stages when a number of changes are occurring as systems interact and inter-connect resulting in growth and maturation of the human body. The stimulation or alternatively 'switching off', of various systems and functions are triggered by neuronal activity in the brain directly affecting target cells with a cascade-like effect on other systems. The introduction of foreign chemicals at these critical periods can have significant impact and effects on the human organism.

Perinatal period: As the blood-brain barrier does not develop until after birth, the developing foetus is highly vulnerable to the effects of maternal ingestion of AOD. The development of the brain is significantly dependent upon the proper neurons being in the right place at the right time, and any changes to brain development, however subtle, can have enduring consequences. For example, research into the effects of cocaine on the developing foetus have demonstrated that such infants are at greater risk of premature birth, low birth weight, smaller head circumferences, and behaviour characterized by social withdrawal (Azmitia 2001: 48). Foetal Alcohol Syndrome has also been recognized as a consequence of alcohol use during pregnancy resulting in mental retardation and developmental delay in motor, cognitive and social skills (Azmitia 2001: 49; Brady, Posner, Lang and Rosati 1994).

Childhood: Children exposed to the effects of AOD in the perinatal period have a greater risk of problems during childhood, given that disruptions to the development of their brains have occurred at a critical developmental period. While some of the damage may be reversed once drugs are withdrawn, it appears that the interactions between neuronal systems may be permanently damaged (Azmitia 2001: 50). For example, mood disturbances during childhood – hyperactivity or withdrawal – may be due to poorly established neuronal connections between brain regions.

Children are also vulnerable to stress, secreting stress hormones from an early age. Should they be living in a stressful environment, for example, in a household where drug abuse exists, their secretions of stress hormones may effect the continued development of the limbic system, altering the chemical balance of the brain (in Chapter 7 for a fuller discussion).

Adolescence: As the child reaches puberty, hormonal and behavioural changes instigated by the brain create surges of chemical activity responsible for the physiological, emotional and cognitive changes characterizing this critical period. It is a time when many young people engage in experimentation with AOD, perhaps prompted by low levels of serotonin in the brain and a commensurate increase in impulsivity. As we have discussed in Chapter 7, there are alterations in the limbic system during adolescence which are associated with the neuroendocrinological changes at puberty. Alterations in 'reward sensitivity' suggest that higher levels of stimulation are required in order to achieve the subjective feelings of pleasure which they earlier enjoyed (Steinberg 2004).

Chambers, Taylor and Potenza (2003) argue that adolescent neurodevelopment occurs in the brain regions associated with motivation, impulsivity and addiction. The impulsivity and novelty-seeking so characteristic of adolescence is, in their view, a transitional behaviour trait which occurs partly because of the maturational changes in the frontal cortical and subcortical monoaminergic brain systems. While these developmental processes are very important for the young person's motivation to adopt adult roles, they simultaneously make the developing adolescent brain more vulnerable to the addictive effects of drugs.

Differences in females' and males' use of and responses to AOD have been linked to the different hormones in their brains which they are exposed to during this period. For example, girls appear less susceptible to the excessive risky behaviours associated with the use of alcohol than are boys, whilst the effects of ecstasy on cognitive functioning appear to be more detrimental to girls (Azmitia 2001: 59). Further, the already impulsive and risk-taking nature of adolescence may place the young person at particular risk of harm if at the same time they are involved with regular substance use. Studies by Martin, Milch, Martin, Hartung and Hengler (1977) and Tapert, Aarons, Georgianna, Sedlar and Brown (2001) point to the increased likelihood of substance-affected females engaging in self-destructive and risky sexual behaviours, for example, having more sexual partners, less consistent use of condoms, more unplanned pregnancies than comparable groups of non-substance using adolescents.

Research examining the impact of high levels of alcohol consumption (Brown and Tapert 2004) on adolescents indicate that individuals' cognitive capacities may be reduced, lowering their performance scores on tests of verbal and non-verbal skills. However, the role of abstinence in achieving recovery of these abilities remains unclear.

Adulthood: After the age of 35, there is a decline in the limbic system with a consequent decline in the pleasure experienced from the use of AOD. However, as Azmitia (2001: 55–56) notes, adults may continue to abuse AOD in order to self-medicate a previously biologically unbalanced brain, for example, using alcohol to counter depression, marijuana to counter anxiety. However, evidence suggests that continued use may increase the very symptoms that the person is trying to alleviate, especially in light of the decline of the limbic system. One explanation for individuals continued usage despite the deleterious effects of AOD abuse is that earlier use has damaged the neuronal connections in the prefrontal cortex (PFC), thereby diminishing the person's capacity to make rational decisions about their behaviour (Azmitia 2001: 56). During the adult years however, the brain appears to retain its plasticity. This offers the possibility that, in the case of alcohol abuse, abstinence may enable the frontal cortex to recover.

Old Age: In later life, the brain enters a period of rapid decline with the loss of neuronal connections, notably in the limbic system. Emotional liability, difficulty in dealing with complex issues, and the declining capacity of the kidneys and liver to process AOD means that an older person becomes highly vulnerable to the toxic and disabling effects of excessive use of AOD.

An understanding of the neurobiology of addiction is crucial to the development of effective treatment strategies and interventions. As Spence, DiNitto and Straussner (2001: 2) point out, this means that social workers practising in the field of AOD will work with an understanding of the brain changes that occur in addiction, not with the intention of changing the brain back to its non-addicted state, but rather placing a focus on devising interventions which compensate for brain deficits and their behavioural manifestations, adopting treatment methods which target the repair of the brain.

Nestler (2002) discusses a range of treatment strategies, many of which remain incompletely researched and evaluated and thus at times speculative. These include medications such as naltrexone which block a drug reaching its target in the brain, vaccines which bind to neurotransporters without affecting the neurotransporter's normal functioning, treating addiction by mimicking the drug action, for example, methadone, which does not give the recipient the same highs and lows as heroin, enabling the person to resume a normal life, nicotine patches and gums which provide a sustained release of the drug without its toxic effects, and dopamine antagonists which inhibit a drug's effects. The possibility of gene therapy is also raised, given the role drug addiction plays in altering gene expression. The utility of naltrexone implants following withdrawal in order to prevent against early relapse, thus enabling those with problematic drug use to develop new 'opiate free cognitive behavioral habits', has received some limited support from recent research (Foster, Brewer and Steele 2003; Kirchmayer, Davoli, Vester, Amato, Ferri and Perucci 2002). More promising however, are research findings of approaches which combine naltrexone with community based supportive interventions (Roozen, Kerkhof, van den Brink 2003). However, as Meijler, Matsushita, Wirshing and Janda (2004) point out, medications currently in use have had only limited success, often with unwanted side effects. These researchers argue that in the near future, immunopharmacotherapy – a treatment process which generates antibodies capable of binding the targeted drug before it reaches the brain – hold promise.

Erickson and Wilcox (2001; see also Zweben 2001; Volpicelli, Pettinati, McLellan and O'Brien 2001) argue for treatments which combine drug therapies with structured non-drug interventions, seeing both approaches as significant in affecting the brain's chemistry in positive ways. CBT, 12-step programs, skills training, and relaxation enable new learning to take place within the limbic system (the emotional brain) which assists people in re-learning patterns of thinking and behaving. Because of the need to 're-set' the chemistry of the brain as a way out of addiction, these combined interventions need to be long term rather than short term, if the risk of relapse is to be minimized. Zweben (2001) makes the case that combined psychosocial and pharmacological interventions offer superior benefit than either intervention alone. Combining these interventions helps to support the change efforts of the person, the medication allowing the brain to return to a non-affected state in which the capacity to think is enhanced, perhaps strengthening the person's motivation to achieve and maintain sobriety or a drug-free state. Volpicelli, Pettinati, McLellan and O'Brien's (2001) model of structured treatment, BRENDA, similarly combines use of medication with 12-step, learning and motivational interventions.

These combined intervention strategies and methods point towards the development of truly effective treatment regimes in the near future. However, as Zweben (2001: 78) notes, more research is needed in order to identify which pharmacological agents are compatible with which particular behavioural modalities, the most effective dosage schedules of both drugs and behavioural treatment, and the most efficacious sequencing of drug regimes and psychosocial treatments.

What is clear from our earlier discussion is that problematic AOD use impacts differently across the life course, raising different treatment and intervention issues for the body cognizant social worker. Very importantly, this enhanced understanding of the effect of AOD on the human brain does not mean that social work's particular emphasis on person-in-environment nexus is diminished or superseded by (what might be perceived as) narrow or reductionist tendencies of neuroscience and neurobiology. On the contrary, as we argue throughout this book, social work brings to the practice arena recognition of the significance of social context and of contextualizing human action within a world characterized by social, political and economic divisions. These divisions structure lived experience, empowering and positioning some members of the social collective to acquire the resources and opportunities which minimize risks to survival and maximize protective factors. For others, perhaps the majority, the opposite is the case.

Corporeal capacity

The concept of corporeal capacity, discussed in Chapter 4, provides a framework for thinking about our location as environmentally embodied beings, adapting, changing and shaping ourselves and the material and social world, in place and across time. On an individual level, it includes amongst other factors, a person's inherited strengths and weaknesses, their developmental stage, prior experiences and self-identity. These individual factors have been considered in the preceding paragraphs and draw our attention to the admixture of neurobiological and situational elements that may account for the propensity of one individual to succumb to addiction whilst another may not.

While we have been concerned so far in this chapter with neurobiological understandings of addiction, sociological perspectives alert us to definitions of addiction which refer both to those behaviours of individuals which have a social effect and to the effect of society at the macro level, influencing and shaping the behaviour of individuals (Adrian 2003). At the macro level the use of AOD is (at least in Western liberal democracies) encouraged, if not promoted, through practices and policies which make them widely available and sanctioned. Contradictions are, of course, readily apparent in regard to distinctions between legal and illegal drugs and acceptable levels of alcohol consumption, evident in limitations on availability and to whom authority is given to provide AODs and to facilitate access to them. As Adrian (2003: 1406) points out, 'Defining a substance as a drug is really defining it as a substance that must be socially controlled through a formal apparatus'.

At the micro level, those whose use of AOD is problematic are frequently those who (come to) occupy positions of marginality and subordination within the social world. It is they – the poor, young people, ethnic minorities, 'drunks', 'addicts', 'junkies' – who more often are the focus of forms of restrictive treatment and legal and health mechanisms of social control. While the social conditions which those labelled as deviant with regard to their use of AOD endure not only serve to exacerbate the individual corporeal problems experienced, they may also play a role in perpetuating the macrolevel effects – crime, social division, family breakdown, divided communities.

Whilst stigmatizing labels are frequently applied to those with problematic AOD use, for some users themselves, their sense of self and identity is closely tied to their usage, the social networks which support them, and the practices and activities entailed in acquiring and using these substances. Many iconic figures of present as well as past popular culture have famously used illicit drugs and/or engaged in problematic alcohol consumption, and in so doing, have acquired a status and infamy coveted and applauded, often both within the mainstream as well as on the 'fringe'. For some, perhaps those whose sense of self and identity may be fragile, acquiring the label of 'junkie' or 'addict' may be positive and sustaining. Indeed, in research with people experiencing dual AOD and serious mental illness, some respondents welcomed the 'junkie' or 'user' label in preference to the stigma and rejection attaching to the label of mentally ill (McDermott and Pyett 1993).

The illegality of AOD use can also have a part to play in reinforcing individual and group identity as subversive or outside the mainstream, factors which may work to strengthen the person's sense of identity as a user and reinforce their bonds to a social network of like-minded others. AOD users, especially where their drug of choice is illegal, remain for obvious reasons as outsiders whose understanding, experiences and knowledge about what using means is not easily accessible and as a consequence may not be included in the policy debates to which they are central. Ethnographic researchers have tackled this issue with attempts to ensure that the voices of users become audible and a part of policy debates (Rowe 2004). Such research is important in providing 'first-person' accounts of the realities and consequences of use, especially by those who live on the margins and whose situations and interpretations of the world may not be registered in policy debate.

The use of AOD remains a prominent public health issue. At various times different beliefs about the nature of addiction, often driven more by ideology and conviction than research, have been reflected in policies and strategies to address problematic use which stretch from prohibition to declarations of war to harm minimization strategies. The choice of appropriate and effective strategies however, would be greatly strengthened by advances in neurobiology. As Nestler (2002: 1079) points out, research efforts which can identify those 'treatment agents that can correct compulsive behaviour towards drug rewards, if they can be developed would represent enormous success, given their potential to treat not only drug addiction, but addictions to non-drug stimuli, such as gambling, food and sex which may be mediated by similar mechanisms'.

In addition, ethical issues with regard to carrying out research, for example, administering illegal and/or psychoactive drugs to research subjects for experimental purposes, complicates the process of knowledge building. There may also be consequences in labelling problematic AOD use as a brain disease, with implications that problematic users are 'automatons whose behaviour is under the control of the drugs acting on the receptor sites in their brains', while at the same time recognizing that social policies and market forces do influence drug use and the behaviour of drug-dependent people (Hall and Morley 1998: 869).

Body cognizant social worker

So, what would a body cognizant social worker do in the field of AOD? In the first instance, social workers need to become knowledgeable about the neurobiology of addictions. As we have sketched in this chapter, there is a considerable amount that is known about the nature and effect of dependence and addiction which has significant consequences for social work interventions. This is also a field in which a range of treatment directions are being investigated which offer hope for success and in which social workers' expertise can contribute significantly. This may mean that body cognizant social workers can usefully provide critique of models of addiction which reinforce stigma and social marginalization, blame and exclusion, for example, the moral model, the degenerative and the deficit model (Rowe 2004: 116), providing in their place information on neurobiology and the potential it holds for effective treatment which 're-sets' brain chemistry (Spence, DiNitto and Straussner 2001).

Body cognizant social workers would develop assessment approaches which take neurobiological insights into account. It would, of course, be important to remain aware of the effects of AOD on the brain and cognitive functioning when undertaking assessments and psychosocial and/or therapeutic interventions, adjusting one's mode of communication – timing, complexity of issues – in order to ensure the meetings are useful. In addition, the assessment needs also to take into account gender differences in responses to AOD use, for example, the lower tolerance of females to alcohol.

SOCIAL WORK, THE BODY AND ALCOHOL **221**

Bearing in mind the fact that potential risk and protective factors change over the life course, the following information might be sought from the client as part of the assessment:

- their perinatal history, for example, their mother's use of AOD when they were *in utero*;
- the client's age, for example, if the client is a child who had been subjected to perinatal damage to their neuronal connections, this may be relevant in understanding such behaviours as social withdrawal or hyperactivity. A consequence of this may be to design programs that gave the child the space and time to work slowly to (re)establish those connections through a program of structured learning and social skills training;
- If an adolescent, it may be important to determine the kinds of behaviours which the person is engaging in when using and work with them to minimize damaging outcomes (Tapert, Aarons, Georgianna, Sedlar and Brown 2001). A consequence of this might be to ensure that the person is adequately informed about the neurobiology of AOD use, its effects on cognitive functioning and behaviour. The development of community-based programs and activities which are stimulating, challenging and risky might provide valid and attractive alternative pursuits;
- If an adult, the assessment may indicate that continued problematic use is an attempt to self-medicate a brain out of balance and subject perhaps to increased anxiety or depression. A consequence of this may be to encourage the person to seek counselling and treatment for these distressing emotional states;
- If an old person, the body cognizant social worker may be aware of the increasing damage that problematic use is causing to the brain. A consequence of this may be to encourage abstinence and focus on the development of social skills and creation of opportunities to reduce isolation.

The body cognizant social worker would utilize intervention programs that combine medications and structured psychosocial methods, for example, skills training and group work and perhaps plan for longer term rather than brief treatments given the time needed to instil and maintain changes in cognitive and neural function.

Given social workers' keen appreciation of the impact of problematic AOD use on families and social networks, case planning would include individual counselling, education programs, including school-based prevention and education programs, as well as practical support such as adequate housing and financial advice.

Findings from neurobiological research indicate that early intervention with children in order to reduce risk factors arising from accumulating stress is vital, especially where children are living within families where parental use of AOD is problematic. This may have an impact in preventing later problematic AOD behaviours, and could include such interventions as making parenting programs available to parents that strengthen bonding and support within the family even while parent(s) continue to use AOD. (For further discussion see Chapter 7.)

At the wider community level, body cognizant social workers might become involved in social action strategies which target misinformation about the origins and effects of problematic AOD use, for example, challenging the notion that AOD can cause the death of the brain, emphasizing instead the plasticity of the brain and its potential to recover when abstinence is combined with psychosocial treatments (Azmitia 2001: 56). Simultaneously, body cognizant social workers might take action at the policy level, providing critique of policies and practices which promote and valorize the use of AOD while simultaneously blaming and punishing those whose use becomes problematic to themselves and to the wider community. Part of such a critique might be the targeting of the pharmaceutical industry to fund and support research into the neurobiology of addictions, where to date a lack of interest prevails (Nestler 2002).

Body cognizant social workers will also actively work to destigmatize those with problematic AOD use, recognizing that their exclusion from the mainstream due to stigma, poverty and homelessness which frequently accompany problematic use will exacerbate the deleterious effects of addiction, for example, increasing their isolation from sources of support, preventing them accessing antenatal care, maintaining a poor lifestyle and self care practices. Social exclusion as we know, also affects the community at large, evident in incidences of drug-related crime, incarceration, extended use of hospital and emergency services. Very importantly, social workers are extremely well placed in a variety of agencies and services where issues of problematic AOD use present. They are amongst the few professionals who may form constructive and long-term relationships with those users who are out of the mainstream, for example, people who are homeless, mentally ill or isolated. They are thus very well positioned to advocate for and to provide a way in which the voices of such individuals may be heard, especially within policy and community debates. As Rowe (2004) points out, for politicians and community leaders to personally hear the voices of users is one very potent way of limiting the extent to which they can be demonized and punished, providing instead a 'human dimension' to debates which challenge prevailing constructions of such people as deviant and dangerous.

In relation to the prevention of damage caused by problematic AOD use, the body cognizant social worker might emphasize the importance of good 'brain health' for everyone, not just those with AOD problems, in order to retain the brain's plasticity, for example, such things as physical and mental exercise to invigorate brain function, eating a nutritious diet, ensuring adequate sleep.

Client profile: The client is a 40-year-old male. He began using marijuana in his early 20s while a student studying Interior Design. He has a family history of alcohol dependence and depression. As a child he was shy and withdrawn and in his early adulthood had a number of unhappy relationships. Presently, he is self-employed, receiving occasional contract work as an interior designer. He is single and somewhat isolated. He has a dependence on marijuana and uses it to deal with anxiety and depression. He shows evidence of some brain damage with poor short-term memory, some paranoia and occasional angry outbursts, mostly directed at family members who attempt to be supportive to him. He referred himself to a social worker at a housing service following a conviction for growing marijuana at the back of his rented house. The crop was destroyed, he received a fine, and the landlord requested him to vacate the house. He is highly anxious, angry and verbally aggressive, experiencing withdrawal from marijuana. He is seeking accommodation and assistance with paying his fines.

	Potential sources of client vulnerabilities/strengths		Targets for amelioration/enhancement	
	Adversive	**Protective**	**Adversive**	**Protective**
Macrosocial factors	**What:** Illegality of drug of choice **How (impact):** Secrecy, danger of criminal charges for growing and possession; life focus on accessing the drug; isolation, withdrawal and restricted social network to other drug users/dealers	**What:** Growing understanding of neurobiology of addiction; harm minimization policies in place in many AOD services **How (impact):** Development of appropriate treatments; possibility of range of treatment approaches being offered as well as establishment of realistic goals and support systems for those with addictions; possibility that blame and rejection feature less prominently in policy debates	**(Address) What:** Sporadic employment and low income **(Address) How:** Possibility of receiving unemployment benefits and assistance with job seeking	**(Address) What:** Professional qualifications and training in Interior Design; skills and experience **(Address) How:** Explore possibilities for extending employment opportunities with employee organizations in Interior Design field
Community scale biological/chemical or physical factors	**What:** Lack of availability of cheap accommodation	**What:** Recent local government initiative to develop community garden	**What:** Finding suitable accommodation; payment of fine	**What:** AOD service in local area

Small scale biological/chemical or physical factors (as afflicting person or home environment)	**How (impact):** Potential to become homeless and/or live in poorly constructed and maintained dwellings; loss of capacity to be self-employed i.e. to work from suitable home premises	**How (impact):** Improvement in air quality, opening up green space within inner city area, opportunities for residents to get involved in self-sufficiency projects	**How:** Access housing; negotiate with court for longer-term fine repayment	**How:** Offers a number of treatment programmes, including harm minimization programme for problematic marijuana users
	What: Addiction to marijuana and continued use of drug **How (impact):** Focusing life around accessing marijuana; some short-term memory loss, occasionally paranoid and angry outbursts. This alienates those who attempt to be supportive to him, which he regrets and which then makes him depressed and anxious	**What:** Professional knowledge of and skills in interior design **How (impact):** Interested in creating positive, safe and comfortable living spaces with emphasis on use of light and colour. This skill can be brought to bear in organising his own living space in manner which aids recovery of brain	**What:** Reduction in use of marijuana **How:** Provide educational materials on effects of drug on brain. Attempt to engage him in appropriate treatment program to reverse damage being experienced	**What:** Relatively good physical health **How:** Encourage attention to nutrition, relaxation and exercise in order to maintain health

Continued

Continued

	Potential sources of client vulnerabilities/strengths		Targets for amelioration/enhancement	
	Adversive	Protective	Adversive	Protective
Intersubjective/interpersonal factors	**What:** Effects of marijuana addiction on brain **How (impact):** Short-term memory loss, occasional paranoid and angry outbursts; social network restricted to other users/suppliers	**What:** Intelligence, skills, friendly personality **How (impact):** Able to present well to employers and clients, and to deliver satisfactory work, even if outside timelines	**What:** Paranoia, forgetfulness, anger and depression **How:** CBT to improve memory and cognitive functioning, target depression and learn new more optimistic patterns of thinking; try out harm minimisation strategies, e.g. not using during weekdays	**What:** Friendliness, intelligence, skills in interior design, supportive family **How:** Encourage identification of these strengths and consideration of ways to re-engage more constructively with family members; encourage involvement with other groups away from drug users/suppliers, e.g. voluntary work on community garden project (given his interest in growing plants)

Intrapersonal/ intrapsychic factors	**What:** Depressed mood, low self-esteem **How (impact):** Poor self-care, tendency to withdraw or seek companionship with others like himself	**What:** Intelligence and capacity to understand effect of his use on brain; **How (impact):** Can make use of educational materials and develop optimistic approach to possibility that treatment strategies will help reverse negative impact on brain	**What:** Depression, isolation and withdrawal **How:** Encourage involvement in CBT and harm minimization approaches	**What:** Capacity to relate warmly to others; creativity; **How:** Encourage self-reflection on these strengths and how he can use them to reach out to others, potential for extending social networks through involvement in artistic relaxation activities, and share his knowledge of interior design and gardening

Conclusion

Throughout this book we have argued that social work – being a profession concerned with the enhancement of human potential – needs to consider that which determines the quality of our humanness, the body. Thinking about the body, or the human as a biological organism, helps us better understand what it means to be an emotional, thinking being that is in constant interaction with its environment. Contemplation of how we use and relate to our bodies assists our understanding of how we form and modify our identities, or senses of self.

The body need not be considered at every turn. Different issues of interest to social work will benefit more or less from specific kinds or levels of analysis. Questions pertaining to how educational policy may be changed, for example, is best answered by considering a society's priorities and those social structures and conventions that have, heretofore, governed provision of public goods. Questions regarding which aspects of work that are the most satisfying for a given individual are best explored through in-depth discussions with the individual himself.

Further, different kinds of knowledge within neuroscience (as with thinking in the social sciences about the body) will continue to undergo marginal or even significant revisions for some time yet. Discoveries in the future may well render some of the contents of this book inaccurate.

Nevertheless, there is an onus upon social work to use any current findings that shed light on such as how emotion impacts decision-making, certain drugs affect cognition and, indeed, anything relevant to quality of life about which social work or the social sciences alone can only learn so much. For social workers *not* to draw on neuroscientific findings that are both relevant to human well-being and, by current research standards, well established, is no less than a dereliction of duty, if not a breach of professional ethics which require the learning of new knowledge.

The biological sciences too, have much to gain from establishing better relationships with social work. Social workers are skilled at considering such matters as the potential consequences, for different groups of individuals, of proposed applications of new scientific knowledge. They are also practiced at providing alternate explanations for kinds of behaviours from which cognitive, behavioural and affective neuroscience frequently draw conclusions. The social work profession's credibility has relied less upon the kinds of empirical evidence on which the biological sciences are so reliant. For this reason, social workers are well placed to critique the usefulness of recommendations emerging from neuroscience upon translating them into practice.

There are a number of forms that a relationship between the social work profession and neuroscience might take. These includes the teaching of cross-disciplinary courses at undergraduate or graduate levels, the establishment of interdisciplinary research teams to examine issues of interest to both professions, regular meetings or conferences during which findings on issues of mutual interest are exchanged and the routine inclusion by each profession, in research advisory panels, members of the other profession.

Likewise, there is no reason that, where relevant, the social work profession cannot build into their current research designs questions about how subjects relate to and use their bodies in everyday life: that is, questions about body and experientiality.

Perhaps one of the first steps towards incorporating the 'new' knowledge which neuroscience provides, is the overcoming of obstacles within social work towards its acceptance. As we have argued in this book, social work's primary conceptual framework – person-in-environment and the biopsychosocial model – has rarely, in the extant literature, explored *how* it is that environment impacts. It is primarily a psychosocial perspective which is offered. What we have attempted to do here is demonstrate the ways in which emotion, behaviour and thinking reflect the 'bio' and indeed *are* biological processes.

In addition, we have put forward two concepts – corporeal capacity and body cognizant social work practice – which are conceptual frameworks designed to move us towards a more integrated neuroscience–social work model. Far from decontextualizing or reducing our understanding of human behaviour, these concepts recognize the central significance which environment (internal and external to the body) hold for understanding and intervening in human social and individual life. Indeed, as we have emphasized throughout, whatever treatment interventions flow from neuroscientific findings, their successful application depends on the social context – social work's theoretical and practical 'home base'. As Johnson (2001) points out, not only does social work have a unique contribution to make within the disciplines, but its potential to go on doing so will be seriously compromised if it denies itself access to the same neuroscientific knowledge that these other professions (medicine, nursing) already have and already are building upon.

In this book, we are urging the development of thinking, conceptualization, practice and research, tantamount perhaps to a paradigm shift in social work. Such efforts will build on the beginning steps made here (and elsewhere), requiring that our colleagues in the profession, firstly, keep informed about contemporary neuroscientific research but more importantly, integrate this knowledge within social work's founding impetus by doing so within a social justice and critical theoretical framework.

Glossary

acetylcholine a classical neurotransmitter found in the basal ganglia and throughout the body, thought to be particularly important for learning

action potential an electrical impulse that sends a signal along the axon of a neuron and allows intercellular communication

adrenal glands glands which produce a variety of hormones that affect most body systems

adrenaline hormone that increases the heart rate, narrows blood vessels and opens up air passages

adrenocorticotropic hormone a hormone produced by the anterior pituitary gland that stimulates the adrenal cortex

amino acids organic compounds that make up peptides and proteins

anterior cingulate cortex a small brain region involved in directing attention, allocating mental resources and decision-making

autonomic nervous system that part of the nervous system that controls bodily functions such as blood pressure and sweating that are not under voluntary control

axons that part of a neuron that transmits electrical impulses away from the cell body to other neurons

brainstem the lowest part of the brain; facilitates communication between the forebrain and the spinal cord and peripheral nerves

cardio-vascular system the circulatory system comprising the heart and blood vessels

cells the smallest units of living matter that can function independently

cerebellum a part of the brain particularly important for balance, posture and the control of muscle tone

cerebral cortex the outer layer of the cerebral hemispheres; required for conscious thought

chromosome a threadlike structure comprised of DNA and associated proteins contained in the nucleus of cells

corpus callosum a bundle of nerve fibres that connect the two hemispheres of the brain

corticotropin releasing hormone a hormone that stimulates release of adrenocorticotropic hormone

cortisol a hormone secreted by the adrenal gland that is important for carbohydrate and protein metabolism and the stress response in humans

cytokines proteins secreted by immune cells that help regulate the immune system

dendrites extensions of the nerve cell body that receive signals from other nerve cells

dopamine a monoamine required for normal functioning of the nervous system; important for the regulation of thought, movement and behaviour

dorsolateral prefrontal cortex an area of the prefrontal cortex involved in the inhibition and control of behaviour; particularly important for decisions that are attentional in nature

endocrine system the system of glands responsible for producing hormones

enzymes protein-based catalysts that effect particular kinds of biochemical reactions

estrogen hormones produced primarily by the ovaries and whose main roles are related to reproductive functions in women

gamma-aminobutyric acid (GABA) the main inhibitory neurotransmitter in the brain

genes sequences of deoxyribonucleic acid that regulates biological activities such as the production of proteins

glucocorticoids a group of steroid hormones that are involved in carbohydrate, protein and fat metabolism, and in anti-inflammatory response and immunosuppression

glutamate the primary excitatory neurotransmitter in the brain

gray matter nerve tissue that consists primarily of nerve cell bodies, dendrites, and unmyelinated axons

gyri folds or raised areas on the surface of the cerebral hemispheres

hippocampus an area inside the temporal lobe crucial to conscious memory formation and emotion

homeostasis the physiological process by which the internal systems of the body (including blood pressure and body temperature) are maintained at equilibrium

hyperarousal over-activation of the autonomic nervous system

hypoarousal under-activation of the autonomic nervous system

hypothalamic-pituitary-adrenal (HPA) axis a major part of the neuro-endocrine system that controls reactions to stress; also central to the regulation of body processes such as digestion and energy usage

hypothalamus a part of the brain that is involved in the control of endocrine activity and plays an integral role in control of body temperature, sleep, appetite and sexual behaviour

immune system that range of cells and organs involved in protecting the body from infection and disease

isoenzymes one of various enzymes that share similar structure and mechanisms but differ chemically or in some other regard

limbic system an imprecise term that refers to those areas of the brain involved primarily in the production of emotion

lymphocytes a type of white blood cell important in immunity and defence against infection

medial prefrontal cortex an area of the prefrontal cortex that, amongst other tasks, is hypothesized to serve as an interface between emotional and cognitive brain systems

meditation a practice that involves focusing the mind to reduce or eliminate conscious thought, or to bring it to rest

mesencephalon that part of the brain between the pons and diencephalons; aids in many sensory and motor functions

metabolism the sum of chemical reactions occurring within a cell or entire organism, including the production of new substances, and the conversion of such into energy for use by the cell or organism

midbrain (see mescencephalon)

molecule two or more atoms joined together by chemical bonds

myelin an insulating layer around neurons that facilitates the conduction of nerve impulses

myelination the forming of myelin

neurogenesis the creation of new neuronal cells

neuroimaging invasive and non-invasive techniques for obtaining images of the nervous system

neurons the primary cells of the nervous system

neuropeptides any of the peptides found in neural tissue

neurotransmitter a substance that transmits a nerve impulse across a synapse

norepinephrine a hormone central to the sympathetic nervous system

opiates (endogenous) a class of peptides that act as the body's natural 'painkillers'

oxytocin a hormone that stimulates contractions of the uterus and secretion of milk, but is also implicated in a range of social bonding behaviours

orbitofrontal cortex a part of brain involved in the inhibition and control of behaviour; particularly important for decisions based on affective information

parasympathetic nervous system (PNS) a division of the autonomic nervous system that is dominant during times where there is little threat to the organism; slows heart rate, lowers blood pressure and slows breathing

peptides a group of two more amino acids that are bound in a particular way

pineal gland a small gland in the brain that produces melatonin

prefrontal cortex (PFC) a significant and complex brain region that allows for problem solving and our most complex of thoughts

progesterone a hormone produced in the corpus luteum that is involved, amongst other things, in regulation of the menstrual cycle in women

receptors molecular structures in or, usually, on the surface of, cells that allow neurotransmitters, hormones and other messenger molecules to bind to cells and, in so doing, trigger specific kinds of physiological changes

serotonin an important transmitter that is involved in, amongst other things, mood, appetite and arousal

serum the fluid component of blood

sulcus grooves in the cerebral hemisphere

sympathetic nervous system (SNS) a division of the autonomic nervous system that, amongst other things, reduces digestive secretions, speeds the heart and contracts blood vessels

synapse the junction between an axon and an adjacent neuron

systolic blood pressure when the heart is contracting

temporal lobe that part of the cerebral cortex involved in the processing of speech, sound and some aspects of memory

testosterone a hormone produced by the testis (and in some other regions) primarily involved in the development of sperm and secondary sexual characteristics in men

thalamus an area of the brain that plays a major role in relaying information from the various sensory receptors to other brain areas

striatum part of the brain important for movement and balance

ventromedial cortex an area of the prefrontal region important to social conduct, emotional processing and decision-making

visceral pertaining to the major internal organs

white matter that part of the nervous system consisting of myelinated fibre tracts

References

Adrian M (2003) 'How can sociological theory help our understanding of addictions?' *Substance Use and Misuse* 38(10): 1385–1423

Aldwin C and Gilmour D (2004) *Health, Illness and Optimal Aging*, Thousand Oaks, CA: Sage

Allen J, Pease B and Briskman L (2003) Critical social work: an introduction to theories and practices, Crows Nest, NSW: Allen and Unwin

American Psychiatric Association (1994) *Diagnostic and Statistical Manual of Mental Disorders: DSM-IV*, Washington, DC: American Psychiatric Association

Andersen B (2002) 'Biobehavioral outcomes following psychological interventions for cancer patients', *Journal of Counseling and Clinical Psychology* 70(1): 591–560

Aronson S (2004) 'Where the wild things are: the power and challenge of the adolescent group', *Mount Sinai Journal of Medicine* 71(3): 174–180

Australian Association of Social Workers (1999) The Development of Competency Standards for Mental Health Social Workers, Report of Australian Association of Social Workers

Australian Psychological Society (1996) Competencies of APS Psychologists, http://www.psychology.org.au/psych/qualifications/competencies_of_aps_psychologists.pdf, accessed on 2.5.2005

Azmitia E (2001) Impact of drugs and alcohol on the brain through the life cycle: knowledge for social workers. In Spence R, DiNitto D and Straussner S (eds) *Neurobiology of Addictions: implications for clinical practice*, New York: Haworth Social Work Practice Press Inc.

Ballmaier M, Sowell E, Thompson P, Kumar A, Narr K, Lavretsky H et al. (2004) 'Mapping brain size and cortical gray matter changes in elderly depression', *Biological Psychiatry* 55(4): 382–389

Bargh J and Chartrand T (1999) 'The unbearable automaticity of being', *American Psychologist* 54(7): 462–479

Bargh J, Gollwitzer P, Lee-Chai A, Barndollar K and Trotschel R (2001) 'The automated will: nonconscious activation and pursuit of behavioural goals', *Journal of Personality and Social Psychology* 81(6): 1014–1027

Batson C, Engel C and Fridell S (1999) 'Value judgments: testing the somatic-marker hypothesis using false physiological feedback', *Personality and Social Psychology Bulletin* 25(8): 1021–1032

Baum A, Garofalo J and Yali A (1999) 'Socioeconomic status and chronic stress: does stress account for SES effects on health?', *Annals of the New York Academy of Sciences* 896: 131–144

Baumeister R, Bratslavsky E and Tice D (1998) 'Ego depletion: is the active self a limited resource?', *Journal of Personality and Social Psychology* 74(5): 1252–1265

Baumeister R, Muraven M and Tice D (2000) 'Ego depletion: a resource model of volition, self-regulation, and controlled processing', *Social Cognition* 18(2): 130–150

Bechara A (2004) 'The role of emotion in decision-making: evidence from neurological patients with orbitofrontal damage', *Brain and Cognition* 55(1): 30–40

Bell C, Hood S and Nutt D (2005) 'Acute tryptophan depletion. Part II: clinical effects and implications', *Australian and New Zealand Journal of Psychiatry* 39(7), 565–574

Bennett A, Lesch K, Heils A, Long J, Lorenz J, Shoaf S et al. (2002) 'Early experience and serotonin transporter gene variation interact to influence primate', *CNS function* 7(1): 118–122

Bennett M, Zeller J, Rosenberg L and McCann J (2003) 'The effect of mirthful laughter on stress and natural killer cell activity', *Alternative Therapies in Health and Medicine* 9(2): 38–45

Bentley K (2001) *Social Work Practice in Mental Health: Contemporary Roles, Tasks and Techniques*, California: Brooks/Cole

Besthorn F (2002) 'Radical ecologisms: insights for educating social workers in ecological activism and social justice', *Critical Social Work* 3(1): 1–19

Birke L (2003) Shaping biology: feminism and the idea of the biological. In Williams S, Birke L, Bendelow G (eds) *Debating Biology: sociological reflections on health, medicine and society*, London: Routledge

Bland R and Renouf N (2001) 'Social work and the mental health team', *Australasian Psychiatry* 9(3): 238–241

Blaxter M (2003) Biology, social class and inequalities in health. In Williams S, Birke L, Bendelow G (eds) *Debating Biology: sociological reflections on health, medicine and society*, London: Routledge

Blum I, Lermana M, Misrachi I, Nordenberg Y, Grosskopf I, Weizman A et al. (2004) 'Lack of plasma norepinephrine cyclicity, increased estradiol during the follicular phase, and of progesterone and gonadotrophins at ovulation in women with premenstrual syndrome', *Neuropsychobiology* 50(1): 10–15

Blumenthal J, Babyak M, Moore K and Craighead E (1999) 'Effects of training on older patients with major depression', *Archives of Internal Medicine* 159(19): 2349–2356

Bodin T and Martinsen E (2004) 'Mood and self-efficacy during acute exercise in clinical depression: a randomized, controlled study', *Journal of Sport and Exercise Psychology* 26(4): 623–633

Booij L, Van der Does W, Haffmans J and Riedel W (2005) 'Acute tryptophan depletion in depressed patients treated with a selective serotonin-noradrenalin reuptake inhibitor: augmentation of antidepressant response?', *Journal of Affective Disorders*, 86: 305–311

Booij L, Van Der Does W, Benkelfat C, Bremmer D, Cowen P, Fava M et al. (2002) 'Predictors of mood response to acute tryptophan depletion: a reanalysis', *Neuropsychopharamcology* 27(5): 852–861

Bordo S (2004) *Unbearable Weight: Feminism, Western Culture, and the Body*, Tenth Anniversary Edition, California: University of California Press

Bourdieu P (1984) *Distinction: A Social Critique of the Judgement of Taste*, London: Routledge

Bowlby, J (1977) 'The making and breaking of affectional bonds. 1. Aetiology and psychopathology in the light of attachment theory', *British Journal of Psychiatry* 130: 201–210

Brady J, Posner M, Lang C, Rosati M (1994) *Prenatal Exposure to Alcohol and Other Drugs*, US Department of Health & Human Services: Education Development Center Inc.

Briggs S (1999) 'Links between infant observation and reflective social work practice', *Journal of Social Work Practice* 13(2): 147–156

Briscoe J, Orwin D, Ashton L and Burditt J (2004) Being there: Report for the Mental Health Workforce Development Programme, Auckland, New Zealand

Brody A, Saxena S, Stroessel P, Gillies L, Fairbanks L, Alborzian S et al. (2001) 'Regional brain metabolic changes in patients with major depression treated with either paroxetine or interpersonal therapy – preliminary findings', *Archives of General Psychiatry* 58(7): 631–640

Brosse A, Sheets E, Lett H and Blumenthal J (2002) 'Exercise and the treatment of clinical depression in adults', *Sports Medicine* 32(12): 741–760

Brown S and Tapert S (2004) 'Adolescence and the trajectory of alcohol use: basic to clinical studies', *Annals of the New York Academy of Sciences* 1021: 234–244

Browne E (2005) Social work in health care settings. In Alston M and McKinnon J (eds) *Social Work Fields of Practice*, Second Edition. South Melbourne: Oxford University Press

Brownlie J (2001) 'The "being-risky" child: governing childhood and sexual risk', *Sociology* 35(2): 519–537

Burkitt I (1999) *Bodies of Thought: embodiment, identity and modernity*, London: Sage

Bury M and Wadsworth M (2003) The 'biological clock?' aging, health and the body across the life course. In Williams S, Birke L, Bendelow G (eds) *Debating Biology: sociological reflections on health, medicine and society*, London: Routledge

Busfield J (1996) *Men, Women and Madness: Understanding Gender and Mental Disorder*, London: Macmillan

Butler, J (1993) *Bodies that matter: on the discursive limits of 'sex'*, New York, Routledge

Butler J (1996) Performativity's social magic. In Schatzki T and Northern W (eds) *The Social and Political Body*, New York: Guildford Press

Cacioppo J, Berntson G, Sheridan J and McClintock M (2000) 'Multilevel integrative analyses of human behavior: social neuroscience and the complementing nature of social and biological approaches', *Psychological Bulletin* 126(6): 829–843

Cameron J (2004) 'Interrelationships between hormones, behavior, and affect during adolescence – understanding hormonal, physical, and brain changes occurring in association with pubertal activation of the reproductive axis', *Annals of the New York Academy of Sciences* 1021: 110–123

Carter S and Pasqualini M (2004) 'Stronger autonomic response accompanies better learning: a test of Damasio's somatic marker hypothesis', *Cognition and Emotion* 18(7): 901–911

Casebeer W (2003) 'Moral cognition and its neural constituents', *Nature Reviews Neuroscience* 4(10): 840–847

Chambers R, Taylor J, Potenza M (2003) 'Developmental neurocircuitry of motivation in adolescents: a critical period of addiction vulnerability', *American Journal of Psychiatry* 160: 1041–1052

Chambon A, Irving A, Epstein L (eds) (1999) *Reading Foucault for Social Work*, New York: Columbia University Press

Charlesworth M, Farrall L, Stokes T, Turnbull D (1989) *Life Among the Scientists: An Anthropological Study of an Australian Scientific Community, Melbourne*: Oxford University Press

Charlesworth S (2000) *A Phenomenology of Working Class Experience*, Cambridge: Cambridge University Press

Chartrand T and Bargh J (1999) 'The chameleon effect: the perception-behavior link and social interaction', *Journal of Personality and Social Psychology* 76(6): 893–910

Chesler P (1974) *Women and Madness*, London: Allen Lane

Chiriboga C (2003) 'Fetal alcohol and drug effects', *Neurologist* 9(6): 267–279

Cirulli F, Berry A and Alleva E (2003) 'Early disruption of plasticity the mother–infant relationship: effects on brain and implications for psychopathology', *Neuroscience And Biobehavioral Reviews* 27(1–2): 73–82

Connell R (2000) *The Men and the Boys*, NSW: Allen and Unwin

Cook C, Becvar D, Pontious S (2000) 'Complementary alternative medicine in health and mental health: implications for social work practice', *Social Work in Health Care* 31(3): 39–57

Cooper B (2001) 'Nature, nurture and mental disorder: old concepts in the new millennium', *British Journal of Psychiatry* 178 (Suppl. 40): S91–S101

Coupland J and Gwyn R (eds) (2003) *Discourse, the Body and Identity*, Hampshire, UK: Palgrave Macmillan

Craft L and Landers D (1998) 'The effect of exercise on clinical depression and depression resulting from mental illness: a meta-analysis', *Journal of Sport and Exercise Psychology* 20(4): 339–357

Creighton (2004) 'Prevalence and Incidence of Child Abuse: International Comparisons', National Society for the Prevention of Cruelty to Children report

Crossley N (1995) Prozac nation and the biochemical self. In Williams S *Medicine and the Body*, Thousand Oaks, CA: Sage

Curtis W and Cicchetti D (2003) 'Moving research on resilience into the 21st century: theoretical and methodological considerations in examining the biological contributors to resilience', *Development & Psychopathology* 15: 773–810

Damasio A (1996) *Descartes' Error*, London: Papermac

Damasio A (2000) *The Feeling of What Happens – Body, Emotion and the Making of Consciousness*, London: Vintage

Dannefer D (2003) 'Cumulative advantage/disadvantage and the life course: cross fertilizing age and social science theory', *Journal of Gerontology Series B: Psychological Sciences & Social Studies* 58: S327–S337

Davidson L, O'Connell M, Tondora J, Staehli M and Evans A (2004) 'Recovery in serious mental illness: paradigm shift or shibboleth', manuscript submitted for publication

Davidson R (2004) 'Well-being and affective style: neural substrates and biobehavioral correlates', *Philosophical Transactions: Biological Sciences* 359(1449): 1395–1411

Davidson R and Slatger H (2000) 'Probing emotion in the developing brain: functional neuroimaging in the assessment of the neural substrates of emotion in normal and disordered children and adolescents', *Mental Retardation and Developmental Disabilities Research Reviews* 6(3): 166–170

Davidson R, Lewis D, Alloy L, Amaral D, Bush G, Cohen J et al. (2002) 'Neural and behavioral substrates of mood and mood regulation', *Biological Psychiatry* 52(6): 478–502

Davidson R, Pizzagalli D, Nitschke J and Putnam K (2002) 'Depression: perspectives from affective neuroscience', *Annual Review of Psychology* 53: 545–574

244 REFERENCES

Davis C, Shuster B, Blackmore E and Fox J (2004) 'Looking good – family focus on appearance and the risk for eating disorders', *International Journal of Eating Disorders* 35(2): 136–144

Davis LJ (1997) 'Nude Venuses, Medusa's body, and phantom limbs: disability and visuality', in DT Mitchell and SL Snyder (eds) The Body and Physical Difference, Ann Arbor, MI: University of Michigan Press

De Bellis M (2001) 'Developmental traumatology: the psychobiological development of maltreated children and its implications for research, treatment and policy', *Development and Psychopathology* 13(3): 539–564

DeCoster V (2000) 'Health care social work treatment of patient and family emotion: a synthesis and comparison across patient populations and practice settings', *Social Work in Health Care* 30(4): 7–23

Denfield D (1996) Old messages: ecofeminism and the alieviation of young people from environmental activism. In Gross P, Livitt N and Lewis M *The Flight from Reason and Science*, United States: Annals of the New York Academy of Sciences

Diseth T (2005) 'Dissociation in children and adolescents as reaction to trauma – an overview of conceptual issues and neurobiological factors', *Nordic Journal of Psychiatry* 59(2): 79–91

Doel M and Marsh P (1992) *Task-centred Social Work*, Aldershot: Ashgate

Ekman P (1993) 'Facial expression and emotion', *American Psychologist* 48(4): 384–392

Elderkin-Thompson V, Kumar A, Bilker W, Dunkin J, Mintz J, Moberg P et al. (2003) 'Neuropsychological deficits among patients with late-onset minor and major depression', *Archives of Clinical Neuropsychology* 18(5): 529–549

Ellis, K and Dean H (eds) (2000) *Social Policy and the Body*, Basingstoke: Palgrave Macmillan

Elstad J (1998) 'The psychosocial perspective on social inequalities in health', *Sociology of Health & Illness* 20(5): 598–618

Eppright T, Sanfacon J, Beck N and Bradley J (1997) 'Sport psychiatry in childhood and adolescence: an overview', *Child Psychiatry & Human Development* 28(2): 71–88

Erickson C and Wilcox R (2001) Neurobiological causes of addiction. In Spence R, DiNitto D and Straussner S (eds) *Neurobiology of Addictions: implications for clinical practice*, New York: Haworth Social Work Practice Press Inc.

Erikson, E (1968) *Identity: Youth and Crisis*, London: Faber and Faber

Evans G and Kantrowitz E (2002) 'Socioeconomic status and health: the potential role of environmental risk exposure', *Annual Review of Public Health* 23: 303–331

Falk L, Nordberg A, Seiger A, Kjaeldgaard A and Hellstrom-Lindahl E (2005) 'Smoking during early pregnancy affects the expression pattern of both nicotinic and muscarinic acetylcholine receptors in human first trimester brainstem and cerebellum', *Neuroscience* 132(2): 389–397

Featherstone M and Hepworth M (1991) The mask of ageing and the postmodern lifecourse. In Featherstone M, Hepworth M and Turner B (eds) *The Body: social processes and cultural theory.* London: Sage

Featherstone M and Wernick A (eds) (1995) *Images of Aging: Cultural Representations of Later Life*, London: Routledge

Field R, Diego M, Dieter J, Hernandez-Reif M, Schanberg S, Kuhn C et al. (2004) 'Prenatal depression effects on the fetus and the newborn', *Infant Behavior & Development* 27(2): 216–229

Finger W and Arnold E (2002) 'Mind–body interventions: applications for social work practice', *Social Work in Health Care* 35(4): 57–78

Foster J, Brewer C, Steele T (2003) 'Naltrexone implants can completely prevent early (1-monthly) relapse after opiate detoxification: a pilot study of 2 cohorts totaling 101 patients with a not on naltrexone blood levels', *Addiction Biology* 8(2): 211–217

Foucault M (1977) *Discipline and Punish: The Birth of the Prison*, New York: Vintage Books

Foucault M (1978) *The History of Sexuality: an introduction*, New York: Random House

Foucault M (1979) Discipline and punish: *the birth of the prison*, New York Random House

Foucault M (1989) *Madness of Civilization: A History of Insanity in the Age of Reason*, London: Routledge

Frank A (1995) 'The self unmade: embodied paranoia', extract from *The wounded storyteller: body, illness, and ethics*, Chicago/London University of Chicago Press

Fraser M and Greco, M (eds) (2005) The body: a reader, London/New York, Routledge

Freund P (2001) 'Bodies, disability and spaces: the social model and disabling spatial organisations', *Disability and Society* 16(5): 689–706

Galambos C and Rosen A (2000) The aging are coming and they are us. In Keigher S, Fortune A and Witkin S *Aging and Social Work: the changing landscape*, New York: NASW Press

Galderisi S and Mucci A (2000) 'Emotions, brain development and psychopathology vulnerability', *CNS Spectrums* 5(8): 44–48

Gardener D and Zodikoff B (2003) Meeting the challenges of social work practice in health care and aging in the 21st century. In Berkman B and Harootyan L (eds) *Social Work and Health Care in an Aging Society: education, policy, practice and research*, New York: Springer Publishing Co.

Germain C and Gitterman A (1996) *The Life Model of Social Work Practice*, Second Edition, New York: Columbia University Press

Geron S and Little F (2003) Standardized geriatric assessment in social work practice with older adults. In Berkman B and Harootyan L (eds) *Social Work and Health Care in an Aging Society: education, policy, practice and research*, New York: Springer Publishing Co.

Giddens (1991) *Modernity and Self-Identity: Self and Society in the Late Modern Age*, Cambridge: Polity Press

Giddens A (1984) *The Constitution of Society: outline of the theory of structuration*, Cambridge: Polity Press

Giddens A (1991) *Modernity and Self-Identity*, Cambridge: Polity Press

Giddens A (1992) *The Transformation of Intimacy: sexuality, love and eroticism in modern societies*, Cambridge: Polity Press

Giedd J (2004) 'Structural magnetic resonance imaging of the adolescent brain', *Annals of the New York Academy of Sciences* 1021: 77–85

Giedke H and Schwarzler F (2002) 'Therapeutic use of sleep deprivation in depression', *Sleep Medicine Reviews* 6(5): 361–377

Gilbert N (ed) (1997) *Combating Child Abuse: International Perspectives and Trends*, New York: Oxford University Press

Gilbert P (1992) *Depression: The Evolution of Powerlessness*, New York: Guilford Press

Gilgun, J (2005) 'Evidence-based practice, descriptive research and the Resilience-Scheme-Gender-Brain Functioning (RSGB) assessment', *British Journal of Social Work* 35: 843–862

Gilleard, C and Higgs, P (2000) *Cultures of ageing: self, citizen and the body*, London: Prentice Hall

Godfrey K (2002) 'The role of the placenta in fetal programming – a review', *Placenta* 23 (Suppl. A): S20–S27

Goffman E (1959) *Presentation of Self in Everyday Life*, New York: Anchor

Goffman, E (1963) *Behavior in public places: notes on the social organization of gatherings*, New York: Free Press of Glencoe, Collier-Macmillan

Gold P and Chrousos G (2002) 'Organization of the stress system and its dysregulation in melancholic and atypical depression: high vs low CRH/NE states', *Molecular Psychiatry* 7(3): 254–275

Goldapple K, Segal Z, Garson C, Lau M, Bieling P, Kennedy S et al. (2004) 'Modulation of cortical-limbic pathways in major depression: treatment specific effects of cognitive behavior therapy', *Archives of General Psychiatry* 61(1): 34–41

Goleman D (1995) *Emotional Intelligence: why it can matter more than IQ*, London: Bloomsbury Publishing

Goswami U (2001) 'Cognitive development: no stages please – we're British', *British Journal of Psychology* 92(1): 257–277

Greenwood J (1994) *Realism, Identity and Emotion*, London: Sage
Grenier A and Gorey K (2000) The effectiveness of social work with older people and their families. In Keigher S, Fortune A and Witkin S *Aging and Social Work: the changing landscape*, New York, NASW Press
Grewen K, Anderson B, Girdler S and Light K (2003) 'Warm partner contact is related to lower cardiovascular reactivity', *Behavioral Medicine* 29(3): 123–130
Gross J (2002) 'Emotional regulation: affective, cognitive and social consequences', *Psychophysiology* 39(3): 281–291
Grosz, E (1994) *Volatile bodies*, Bloomington: Indiana University Press
Grosz E (1995) *Space, Time and Perversion*, New York: Routledge
Hagenstad G and Dannefer D (2001). Concepts and theories of aging. In Binstock R and George L *Handbook of Aging and the Social Sciences*, Sandiego, CA: Academic Press
Hall T, Kaduson H and Schaefer C (2002) 'Fifteen effective play therapy techniques', *Professional Psychology: Research and Practice* 33(6): 515–522
Hall W, Carter L and Morley K (1998) 'Editorial: addiction, neuroscience and ethics', *Addictions* 93(6): 867–870
Hareven T (1995) Changing images of aging and the social construction of the life course. In Featherstone M and Wernick A (eds) *Images of Aging: cultural representations of later life*, London: Routledge
Harms, L (2005) *Understanding Human Development: A Multidimensional Approach*, Melbourne: Oxford
Harris J (2000) 'Socialization, personality development, and the child's environments: comments on Vandell', *Developmental Psychopathology* 36(6): 711–723
Haustein K, Haffner S and Woodcock B (2002) 'A review of the pharmacological and psychopharamacological aspects of smoking and smoking cessation in psychiatric patients', *International Journal of Clinical Pharmacology and Therapeutics* 40(9): 404–418
Hawthorne S (2002) *Wild Politics*, North Melbourne Australia: Spinifex Press
Heikkinen R (2003) 'The experience of aging and advanced old age: a ten-year follow up', *Aging and Society* 24: 567–582
Heim C, Newport D, Wagner D, Wilcox M, Miller A and Nemeroff C (2002) 'The role of adverse experience and adulthood stress in the prediction of neuroendocrine stress reactivity in women: a multiple regression analysis', *Depression and Anxiety* 15(3): 117–125
Heim C, Newport D, Wagner D, Wilcox M, Miller A and Nemeroff C (2002) 'The role of adverse experience and adulthood stress in the prediction of neuroendocrine stress reactivity in women: a multiple regression analysis', *Depression and Anxiety* 15(3): 117–125

Heinrichs M, Baumgartner T, Kirschbaum C and Ehlert U (2003) 'Social support and oxytocin interact to suppress cortisol and subjective responses to psychosocial stress', *Biological Psychiatry* 54(12): 1389–1398

Henderson L (2000) 'The knowledge and use of alternative therapeutic techniques by social work practitioners: a descriptive study', *Social Work in Health Care* 30(3): 55–71

Hepworth M (2003) Aging bodies: aged by culture. In Coupland J and Gwyn R (eds) *Discourse, the Body and Identity*, Hampshire: Palgrave Macmillan

Hepworth D, Rooney R, Rooney G, Strom-Gottfried K and Larson J (2006) *Direct Social Work Practice*, Seventh Edition, Pacific Grove, CA: Brooks/Cole

Hochschild R (1983) 'Laboring the emotions: expanding the remit of nursing work?', *Journal of Advanced Nursing*, 24(1): 139–143

Hokenstadt M (2000) Towards a society for all ages: the international year of older persons. In Keigher S, Fortune A and Witkin S *Aging and Social Work: the changing landscape*, New York: NASW Press

Howson A (2004) *The Body in Society*, Cambridge: Polity Press

Hsu H and Fogel A (2003) 'Stability and transitions in mother-infant face-to-face communication during the first 6 months: a microhistorical approach', *Developmental Psychology* 39(6): 1061–1082

Hudson C (2005) 'Socioeconomic status and mental illness: tests of the social causation and selection hypotheses', *American Journal of Orthopsychiatry* 75(1): 3–18

Isaacowitz D and Smith J (2003) 'Positive and negative affect in very old age', *Journal of Gerontology Series B Psychological Sciences and Social Sciences* 58: P143–P152

Jaeger J, Lockwood A, Van Valin R, Kemmerer D, Murphy B and Wack D (1998) 'Sex differences in brain regions activated by grammatical and reading tasks', *Neuroreport* 9(12): 2803–2807

Johnson H (2002) Emerging knowledge and future trends in mental health: implications for social work. In K Bentley (ed) *Social Work Practice in Mental Health*, California: Brooks/Cole

Johnson H (2001) Neuroscience in social work practice and education. In Spence R, DiNitto D and Straussner S (eds) *Neurobiology of Addictions: implications for clinical practice*, New York: Haworth Social Work Practice Press Inc.

Johnson H, Atkins S, Battle S, Hernandez-Arata L, Hesselbrock M, Libassi M et al. (1990) 'Strengthening the "bio" in the biopsychosocial paradigm', *Journal of Social Work Education*, 26(2): 109–123

Johnson M (2001) 'Functional brain development in humans', *Nature Reviews Neuroscience* 2(7): 475–483

Kagan J (1999) Born to be shy. In R Conlan (ed.) *States of Mind: New Discoveries About How Our Brains Make Us Who We Are*, New York: Wiley

Kagan J (2001) 'Biological constraint, cultural variety, and psychological structures', *Annals of the New York Academy of Sciences* 935: 177–190

Kagan J, Snidman N and Arcus D (1998) 'Childhood derivatives of high and low reactivity in infancy', *Child Development* 69(5): 1483–1493

Kandel E (1998) 'A new intellectual framework for psychiatry', *American Journal of Psychiatry* 155(4): 457–469

Kandel E (2001) 'The molecular biology of memory storage', *Science* 294(5544): 1030–1038

Kandel E and Squire L (2001) 'Neuroscience – breaking down scientific barriers to the study of brain and mind', *Annals of the New York Academy of Sciences* 935: 118–135

Kandel E, Schwartz J and Jessell T (2000) *Principles of Neural Science*, Fourth Edition, New York: McGraw-Hill

Kanel K (2003) *A Guide to Crisis Intervention*, Pacific Grove: Brooks/Cole

Kaplan A (2005) 'Advances in pharmacogenomics reduce side effects and save lives', *Psychiatric Times*, 22(7): 4–7

Kataria, M (1999) *Laugh for No Reason*, India: Madhuri International

Kaye J (2002) 'Health brain aging', *Archives of Neurology* 58(11): 1721–1723

Keigher S, Fortune A and Witkin S *Aging and Social Work: the changing landscape*, New York, NASW Press

Kemp S (2001) 'Environment through a gendered lens: from person-in-environment to woman-in-environment', *Journal of Women and Social Work* 16(1): 1–16

Kendler K (2001) 'A psychiatric dialogue on the mind–body problem', *American Journal of Psychiatry* 158(7): 989–1000

Kennardy J, Mensch M, Bowen K, Green B, Walton J (2002) 'Group therapy for binge eating in Type 2 diabetes: a randomized trial', *Diabetic Medicine* 19 (1): 243–242

Kiecolt-Glaser J and Newton T (2001) 'Marriage and health: his and hers', *Psychological Bulletin* 127(4): 472–503

Kirchmayer V, Davoli M, Vester A, Amato L, Feerri A, Perucci C (2002) 'A systematic review of the efficacy of naltrexone maintenance treatment on opioid dependence', *Addiction* 97(10): 1241–1249

Kleinman, A 'Hypochondriasis: the ironic disease' from Geertz, C (1986) 'Making experiences, authorizing selves'. In Turner VW and Brunes EM (eds) *The Anthropology of Experience*, Urbana: University of Illinois Press

Koger S, Schettler T and Weiss B (2005) 'Environmental toxicants and developmental disabilities: a challenge for psychologists', *American Psychologist* 60(3): 243–255

Kondrat M (2002) 'Actor centered social work', *Social Work* 47(4): 435–449

Kontos P, (1999) 'Local biology: bodies of difference in aging studies', *Aging and Society* 19: 677–689

Kornstein, S (2001) 'The evaluation and management of depression in women across the lifespan', *Journal of Clinical Psychiatry* 62(1): 11–17

Kosslyn S, Cacioppo J, Davidson R, Hugdahl K, Lovallo W, Spiegel D et al. (2002) 'Bridging psychology and biology – the analysis of individuals in groups', *American Psychologist* 57(5): 341–351

Kraemer A, Bherer L, Colcombe S, Dong W, Greenough W (2004) 'Environmental influences on cognitive and brain plasticity during aging', *Journal of Gerontology Series A: Biological Sciences and Medical Sciences* 59: M940–M957

Kuehner C and Buerger C (2005) 'Determinants of subjective quality of life in depressed patients: the role of self-esteem, response styles and social support', *Journal of Affective Disorders* 86(2–3): 205–213

Kuh D and Ben-Shlomo Y (eds) (1997) *A Life Course Approach to Chronic Disease Epidemiology*, Oxford: Oxford University Press

Kuh D and Hardy R (eds) (2002) *A Life Course Approach to Women's Health*, New York: Oxford University Press

Kunkel S (2003) 'Mapping the field: shifting contours of social gerontology', *The Gerontologist* 43: 128–132

Lachman L (2002) 'Group therapy for cancer patients: examining the impact on quality and quantity of life', *Psychology Today* (Sept–Oct): 27

Lamberts S (2003) 'The endocriniligy of aging and the brain', *Archives of Neurobiology* 59(11): 1709–1712

Latour B and Woolgar S (1979) *Laboratory Life: the social construction of scientific facts*, Beverly Hills: Sage

Le Doux J (1999) *The Emotional Brain*, London: Phoenix

Le Doux J (2002) *The Synaptic Self: How Our Brains Become Who We Are*, New York: Penguin

Lerner D, Adler D, Chang H, Lapitsky L, Hood M, Perissinotto C et al. (2004) 'Unemployment, job retention, and productivity loss among employees with depression', *Psychiatric Services* 55(12): 1371–1378

Lewis M (1996) Radical environmental philosophy and the assault on reason. In Gross P, Livitt N and Lewis M *The Flight from Reason and Science*, United States: Annals of the New York Academy of Sciences

Lillquist P and Abramson J (2002) 'Separating the apples and oranges in the fruit cocktail: the mixed results of psychosocial interventions on cancer survival', *Social Work in Health Care* 36(2): 65–79

Link B, Cullen F, Stuening E, Shrout P and Dohrenwend B (1989) 'A modified labeling theory approach to mental disorders: an empirical assessment', *American Sociological Review* 54: 400–423

Link B, Lennon M and Dohrenwend B (1993) 'Socioeconomic status and depression: the role of occupations involving direction, control and planning', *American Journal of Sociology* 98(6): 1351–1387

Lock, M (2002) Twice dead: organ transplants and the reinvention of death, Berkeley, CA: University of California Press

Longo V and Finch C (2002) 'Genetics of aging and disease: from rare mutations and model systems to disease prevention', *Archives of Neurobiology* 59(11): 1706–1709

Lopez F (1995) 'Contemporary attachment theory: an introduction with implications for counseling psychology', *Counseling Psychology* 23(3): 395–416

Loving T, Heffner K, Kiecolt-Glaser J, Glaser and Malarkey W (2004) 'Stress hormone changes and marital conflict: spouses' relative power makes a difference', *Journal of Marriage and the Family* 66(3): 595–612

Lupien S and McEwen B (1997) 'The acute effects of corticosteroids on cognition: integration of animal and human model studies', *Brain Research Reviews* 24(1): 1–27

Lupien S and McEwen B (1997) 'The acute effects of corticosteroids on cognition: integration of animal and human model studies', *Brain Research Reviews* 24(1): 1–27

Lupien S, King S, Meaney M and McEwen B (2001) 'Can poverty get under your skin? Basal cortisol levels and cognitive function in children from low and high socioeconomic status', *Development and Psychopathology* 13(3): 653–676

Lutz A, Greischer L, Rawlings N, Ricard M and Davidson R (2004) 'Long-term meditators self-induce high-amplitude gamma synchrony during mental practice', Proceedings of the National Academy of Sciences 101(46): 16369–16373

Lyon M (2003) 'Immune' to emotion: the relative absence in PNI, and its centrality to everything else. In Wilce J (ed) *Social and Cultural Lives of Immune Systems*, London: Routledge

Macijewski P, Prigerson H and Mazure C (2001) 'Sex differences in event-related risk for major depression', *Psychological Medicine* 31(4): 593–604

Maclean, K (2003) 'The impact of institutionalisation on child development', *Development and Psychopathology* 15(4): 853–884

Martin C, Milch R, Martin W, Hartung C, Hengler E (1997) 'Gender differences in adolescent psychiatric outpatient substance use: associated behaviors and feelings', *Journal of the American Academy of Child and Adolescent Psychiatry* 36(4): 486–494

Martin, E (1994) 'Complex systems', in *Flexible Bodies: tracking immunity in American culture – from days of polio to the age of AIDS*, Boston, MA: Beacon Press

Massey D (2002) 'A brief history of human society: the origin and role of emotion in social life', *American Sociological Review* 67(1): 1–29

Mattaini, M and Kirk, SA (1991) 'Assessing assessment in social work', *Social Work*, (May) 36(3): 260–266

Mattaini, M, Lowery, CT and Meyer, CH (2002) Foundations of social work practice: a graduate text, Washington, DC: NASW

Mayberg H (2003) 'Modulating dysfunctional limbic-cortical circuits in depression: towards development of brain-based algorithms for diagnosis and optimised treatment', *British Medical Bulletin* 65: 193–207

McDermott F and Pyett P (1993) *Not Welcome Anywhere: people with serious mental illness and problematic drug or alcohol use*, Melbourne: VICSERV

McEwan B and Lesley E (2004) The End of Stress *as we know it*, New York: Joseph Henry and Dana Presses

McEwen B (1998) 'Stress, adaptation and disease – allostasis and allostatic load', *Annals of the New York Academy of Sciences* 840: 33–44

McEwen B and Seeman T (1999) 'Protective and damaging effects of mediators of stress – elaborating and testing the concepts of allostasis and allostatic load', *Annals of the New York Academy of Sciences* 896: 30–47

McKenzie L (1994) 'Psychiatric disability or mental illness: is there a difference?', *New Paradigm* (June), 582–601

Meaney M (2001) 'Nature, nurture and the disunity of knowledge', *Annals of the New York Academy of Sciences* 935: 50–61

Meijler M, Matsushita M, Wirshing P, Janda K (2004) 'Development of immunopharmacotherapy against drugs of abuse', *Current Drug Discovery Techniques*, 1(1): 77–89

Merleau-Ponty, M (2005) *Phenomenology of Perception*, London and New York: Routledge

Meuret A, Ritz T, Wilhelm F and Roth W (2005) 'Voluntary hyperventilation in the treatment of panic disorder – functions of hyperventilation, their implications for breathing training, and recommendations for standardization', *Clinical Psychology Review* 25(3): 285–306

Meyer S, Chrousos G and Gold P (2001) 'Major depression and the stress system: a life span perspective', *Development and Psychopathology* 13(3): 565–580

Miehls D and Moffatt K (2000) 'Constructing social work identity based on the reflexive self', *British Journal of Social Work* 30: 339–348

Mikulincer M, Shaver P and Pereg D (2003) 'Attachment theory and affect regulation: the dynamics, development, and cognitive consequences of attachment-related strategies', *Motivation and Emotion* 27(2): 77–102

Milligan R and Andrews B (2005) 'Suicidal and other self-harming behaviour in offender women: the role of shame, anger and childhood abuse', *Legal and Criminological Psychology* 10(1): 13–25

Mishler, E and AmaraSingham, L (1981) *Social Contexts of Health, Illness and Patient Care*, New York: Cambridge University Press

Moll J, de Oliveira-Souza R, Eslinger P, Bramati I, Mourao-Miranda J, Andreiuolo P et al. (2002) 'The neural correlates of moral sensitivity: a functional magnetic resonance imaging investigation of basic and moral emotions', *Journal of Neuroscience* 22(7), 2730–2736

Mrak R, Griffin S and Graham D (1997) 'Aging-associated changes in human brain', *Journal of Neuropathology and Experimental Neurology*, 56(12): 1269–1276

Mullaly, B (1997) *Structural Social Work: Ideology, Theory and Process*, Second Edition, Toronto: Oxford University Press

Mulvany J (2000) 'Disability, impairment or illness? The relevance of the social model of disability to the study of mental disorder', *Sociology of Health and Illness* 22(5): 582–601

Mutaner C, Eaton W, Miech R and O'Campo P (2004) 'Socioeconomic position and major mental disorders', *Epidemiological Review* 26: 53–62

Nasser E and Overholser J (2005) 'Recovery from major depression: the role of support from family, friends and spiritual beliefs', *Acta Psychiatrica Scandinavica* 111 (2): 125–132

National Inquiry into the Separation of Aboriginal and Torres Strait Islander Children from their Families (Australia) (1997) *Bringing Them Home: Report of the National Inquiry into the Separation of Aboriginal and Torres Strait Islander Children from their Families*, Sydney: Human Rights and Equal Opportunity Commission

Nelson C, Bloom F, Cameron J, Amaral D, Dahl R and Pine D (2002) 'An integrative, multidisciplinary approach to the study of brain-behavior relations in the context of typical and atypical development', *Development and Psychopathology* 14(3): 499–520

Neppl T and Murray A (1997) 'Social dominance and play patterns among preschoolers: gender comparisons', *Sex Roles* 36(5–6): 381–394

Nestler E (2002) 'From neurobiology to treatment: progress against addiction', *Nature Neuroscience* (Suppl. 5): 1076–1079

Nettleton S and Gustafsson V (2002) *The Sociology of Health and Illness Reader*, Cambridge: Polity Press

Nettleton S and Watson J (1998) *The Body in Everyday Life*, London: Routledge

Newport D, Owens M, Knight D, Ragan K, Morgan N, Nemeroff C and Stowe Z (2004) 'Alterations in platelet serotonin transporter binding in women with postpartum onset major depression', *Journal of Psychiatric Research* 38(5): 467–473

Neysmith S (ed.) (1999) *Critical Issues for Future Social Work Practice with Aging Persons*, New York: Columbia University Press

O'Neal H, Dunn A and Martinsen E (2000) 'Depression and exercise', *International Journal of Sport Psychology* 31: 110–135

Orbach I, Stein D, Shani-Sela M and Har-Even D (2001) 'Body attitudes and body experiences in suicidal adolescents', *Suicide and Life-threatening Behavior* 31(3): 237–250

Ornish D (1990) *Dr Dean Ornish's Program for Reversing Heart Disease*, New York: Random House

Ornoy A (2002) 'The effects of alcohol and illicit drugs on the human embryo and fetus', *Israel Journal of Psychiatry And Related Sciences* 39(2): 120–132

Panksepp J (1998) *Affective Neuroscience: The Foundations of Human and Animal Emotions*, New York: Oxford University Press

Paton C and Beer D (2001) 'Caffeine: the forgotten variable', *International Journal of Psychiatry in Clinical Practice* 5(4): 231–236

Paul R, McDonnell A and Kelly C (2004) 'Folic acid: neurochemistry, metabolism and relationship to depression', *Human Psychopharmacology: Clinical and Experimental* 19(7): 477–488

Payne M (1998) Social work theories and reflective practice. In Adams R, Dominelli L, Payne M (eds) *Social Work: themes, issues and critical debates*, London: Macmillan

Pease B and Fook J (eds) (1999) *Transforming Social Work*, London: Routledge

Pecukonis E, Cornelius L and Parrish M (2003) 'The future of health social work', *Social Work in Health Care*, 37(3): 1–16

Pederson S and Seidman E (2004) 'Team sports achievement and self-esteem development among urban adolescent girls', *Psychology of Women Quarterly* 28(4): 412–422

Pilgrim D and Rogers A (1999) *A Sociology of Mental Health and Illness*, Buckingham: Open University Press

Powell J (2001) 'Theorising social gerontology: the case of social philosophies of age', *Sincronia* Summer 1–9

Powell J and Biggs S (2003) 'Foucauldian gerontology: a methodology for understanding', *Electronic Journal of Sociology*, 7: 2–3

Putnam M (2002) 'Linking aging theory and disability models: increasing the potential to explore aging with physical impairment', *The Gerontologist* 42(6): 779–786

RANZCP (1998) The RANZCP Code of Ethics (1998), Melbourne, Australia: RANZCP

Reason J (2000) 'Human error: models and management', *British Medical Journal* 320(7237): 768–770

Richards J (2004) 'The cognitive consequences of concealing feelings', *Current Directions in Psychological Science* 13(4): 131–134

Richman E and Shaffer D (2000) 'If you let me play sports' – how might sport participation influence the self-esteem of adolescent females?', *Psychology of Women Quarterly* 24(2): 189–199

Roberts G, Williams G, Lawrence J and Raphael B (1998) 'How does domestic violence affect women's health?', *Women's Health* 28(1): 117–1129

Robinson L (1998) Social work through the life course. In Adams R, Dominelli L and Payne M (eds) *Social Work: themes, issues and critical debates*, London: Macmillan

Robles T, Glaser R and Kiecolt-Glaser J (2005) 'Out of balance – a new look at chronic stress, depression, and immunity', *Current Directions in Psychological Science* 14(2): 111–115

Rogers, Lesley (1999) *Sexing the brain*, London: Weidenfeld & Nicolson

Romero A (2005) 'Low-income neighborhood barriers and resources for adolescents' physical activity', *Journal of Adolescent Health* 36(3): 253–259

Roozen H, Kerkhof A, van den Brink W (2003) 'Experience with an outpatient relapse program (Community Reinforcement Approach) combined with naltrexone in the treatment of opioid dependence: effects on addictive behaviors and the predictive value of psychiatric comorbidity', *European Addiction Research* 9: 53–58

Rose N (1996) *Inventing Ourselves: psychology, power and personhood*, Cambridge: Cambridge University Press

Rosenberg R (2002) 'Time and memory', *Archives of Neurology* 59(11): 1699–1700

Rowe J (2004) Towards a 'thoughtful' sociology of drug use. Involving drug users in policy making. In Mendes P and Rowe J (eds) *Harm Minimization: zero tolerance and beyond*, Australia: Pearson Education

Saleeby D (1992) 'Biology's challenge to social work: embodying the person-in-environment perspective', *Social Work* 37: 112–118

Saleeby D (1996) 'The strengths perspective in social work practice: extensions and cautions', *Social Work* 1(3): 296–305

Salih S (ed) (2004) *The Judith Butler Reader*, Oxford: Blackwell

Salovey P, Rothman A, Detweiler J, Steward W (2000) 'Emotional states and physical health', *American Psychologist* 55(1): 110–121

Sampson W (1996) Antiscience trends in the rise of the 'alternative medicine' movement. In Gross P, Livitt N and Lewis M *The Flight from Reason and Science*, United States: Annals of the New York Academy of Sciences

Scaer R (2001) 'The neurophysiology of dissociation and chronic disease', *Applied Psychophysiology and Biofeedback* 26(1): 73–91

Scharlach A, Damron-Rodriguez J, Robinson B, Feldman R (2000) 'Educating social workers for an aging society: a vision for the 21st century', *Journal of Social Work Education*, 36(3): 521–538

Schatzki T and Northern W (eds) (1996) *The Social and Political Body*, New York: Guildford Press

Scheff T (1974) 'The labelling theory of mental illness', *American Sociological Review* 39(3): 444–452

Scheper-Hughes, N (2000) 'The global traffic in human organs', *Current Anthropology* 41(2): 191–224

Shilling C (2003) *The Body and Social Theory*, Newbury Park: Sage

Schlesinger S (1985) *Health Care Social Work Practice: concepts and strategies*, St Louis Missouri: Times/Mirror/Masby College Publishing

Schore A (2001a) 'Effects of a secure attachment relationship on right brain development, affect regulation, and infant mental health', *Infant Mental Health Journal* 22(1–2): 7–66

Schore A (2001b) 'The effects of early relational trauma on right brain development, affect regulation, and infant mental health', *Infant Mental Health Journal* 22(1–2): 201–269

Schore A (2003) *Affect Dysregulation and Disorders of the Self*, New York: WW Norton and company

Schulkin J, Thompson B and Rosen J (2003) 'Demythologizing the emotions: adaptation, cognition, and visceral representations of emotion in the nervous system', *Brain and Cognition* 52(1): 15–23

Scott D and Swain S (2002) *Confronting Cruelty: Historical Perspectives on Child Protection in Australia*, Melbourne: Melbourne University Publishing

Scott S, Jackson S and Backett-Milburn K (1998) 'Swings and roundabouts: risk anxiety and the everyday worlds of children', *Sociology* 32(4): 689–705

Seeman T (2000) 'How do others get under our skin: social relationships and health'. In C Ryff and B Singer (eds), *Emotion, Social Relationships and Health*, New York: Oxford Press

Sharlach A, Damron-Rodriguez J, Robinson B, Feldman R (2000) 'Educating social workers for an aging society: a vision for the 21st century', *Journal of Social Work Education* 36(3): 521–538

Shenal B, Harrison D and Demaree H (2003) 'The neuropsychology of depression: a literature review and preliminary model', *Neuropsychology Review* 13(1): 33–42

Siefert K, Heflin C, Corcoran M and Williams D (2004) 'Food insufficiency and physical and mental health in a longitudinal survey of welfare recipients', *Journal of Health and Social Behavior* 45(2): 171–186

Solomon A (2002) *The Noonday Demon: An Atlas of Depression*, New York: Touchstone

Spence R, DiNitto D and Straussner S (eds) (2001) *Neurobiology of Addictions: implications for clinical practice*, New York: Haworth Social Work Practice Press Inc.

Steinberg L (2004) 'Risk taking in adolescence: what changes, and why?', *Annals of the New York Academy of Sciences* 1021: 51–58

Steiner M, Dunn E and Born L (2003) 'Hormones and mood: from menarche to menopause and beyond', *Journal of Affective Disorders* 74(1): 67–83

Sternberg E (1999) Emotions and disease: a balance of molecules. In R Conlan (ed.) *States of Mind: New Discoveries About How Our Brains Make Us Who We Are*, New York: Wiley

Stone S (1995) 'The Myth of Bodily Perfection', *Disability in Society* 10: 413–434

Stoppard J (2000) *Understanding Depression: Feminist Social Constructionist Approaches*, London: Routledge

Strongman K (1996) *The Psychology of Emotion*, West Sussex, England: Wiley

Suzuki A, Hirota A, Takasawa N and Shigemasu K (2003) 'Application of the somatic marker hypothesis to individual differences in decision making', *Biological Psychiatry* 65(1): 81–88

Taleporas G and McCabe M (2001) 'The Impact of Physical Disability on Body Esteem', *Sexuality and Disability* 19(4): 293–308

Tangenberg K and Kemp S (2002) 'Embodied practice: claiming the body's experience, agency and knowledge for social work', *Social Work* 47(1): 9–18

Tapert S, Aarons G, Georgianna R, Sedlar B, Brown S (2001) 'Adolescent substance use and sexual risk-taking behavior', *Journal of Adolescent Health*, 28: 181–189

Thayer J and Lane R (2000) 'A model of neurovisceral integration in emotion regulation', *Journal of Affective Disorders*, 61(2): 201–216

Thompson N (1998) 'The ontology of aging', *British Journal of Social Work*, 28: 695–707

Tlauka M, Brolese A, Pomeroy D and Hobbs W (2005) 'Gender differences in spatial knowledge acquired through simulated exploration of a virtual shopping centre', *Journal of Environmental Psychology* 25(1): 111–118

Tomison A (2001) 'A history of child protection: back to the future', *Family Matters* 60: 46–57

Tulle-Winton E (1999) 'Growing old and resistance: towards a new cultural economy of old age?', *Ageing and Society* 19: 281–299

Turner B (1995) Aging and Identity: some reflections on the somatization of the self. In Featherstone M and Wernick A (eds) *Images of Aging: cultural representations of later life*, London: Routledge

Uchino B, Holt-Lunstad J, Uno D and Flinders J (2001) 'Heterogeneity in the social networks of young and older adults: prediction of mental health and cardiovascular reactivity during acute stress', *Journal of Behavioral Medicine* 24(4): 361–382

Ungar M (2002) 'A deeper more social ecological social work practice', *Social Services Review* 76(3): 480–499

Urry H, Nitschke J, Dolski I, Jackson D, Dalton K, Mueller C et al. (2004) 'Making a life worth living – neural correlates of well-being', *Psychological Science* 15(6): 367–372

Van den Bergh B, Mulder E, Mennes M and Glover V (2005) 'Antenatal maternal anxiety and stress and the neurobehavioral development of fetus and child: links and possible mechanisms. A review', *Neuroscience And Biobehavioral Reviews* 29(2): 237–258

Van Wormer K (1995) *Alcoholism Treatment: A Social Work Perspective*, Chicago: Nelson-Hall

Viner R, Christie D, Taylor V and Hey S (2003) 'Motivational/solution-focused intervention improbes HbA1c in adolescents with Type 1 diabetes: a pilot study', *Diabetic Medicine* (Sept.) 20(9): 739–742

Volland R, Berkman B, Phillips M, Stein G (2003) 'Social work education for health care: addressing practice competencies', *Social Work in Health Care* 37(4): 1–17

Volpicelli J, Pettinati H, McLellan, A, O'Brien C (2001) *Combining Medication and Psychosocial Treatments: the BRENDA Approach*, New York: Guildford Press

Voss S (2000) Descartes, Heart and Soul. In J Wright and P Potter (ed.) *Psyche and Soma: Physicians and Metaphysicians on the Mind–Body Problem from Antiquity to Enlightenment*, Oxford: Clarendon

Wahidin A and Powell J (2003) 'Reconfiguring old bodies: from the biomedical model to a critical epistemology', *Sincronia* Summer: 1–11

Wainwright S and Turner B (2003) 'Reflections on embodiment and vulnerability', *BMJ Publishing Group & Institute of Medical Ethics*, 29: 4–7

Waldby, C (1999) 'IatroGenesis: the Visible Human Project and the reproduction of life' *Australian Feminist Studies*, 14(29)

Warin J (2000) 'The attainment of self-consistency through gender in young children', *Sex Roles* 42(3–4): 209–231

Weaver I, Cervoni N, Champagne F, D'Alessio A, Sharma S, Seckl J et al. (2004) 'Epigentic programming by maternal behaviour', *Nature Reviews Neuroscience* 7(8): 847–854

Weich S and Lewis G (1998) 'Poverty, unemployment and common mental disorders: population based cohort study', *British Medical Journal* 317: 115–119

Wendell, S (1996) The rejected body: feminist philosophical reflections on disability, New York/London, Routledge

Weissman G (1996) 'Sucking with vampires': the medicine of unreason. In Gross P, Livitt N and Lewis M *The Flight from Reason and Science*, United States: Annals of the New York Academy of Sciences

Wilce J (ed) (2003) *Social and Cultural Lives of Immune Systems*, London: Routledge

Williams S (ed) (1995) *Medicine and the Body*, Thousand Oaks, CA: Sage

Williams S (2003) 'Reason, emotion and embodiment: is "mental" health a contradiction in terms?' *Sociology of Health and Illness*, 22: 559–581

Williams S, Birke L and Bendelow G (eds) (2003) *Debating Biology: Sociological Reflections on Health, Medicine and Society*, London: Routledge

Wisner K and Stowe Z (1997) 'Psychobiology of postpartum mood disorders', Seminars in Reproductive Endocrinology 15(1): 77–89

Witkin S (2000) How 'ripened' are you? In Keigher S, Fortune A and Witkin S *Aging and Social Work: the changing landscape*, New York: NASW Press

Wittling W (1997) 'The right hemisphere and the human stress response', *Acta Physiologica Scandinavica* 161 (Suppl. 640): 55–59

Woodside D, Bulik C, Halmi K, Fichter M, Kaplan A, Berrettini W et al. (2002) 'Personality, perfectionism and attitudes toward eating in parents of individuals with eating disorders', *International Journal of Eating Disorders* 31(3): 290–299

World Health Organisation Department of Mental Health and Substance Abuse (2004) Prevention of Mental Disorders: Effective Interventions and Policy Options, a summary report, Geneva: World Health Organisation

Wu J, Buchsbaum M and Bunney W (2001) 'Clinical neurochemical implications of sleep deprivation's effects on the anterior cingulate of depressed responders', *Neuropsychopharmacology* 25 (Suppl. 5): S74–S78

Zajonc R (2001) 'Mere exposure: a gateway to the subliminal', *Current Directions in Psychological Science* 10(6): 224–228

Zhu J and Thagard P (2002) 'Emotion and Action', *Philosophical Psychology* 15(1): 19–36

Ziguras S, Henley K, Conron W and Catford N (1999) 'Social work in mental health services: a survey of the field', *Australian Social Work* 52(2), 27–34

Zweben A (2001) Integrating pharmacotherapy and psychosocial interventions in the treatment of individuals with alcohol problems. In Spence R, DiNitto D and Straussner S (eds) *Neurobiology of Addictions: implications for clinical practice*, New York: Haworth Social Work Practice Press Inc.

Index

abuse 45, 124, 141–3, 150–1, 158,
   160–1, 197
actors, embodied human 86, 90, 92
addictions 210–11, 213–16, 218–20,
   222, 224–5, 239, 244, 247–9,
   253, 257, 259
   neurobiology of 215, 220, 222, 224
adolescence 70, 143–4, 152–3,
   160–1, 167, 180, 196, 214–15,
   241–4, 255–6, 258
adolescent
   brain, developing 153, 214, 246
   health 107, 255, 257
affective research 31
age – *see also* late life 3, 12, 48, 71,
   144, 151–2, 158–60, 165,
   167–9, 171–2, 174–6, 180–1,
   197, 215, 247–8
ageing process 44, 172–4, 176–9,
   182, 185, 242, 245, 247, 250–1,
   254, 257
aging
   brain 178, 249
   and Social work 245, 247–9, 259
   society 245–6, 256
alcohol 21, 111, 118, 137–8, 146,
   153, 209, 211–15, 217, 219–21,
   223, 239, 241, 254
   brain 210, 217
Aldwin C and Gilmour D 82, 171,
   174–5, 177–8, 180
allostatic load 48, 64, 182, 197–8,
   203, 252
amygdala 39, 41, 52–3, 57–8, 120,
   122, 149
anxiety 3, 37, 40, 43, 71, 85–6,
   101, 104, 113, 119–20, 134–6,
   138–9, 160, 185–8, 247
assessments 16, 91, 99, 100, 161,
   169, 182, 220–1, 243, 246, 252

attachment 45, 143, 147–50, 256
   theory 143–4, 241, 252
Australia 115, 142, 189, 209, 253–5
awareness 11, 26, 68, 70, 79, 84–7,
   92, 105, 159, 161, 163, 172,
   183, 194
axons 29, 30, 233, 237
Azmitia E 211, 213–15, 222

Bargh J and Chartrand T 26, 54–5
Bargh J, Gollwitzer, P et al. 54, 157,
   239, 242
BCAG (Body Cognizant Assessment
   Guide) 21–2, 91–2, 99–101,
   136, 162, 184, 205
behaviours, new 59, 60, 98, 102
beings, embodied 21, 88, 141, 194,
   217
biological
   body 17–18, 62–3, 70, 73, 79, 132
   perspectives 12, 14, 25–6, 35, 60,
      62, 143, 191
biology 4, 13–15, 20, 22–3, 25–6,
   37, 64, 77, 79, 80, 82–3, 118,
   133, 190, 195, 198
Birke L 183, 195, 197, 240, 242,
   259
Blumenthal J, Babyak M et al. 129,
   240–1
Bodies, ageing 172–3, 181–2
Body cognizant 20–1, 87–8, 90, 92,
   97, 99–102, 104–7, 133–6, 181,
   183, 198, 202–3, 210, 213,
   220–3
   social worker 21, 87, 91, 97, 99,
      101, 103, 105–7, 133, 158,
      181–2, 198, 203, 220, 222
Booij L, Van Der Does W et al. 125,
   241
Bowlby J 45, 143, 161, 241

brain
  activity   25, 30–1, 59, 145
  areas   28, 32–3, 50, 128, 149, 237
  changes   34, 215, 242
  damage   36, 53, 81, 211, 220, 223
  developing   147–8, 213, 243, 245, 256
  functions   25, 29, 32, 148, 176, 210
  health   149, 175, 177, 223
  regions   21, 27, 29, 31–3, 51, 119, 128, 145, 149, 212–14, 233, 236, 248
brainstem   33, 128, 145, 233
breast cancer   201, 206–8
Butler J   18, 20, 74–5, 242

Cacioppo J, Bernston G et al.   36, 43, 45–6, 48, 55, 250
caffeine   125, 254
caregivers   45, 48, 143, 148, 151, 154
CBT (Cognitive Behavioural Therapy)   19, 102, 216, 226–7
cells   26, 29–32, 34, 47–8, 53, 211, 233, 235–6
cerebellum   33, 145, 233, 245
cerebrum   32–3
Chambon A, Irving A, Epstein L   5, 72, 242
child
  development   143, 146, 153, 158, 161, 249, 251
  protection   21, 111, 141–3, 145, 147, 149, 151, 153, 155, 157, 159, 161, 209, 256–7
childhood   9, 44, 154, 157, 180, 196, 213, 241, 244
cognition   12, 14, 20, 23, 39, 70, 92, 113–14, 118, 120, 153, 175–6, 229, 251, 256
communities   37, 73, 85, 113, 115, 117, 125, 136–7, 168, 192, 203, 209–10, 216, 222
Connell R   155–6, 243
Cooper B   37, 80, 119, 243
corporeal capacity   21, 88–92, 100, 133, 157, 173–4, 179, 183, 194–5, 202, 205, 210, 217, 230

cortex, cerebral   33, 233, 237
cortisol   31, 46–8, 86, 123–4, 146–7, 152, 234
counselling   150, 159, 163, 202–4, 208, 222
critical periods   213–14, 242
culture   10–11, 38, 67, 74–5, 81, 85–6, 90, 114, 130, 172, 179, 190, 246, 248
Curtis W and Cicchetti D   89, 199, 200, 202

Damasio A   39, 40, 53, 81, 150, 242
Davidson R   27, 41–3, 48, 58–9, 115, 120–1, 145, 243, 250–1
decision-making   33, 40, 55–6, 83, 104, 161, 229, 233, 237, 240
dendrites   29, 30, 234
depression   40, 49, 98, 117, 119–26, 128–30, 132, 134–6, 138–9, 223, 226–7, 240–1, 243–4, 246–7, 250–6
  clinical   120, 241, 243
  sufferers   120, 129
depressive episodes   125–6, 128–9
Descartes R   24
diet   43, 48, 81, 101–2, 135, 172, 178, 197, 203
disability   10, 13, 32, 66, 68–9, 85, 115, 120, 132, 141, 160, 180–1, 192, 244–5, 257–8
discourse   18, 20, 72, 74–6, 85, 117, 172, 179, 190, 243, 248
disease   49, 70–1, 85, 94, 164, 177–8, 180, 182, 189–90, 196–7, 199, 201–2, 205, 235, 251–2
disorders   27–8, 80, 89, 113, 115, 134, 145, 150, 256
distress   98, 148–50
diversity   12, 142, 171–3
dopamine   31, 147, 149, 212, 234

eating disorders   244, 259
embodied   16, 86, 91
emotion   6, 7, 25–7, 38–40, 42–6, 52, 57–60, 67–8, 81–3, 86–8,

emotion – *continued*
144–6, 148–9, 151–3, 200–1,
242–5, 256–7
emotional
brain 44, 81, 216, 250
development 45, 123, 147, 158
disorders 124, 126, 159
dysregulation 159, 165
health 66, 113, 133
memory 52, 150
processing 38, 161, 237
regulation 46, 57, 59, 128, 148,
158, 247
responses 32, 43, 70, 98, 101, 150
states 42, 45, 57, 67, 99, 104,
145–6, 148, 150, 158–9,
198–200, 211, 255
support 150, 152, 165, 201
well-being 21, 87, 113, 158, 177
environment 6, 8–11, 13, 16, 20–1,
35–7, 51, 56–7, 63–4, 67, 80,
82–3, 89, 90, 97, 179
environmental factors 9, 12, 16, 32,
34, 36–7, 89, 102, 113, 150,
177, 182, 191, 195, 203
enzymes 127, 234–5
Erikson E 82, 143–5
exercise 19, 43, 48, 102, 129,
135–6, 172, 174, 177–8, 182,
187, 197, 203, 225, 241

facial expressions 7, 8, 45, 66–7, 98,
131, 135, 145, 147
Featherstone M 71, 168, 172–3,
245, 247, 257
feelings 24–6, 43, 65, 97–9, 103–4,
139–40, 155, 197, 212
female brains 34–5
foetus 145–6, 158
forebrain 233
Foucault M 20, 72–4, 130–1, 245
Fraser M and Greco M 64–5, 69,
70, 73

GABA (gama-aminobutyric acid)
30–1, 234
gender 10, 12, 18, 56, 74–5, 86, 98,
157, 169, 180–1, 196, 258

genes 28, 31–2, 34, 36, 48, 83, 90,
119, 174, 211
genetic 6, 12, 34, 36, 174, 177–8,
192
Germain C and Gitterman A 10–11,
79, 118, 170
gerontology 169–71
girls 75, 157, 214
glossary 234–7
Goffman E 7, 20, 66–7, 72, 246
Goldapple K, Segal Z et al. 127–8,
246
Grosz E 18, 20, 65, 72, 75, 247

hazards, environmental 35, 37, 155
health 4, 21, 44–5, 50, 70, 76, 87,
111, 123, 152, 154, 168–9,
178–80, 189–96, 202–4
behaviours 179, 199, 208
capital 196–7
holistic 192, 194
inequalities 192, 196–7
professionals 106, 115–16, 133,
193, 200, 204
services 76, 115, 117, 192–3, 259
heart disease 49, 199
hemispheres, cerebral 33, 233–4, 236
hippocampus 52, 121–2, 127, 149,
176, 179, 212, 234
holistic 10, 19, 169–70, 194
hormones 23, 31, 39, 46, 48, 89,
119, 124–6, 128, 214, 233–4,
236–7, 242, 257
Howson, C 17, 65–71, 73, 154
human
bodies 3, 5, 6, 9, 13, 17–18, 63,
66, 76–7, 79–81, 86–8, 168,
179, 213
brain 27, 29, 32, 53, 56, 88, 173,
176, 179, 202, 217, 253
life 13, 28, 86, 133

illness 4, 13, 18, 36–7, 46, 70, 94,
116–17, 119, 123–4, 134–5,
189, 191–2, 201, 253–4
immune system 11, 23, 46–8, 86,
124, 175, 197, 202, 234–5, 251,
259

infant 41, 43, 45, 66, 85, 143–4,
147–51, 159, 161–2, 213, 241,
256
brain 147
institutions 18, 72–3, 75, 192
isolation 69, 85, 122, 172, 184,
186–7, 198, 222, 224, 227

Johnson H 118–19, 147, 231, 248

Kagan J 41–2, 44, 249
Kandel E 25–6, 28, 58, 249
Kaye J 173–6, 178, 181
Keigher S 168, 245, 247–9, 259
Kiecolt-Glaser J 47, 124, 249, 251,
255
Kosslyn S, Cacioppo J, Davidson R et al.
43, 48, 60, 250
Kraemer A, Herer L, Colcombe S et al.
174, 176–9, 250
Kuh D 49, 180, 195–6
Kunkel S 168, 170

Lamberts S 174–6, 181, 250
late life 6, 11, 70, 167–72, 174,
177–80, 182 – *see also* age
Le Doux J 27, 38, 52–3, 58, 60
learning 32, 57–8, 60, 66, 82–3, 85,
88, 105–6, 135, 164, 172, 178,
183, 198, 216–17
life trajectories 13, 171
lifespan 174, 202, 250
limbic system 146, 152, 214–16, 235
Lupien S et al. 50, 152
lymphocytes 47–8, 235

males 34–5, 125, 132, 156, 170,
175, 214
marijuana 212, 215, 223, 225
Martin E 173–4, 214
material bodies 4, 18, 64–5, 69,
71–2, 74–5, 193, 203
Mattaini M 8, 15–16, 252
Mayberg H 120
McEwan B 48–50, 197–8
medications 35, 73, 98, 125, 127–9,
136, 216–17, 221

meditation 19, 58–9, 127, 174, 194,
207, 235
memory 20, 27, 31, 33, 35, 52–3,
57–8, 80, 87–8, 122–3, 127,
175–6, 179, 212, 237
mental
disorders 21, 117–19, 239, 242–3,
251, 253, 259
health 21, 73, 76, 111, 113,
115–17, 119, 121, 123, 125,
131–3, 135, 169, 248, 256–7
illness 21, 25, 111, 113–20, 123,
125, 130–6, 144, 153, 219,
243, 248, 252, 256
mind 6, 7, 10, 12, 16–17, 19–21,
23–6, 38, 52–3, 55, 58, 69, 87,
194, 249, 257–8
models
biopsychosocial 191, 193, 230
life stage 82–3
monoamines 31, 234
Mrak R, Griffin S and Graham D
173, 175–6, 178, 253

negative emotion 41, 44, 46, 57–8,
127, 155, 159
neglect 45, 62, 141, 151, 157–8,
160, 168, 205
nervous system 27, 41, 45, 47, 86,
175, 233–7, 256
Nestler E 123, 211–12, 216, 219,
222
Nettleton S 17, 69, 70, 172, 192–3,
253
neural circuits 32, 38, 52, 54, 119
neurobiology 50, 210, 217, 219–20,
250–1, 253
neurons 28–30, 32, 58, 176, 213,
233, 235–6
neuroscience 4, 17, 20–1, 23, 26–9,
35, 38, 42, 51–2, 57, 60–1,
79–81, 118–19, 160–1, 229–31
neurotransmitters 29–31, 124–6,
149, 212, 236

organism, biological 11–13, 179, 229
oxytocin 49, 236

Payne, M   7, 254–5
peptides   31, 233, 236
perceptions   12, 31, 50–1, 54, 57,
    62, 70, 81, 83, 133–5, 154, 252
person-in-environment   9–11, 13,
    15, 19, 65, 69, 77, 79, 89, 90,
    170, 173, 180, 210, 230, 249
personality   32, 177–8, 239–40, 242,
    259
physical
    factors   84, 93–4, 103, 118,
        137–8, 163–4, 185–6, 206–7,
        224–5
    health   178, 182, 210, 225, 255
physiological perspective   45, 49,
    61–2, 134
Piaget J   143–5
plasticity   58, 88, 158, 174, 176,
    179–82, 202, 211, 215, 222–3,
    242
postmodernism   5, 7
power   8, 11, 18, 47, 73–4, 163,
    204, 239, 255
practice, self-reflexive   56–7
prefrontal cortex   41, 121, 146, 215,
    234–6
pregnancy   145–6, 213
protection   12, 46, 143, 151, 154,
    163, 168
proteins   32, 47, 233–4
psyche   24, 65, 258
psychiatric disability   114, 198
psychopathology   6, 149, 151, 202,
    241–2, 244, 251–3
psychotherapy   58, 127–8, 199, 202
puberty   70, 125–6, 152, 214

reason   8, 13, 24, 26–7, 30–1, 39,
    82, 111, 116, 127, 230, 244–5,
    249–50, 254–5, 258–9
recovery   12, 41, 88, 98, 114–15,
    133, 135, 153, 178, 199, 202,
    215, 243, 253
relaxation   19, 134–5, 161, 197,
    203, 206–7, 216, 225
resilience   12, 16, 63–4, 83, 89, 103,
    170, 182, 199, 200, 202, 243, 246

right-brain   45–6
risks   4, 12, 37, 46, 50, 123–4,
    137–8, 152–3, 155, 159–61,
    180, 193, 196, 213, 216–17

schizophrenia   86, 119, 125
Schore A   44–6, 98, 147–50, 158,
    256
self   4, 6, 7, 20, 55, 57, 65–6,
    68–70, 73, 75–6, 87–8, 131–2,
    154, 218–19, 246, 256–7
self-confidence   102
self-esteem   35, 42, 56, 92, 101–2,
    155–8, 160, 227, 250, 255
self, professional   56–7
self-reflexive   56
skills   4, 7, 58, 85, 89, 100, 133,
    148, 158, 170, 182, 195, 224–6
social
    bodies   20, 23, 63, 65, 67, 69,
        71–3, 75, 77, 87, 132
    constructionism   5, 15–17, 91
    environments   10, 34–5, 51, 116,
        118–19, 147, 150
    life   5, 8, 63, 73, 131, 252
    order   73–4, 130
    relationships   35, 40, 46, 49, 50,
        68, 113, 150, 157, 177, 190,
        200, 203, 209, 256
    sciences   27, 64, 229, 247–8
    support   42, 45, 49, 85, 126, 128,
        174, 178, 182, 199, 200, 248,
        250
social work   3–10, 12–14, 17, 19,
    20, 23, 35, 75–7, 82–3, 86–7,
    116–17, 168–71, 189–91,
    204–5, 217, 229–31
    practice   3, 6, 14–15, 21–2, 77,
        83, 92, 111, 168–9, 193–4,
        202, 204, 230, 241
    theory   3–5, 12–13, 20, 23, 28,
        35, 63–4, 79, 82, 89, 117–18,
        173, 254
social world   3, 72, 88, 194, 218
society   4, 17–18, 44, 73, 81, 114,
    154–6, 171–2, 179, 195–6, 198,
    209–10, 240, 245–8, 257

sociology   20, 22, 28, 64–5, 76–7,
  80, 82, 111, 117, 158, 168,
  170–3, 181, 190, 254–6
souls   24, 258
Stoppard J   131–2, 257
strengths   12, 82, 91, 93–4, 96, 100,
  137–8, 140, 148, 150, 163–4,
  185–6, 188, 206, 208
stress   9, 11–12, 46–8, 50, 53, 64,
  83, 94–5, 122–5, 134, 158,
  177–8, 197, 202–3, 234–5
stressors   11–12, 63–4, 122, 126,
  147, 150, 189
synapse   29, 30, 176, 236–7

teams   193, 204
temperaments   36–7, 41–2, 57
temporal lobe   33, 52, 122, 234, 237
theories, critical   5, 7, 8, 15, 17–18,
  91, 171

thought patterns   25, 57, 59, 60, 101
thoughts   24–7, 38–9, 56, 60, 69,
  102, 104, 113–14, 128, 130–1,
  140, 182, 233–6
trauma   9, 12, 88–9, 149, 244
Turner B   15, 71, 88, 132, 167–8,
  172, 192, 245, 257–8

unconscious   7, 26, 38, 52, 54–5,
  57, 67, 114, 183

well-being   35–6, 42–5, 50, 98, 101,
  104, 106–7, 132, 152, 154–5,
  157, 160, 169, 179, 182
Williams S   240, 242–3, 259
Witkin S   167–9, 172, 245, 247–9,
  259
women   10, 14, 34–5, 47, 65, 74–5,
  86, 125–6, 132, 158, 167, 169,
  175, 234, 236